TOP OF THE MOUNTAIN

TOP OF THE MOUNTAIN

THE BEATLES AT SHEA STADIUM 1965

LAURIE JACOBSON

Backbeat Books

GUILFORD, CONNECTICUT

An imprint of Globe Pequot, the trade division of
The Rowman & Littlefield Publishing Group, Inc.
4501 Forbes Blvd., Ste. 200
Lanham, MD 20706
www.rowman.com

Distributed by NATIONAL BOOK NETWORK

Copyright © 2022 by Laurie Jacobson

All rights reserved. No part of this book may be reproduced in any form or by any electronic or mechanical means, including information storage and retrieval systems, without written permission from the publisher, except by a reviewer who may quote passages in a review.

Images appearing on pages 147 to 151 are © 2012 Adam Kushner photographed by Marc Weinstein.

Image of Brian Epstein on page 23 is licensed under the Creative Commons Attribution CC0 1.0 Universal (CC0-1.0) Public Domain Dedication. [https://creativecommons.org/publicdomain/zero/1.0/legalcode]

Image of a NEMS store on page 23 and of the Beatles exiting a plane in Madrid on page 75 are licensed under the Creative Commons Attribution 2.0 Generic license (CC BY 2.0). [https://creativecommons.org/licenses/by/2.0/legalcode]

Unless otherwise noted, all images are from the author's personal collection.

British Library Cataloguing in Publication Information available

Library of Congress Cataloging-in-Publication Data available

Names: Jacobson, Laurie, author.
Title: Top of the mountain : the Beatles at Shea Stadium 1965 / Laurie Jacobson.
Description: Lanham : Backbeat Books, 2022. | Includes bibliographical references and index. | Summary: ""That concert in 1965 at Shea Stadium . . . I saw the top of the mountain on that unforgettable night." -John Lennon"— Provided by publisher.
Identifiers: LCCN 2021057569 (print) | LCCN 2021057570 (ebook) | ISBN 9781493065288 (cloth) | ISBN 9781493065295 (epub)
Subjects: LCSH: Beatles. | Beatles—Performances—New York (State)—New York. | Rock music—New York (State)—New York—1961-1970—Performances. | Rock concerts—New York (State)—New York—History—20th century. | Shea Stadium (New York, N.Y.)
Classification: LCC ML421.B4 J36 2022 (print) | LCC ML421.B4 (ebook) | DDC 782.42166092/2—dc23
LC record available at https://lccn.loc.gov/2021057569
LC ebook record available at https://lccn.loc.gov/2021057570

♾™ The paper used in this publication meets the minimum requirements of American National Standard for Information Sciences—Permanence of Paper for Printed Library Materials, ANSI/NISO Z39.48-1992

To the late, great Marc Weinstein, whose sense of adventure took him to exciting places including the edge of the stage at Shea. What chutzpah! What photos! What a guy.

CONTENTS

Acknowledgments	ix
Introduction	xi
1. **LIFE BEFORE SHEA**	1
2. **THE WAY TO SHEA**	17
3. **GOING FOR BROKE**	37
4. **THE BEATLES TAKE NEW YORK**	89
5. **THE CONCERT**	101
6. **AFTER SHEA AND BEYOND**	161
Cast of Characters	183
Index	189
Quotes	197

ACKNOWLEDGMENTS

The story of The Beatles at Shea Stadium lies in the many voices of the people who were lucky enough to be there. Endless thanks for your help and contributions . . . yeah, yeah, yeah.

Eric J. Adams, Jeffrey Ainis, Bill Angelos, Tony Barrow, John Bezzini, Steve Boone, Al Bunetta, Dawn Bunetta, Vince Calandra, Tracy Campbell, Felix Cavaliere, Joy Musiker Cohen, Melissa Davis, Jim Freyler, Dave Glyde, Whoopi Goldberg, Debbie Greenberg, Deborah Levine Herman, Jeff Herman, John Kane, Buz Kohan, Linda LaFlamme, Michael Lang, Bob Lefsetz, Tom Leonardis, John Lociano, Jim McCarty, Linda Ghignone Marotte, Melanie from Low 302 NSW, Dawn Michaels, Bobbie Molina, Chip Monck, Cousin Brucie Morrow, Denise Mourges, George Orsino, John Orsino, David Pelletier, Renee Perst, Bob Precht, Ronnie Schneider, Kurt Schreiner, John Sebastian, Susan Silva, Ronni Simon, Meryl Streep, Adrienne Steinbaum, Judi Tulini-Sims, Steve Van Zandt, Bobby Vinton, Mary Wilson, Seth Zimmerman.

    Special thanks to Anne McDermott and Elliott Gordon.

    Very special thanks to Marc Weinstein.

    Love to my forever "Beatle People" Cristie Krauss, Cyndi Trauernicht, and Colin Gardner.

    Love and thanks to my husband, Jon Provost, smart, fun, and totally fab.

And my deep gratitude to John, Paul, George, and Ringo, without whom this world would be a very different place.

INTRODUCTION

In August 1965, during a sweltering heat wave, fifty-six thousand people traveled by plane, car, bus, ferry, and subway train to pack New York's Shea Stadium on a Sunday evening—not for a baseball game, but for a rock and roll concert. No rock band had ever played a baseball stadium, and no one believed it could be pulled off. But on that glorious night, The Beatles sold out Shea Stadium, shattering all existing box office and attendance records in show business history. Oh, and they also changed the world.

I am pinching myself that I wrote a book about The Beatles. I'm your average devoted Beatle fan. I have all their albums and 45s original from the day—mono—and even some rarities. I have a literal trunkful of scrapbooks about them, which I began in 1964 and ended only recently, and many pieces of memorabilia. I was so lucky to see them in St. Louis in 1966, and I've seen Ringo and Paul solo every tour and George in '74. I can barely stand to mention that I went a different way in Central Park one spring afternoon in 1974 and missed John giving an impromptu concert for a fortunate few. Hands down, biggest life regret. I know a fair amount about them, but there are many who know so much more. No matter—The Beatles had an enormous impact on me. They got me through the best and the worst times of my life. They influenced me on every level. I deeply love them. And I will carry them in my heart and soul forever.

That said, quite some time ago, I tucked away the feelings that went with the music. I had the image of me curled up in front of the speaker of my parents' hi-fi listening to every note, but I had not reconnected with the wonder of it in a very long time: the thrill of a new Beatle album coming out, the rush to the store on release day to buy it, running home to listen to it alone or with friends to talk about each song and to play it over and over—without smoking pot.

Working on this book has reawakened that dormant exuberance in me. And I couldn't be happier about it, because those were among the best times of my life. To have them back is a tremendous gift. I don't intend to ever lose touch with them again.

INTRODUCTION

Author with John Lennon statue in Havana, Cuba. PHOTO BY JON PROVOST

I have spent years gathering stories from people who were involved with Shea on every level. I learned things about The Beatles and the craziness that surrounded them in those days that gave me insight into them as young men and the solo paths they would take in the future. The treasure trove of photos I found captured this magic time. And I met some fab Beatle People along the way. I am a Beatlemaniac all over again.

Beatlemania is contagious. I hope you catch it reading *Top of the Mountain*. Whether you recapture a wonderful time in your life or discover The Beatles for the first time, you will never read another story like this—because it only happened once.

Laurie Jacobson

Santa Rosa, California

August 2021

That concert in 1965 at Shea Stadium . . . I saw the top of the mountain on that unforgettable night.
—John Lennon

1

LIFE BEFORE SHEA

THE BEGINNING

To know where you're going, you've got to know where you've been.

In the early 1960s, the Rat Pack was cool, Elvis was hot, and Annette and Frankie ruled the beach.

Bobby Vinton is an American singer, songwriter, and actor.

Bobby Vinton: I was a Las Vegas performer. I wanted to hang out with Sinatra, Sammy Davis Jr., and Dean Martin. Those were my idols. Those were the guys to know.

John and Jacqueline Kennedy, the nation's youngest president and his beautiful wife, seemed more like movie stars than politicians. Gorgeous, charming, and fashionable, they ushered in a new era with the focus on youth. JFK inspired high school and college graduates with hope and confidence for a future they could help to shape and build. By 1964, ten thousand Americans—mostly people in their twenties—had volunteered for JFK's Peace Corps to aid developing countries in the struggle against poverty, illiteracy, and disease. Baby boomers were encouraged to make the world a better place, to dream and dream big. Reach for the stars, and one day we'll even walk on the moon. All things were possible.

But in November 1963, the nation's dreams, big and small, were crushed with Kennedy's assassination. It was a harsh reality for all, but hardest on the young. They had seen a light—what they could be if they dared, what the world could be. A generation had been awakened, but evil had won—or had it? The answer came back: only if they let it. The boomers were not going to let it; no, not this generation.

They began to turn away from the establishment and their parents' "five o'clock" way of life. Hollywood was still dishing up pablum: a flag-waving John Wayne or Sandra Dee's virginal Gidget and her beach scene, where no one ever drank or took drugs or had sex—ever. Boomers were choosing instead to search for something of their own, something real. And that meant music. Sure, there was Elvis, but the army had taken the bite out of him. And prior to The Beatles' first appearance on *Ed Sullivan*, the number-one spot on the Billboard Top 100 had been held for eleven weeks by the Singing Nun. Something had to give.

Steve Boone played bass for the Lovin' Spoonful.

Steve Boone. COURTESY STEVE BOONE

Steve Boone: The formula had worn out, the formula being: a record producer goes to 1650 Broadway—the Brill Building—and says, "I need a medium-tempo song about boy-meets-girl-and-falls-in-love." Then they take some artist they're developing . . . into the studio. They hire the musicians, bring in a songwriter who has written this song according to the producer's dimensions, and then they produce it. And the artist is really a "come in and sing the song and go home. We'll take care of the rest of it." That formula was getting tired.

In the '50s, you were expected to leave music behind when you got out of high school. The '50s were very buttoned-down. Once high school was over, you stopped having fun. You went to college or got married or both in some cases. Rock and roll was for kids. But all that was changing . . . in the American post–high school scene. The entertainment at college was mostly jazz and folk and poetry. The Lovin' Spoonful was the first rock band to tour extensively on college campuses. But somebody else would have done it if we hadn't. That's what I mean. [Change was to be expected] because the whole mood of how young people listened to music and participated in the culture was changing.

Not that I wasn't impressed by The Beatles' talent—I certainly was—and their records, their songs, and the change they made in the entire record industry, but it was an inevitable change. It was going to happen whether it was The Beatles, the Lovin' Spoonful, the Searchers, the Rolling Stones, or the Byrds. Somebody was going to come along and be a self-contained music machine—[a group who] writes their own songs, plays all their own instruments on their records. The Beatles just got there first—and more power to them.

The Lovin' Spoonful. COURTESY STEVE BOONE

In other words, the stage was set for something different, and John, Paul, George, and Ringo were in the right place at the right time and—most importantly—primed and ready for the moment. They had played more gigs in Hamburg, Germany, and at the Cavern Club in Liverpool than many artists play in their entire careers. That's where they developed style and presence and moves. And that's where they learned to make enthusiastic fans of complete strangers.

Peter Asher is a music producer, half of the successful pop duo Peter and Gordon, and the brother of Jane Asher, Paul's longtime girlfriend.

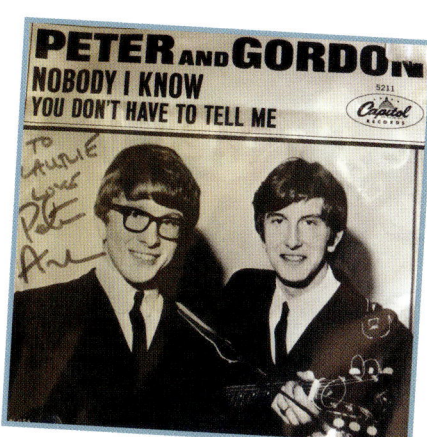

Peter Asher: It's like that sort of perfect storm period: if everything falls into place in exactly the right direction and exactly the right people and exactly the right time, it's one of those miraculous events. And something about the coincidence or whatever it was that got those musical talents to form a band, there's never been anything like it. Because as remarkable as they were individually—and that's terribly important to remember—if George Harrison was in any other band, he would have been the leader and a gigantic star.

Bill Angelos—with his partner Buz Kohan—won an Emmy for his work on *The Carol Burnett Show*. This prolific team wrote and produced hundreds of songs and shows of all genres during their decades-long careers.

Bill Angelos: Martin Block used to have something called *The Battle of the Baritones*. It was a battle between Frank Sinatra and Bing Crosby. That's what the music was. Prior to rock and roll, there was jazz. And prior to that was swing. And prior to that was ragtime. Once rock and roll took over, it morphed into hip-hop, but rock and roll still is here. And that's fifty years later. To my knowledge no musical genre, with the possible exception of classical, of course, has lasted that long.

It was the beginning of an entire culture of change, first of all, beginning with the music. At the time we were working for Perry Como and that element of the music business got scared. Oh yeah. Oh yeah. You could just sense it. And we were at the time very much looking forward to writing for Broadway. But even that started to change.

My sister was a bobby-soxer and she took me to see Frank Sinatra at the Paramount Theater when he was really at the beginning of his career. And the major difference between the bobby-soxers and The Beatle fans [was that] the bobby-soxers would never think of even shouting when Sinatra was singing. The bobby-soxers *swooned*. . . . They kind of sighed. But it would be almost sacrilegious to do anything to him when he was singing.

I actually went to an Elvis Presley concert in Texas when I was in the air force. This had to be in 1955, '56, when he was just starting out. And for all of his gyrations and machinations, he was really extraordinary. You had never seen anything like it. But the audience was respectful. They listened to him and watched him.

It was this screaming and shouting that, as far as I know, The Beatles were the first ones to experience that. Whether that was initially manufactured or not, I don't know. I doubt it. I think that may have been an actual change in the evolution of humanity. Suddenly we had to scream when things like that happened.

Buz Kohan: I had a partner named Bill Angelos. We had gone to high school together—the Bronx High School of Science. I had a band called the Blue Notes and he was my vocalist. Then I went on to the Eastman School of Music. I played piano. Bill was the vocalist. He didn't play an instrument. He went on to Syracuse. And he got involved in a number of shows with a number of people whose names you would probably be familiar with because it was a very good time there for theater and things.

We had never really written together but I said, "You want to try it? Let's try a partnership." So, when we finally got together, we decided we would focus on writing material; and we got signed by the William Morris office as a team. One of the first things we did was . . . Arthur Godfrey. And we were writing stuff for his radio show and his personal appearances.

Bill Angelos: The first time I actually heard them [The Beatles], I was in Florida driving down Arthur Godfrey Boulevard—with Arthur Godfrey. We heard, "She loves you—yeah, yeah, yeah," and I said, "What is that?" It was just a foreign sound. Literally a foreign sound because it wasn't Chuck Berry. It wasn't the rock and roll we were aware of. I'm telling you, it scared people. Here's a quick story. This is a true story. When we were working with Perry Como, we came across a song we wanted Perry to sing. We knew that if he knew who had written it, he wouldn't sing it. So, one day Buz and I went into the room next door to Perry's office and there was a piano there. Buz started playing and I started singing, "Yesterday . . . Dah dah dah da." And Perry came in and the sheet music was on the piano turned over. And he stood next to me and he listened to me singing this song. He turned over the sheet music, saw who wrote it and then started singing with me. We had to ease him into the fact that these are the guys who are taking over. And they did.

1964: THE BEATLES ON *ED SULLIVAN* AND THE LAUNCH OF BEATLEMANIA

The Ed Sullivan Show was the national cultural touchstone. You could see the greats of popular song, comedy, opera, ballet, Broadway, jazz, jugglers, unicyclists, plate spinners, dog acts, puppets, bell ringers—there is no act that you could name that wasn't on his show. There was something for every member of the family, so families watched together, often gathered around the only television in the house. If you didn't like one act, wait three or four minutes for the next one. It was all held together by the stiff, awkward Sullivan, who often mispronounced names, but who had the goods week after week in every color and nationality.

Robert E. Precht is the eldest of Sullivan's five grandchildren.

Robert E. Precht: When people think of him, they think of family togetherness—watching his show together. It's a legacy of shared experience that's a unique, vanished part of America.

Robert's brother Vincent was a Los Angeles schoolteacher. In 1964, he was six years old.

Vincent Precht: Maybe having The Beatles on his show seemed like the only thing to do, to my grandfather. The country was reeling after Oswald shot Kennedy. It needed something to sing about. It needed hope.

Cousin Brucie Morrow was the nighttime deejay on New York's WABC, making him the highest profile deejay in the country.

Cousin Brucie. COURTESY BRUCE MORROW

Cousin Brucie: The Beatles weren't very sophisticated. Never mind young, talk about sophisticated. They had no sophistication. These guys came from a working-class environment. They went all over Europe, which was fine. They had a little bit of education. But they did not have what they got when they came here. It [the experience] was tenfold, maybe even more than that. So that's why I say they were not ready for what they were to garner in this place.

Not only were they good, but let's think about this thing, this is very important too. What was going on in our lives as Americans in the United States? In the United States at that time, we went through an assassination. We were going through terrible racial strife. Economics were not good. Politics were terrible, as they are now. Awful. We were in a real bad ball of wax. So we needed something very badly. So our reaction probably was ten times the amount that it would have been during a normal time. So because of this angst that we all had and this desire for something to relax with, we reacted to them even more. They were giving us something different. They took the American music idiom of rock and roll. Let's face it. They took the Everly Brothers and Chuck Berry and Elvis and all the people they loved, and they added a little excitement to it. Some energy, which we needed, because we were out of energy. But here were these mop tops who were then followed by all these other mop tops at that time, and they were giving us this new energy. And we needed something to hook onto. We needed a smile. We needed a laugh. We needed something to look forward to with a little bit of positive energy.

Though the group had been rapidly gaining popularity in America since the December 1963 release of "I Want to Hold Your Hand," their *Ed Sullivan* appearance confirmed that Beatlemania was sweeping the country.

Bob Precht, Ed Sullivan's son-in-law, produced *The Ed Sullivan Show*.

Bob Precht: I met Epstein at my father-in-law's apartment at the Delmonico Hotel in November of '63. Peter Prichard, our representative at the Grade organization in London, had set up the meeting. The deal for the appearances for the following February was made at that time. Brian was a cool, confident, immaculately dressed Brit. He knew what he wanted for his boys and made sure he got it. We got along well, and I think he was pleased with how the boys were presented.

About seventy-three million people watched when *The Ed Sullivan Show* went on the air the night of February 9, 1964. That's twenty million more than the 1964 population of England. CBS received fifty thousand requests for 728 tickets to see them live inside what was then CBS Studio 50, a former Broadway house later renamed the Ed Sullivan Theater. That's an acceptance rate of 1.45 percent. The odds of getting into an Ivy League college were better. The Beatles didn't know from Ivy League. And Sullivan's show didn't either. It went into living rooms across the country regardless of race, color, or economic standing.

Vincent Precht: I know they're important—my father has informed me—and I'm a little nervous about meeting them. . . . It's sound check time. My father seats my brother and me in the audience a few rows back. The Beatles start playing "I Want to Hold Your Hand." It's the most beautiful thing I have ever heard.

Bob Lefsetz is an American music industry analyst and critic. He is the author of *The Lefsetz Letter*, an email newsletter and blog.

Bob Lefsetz: Fifty years ago, our nation was changed literally overnight. Guitar sales burgeoned and barbershops closed. Because we'd all seen The Beatles on *Ed Sullivan*.

TOP OF THE MOUNTAIN

Mikal Gilmore is a famed writer and music journalist.

Mikal Gilmore: Their American debut, on *The Ed Sullivan Show* on February 9, 1964, coincided with my thirteenth birthday. I certainly didn't understand everything I was seeing—the girls in the audience sticking their tongues out leeringly at the group, the whole shock-of-the-new effect of these four men who looked so foreign and who commanded their melodies with such assurance and their instruments with such synchronous force—but I knew, as millions of others did, that I was witnessing something seismic.

The next day, The Beatles' performance was the only thing we talked about at school. The girls loved the band members' long hair, the boys seemed unnerved by it, but everyone agreed that The Beatles and their music was an awakening.

In the days following, the arguments and reactions around the country only grew. While Elvis Presley had already shown us something about using rebellious style as a means of change, The Beatles helped incite something stronger in American youth that night—something that started as a consensus, as a shared joy, but that in time would seem like the prospect of power—a new kind of youth mandate.

Bobbie Molina is a Beatle fan.

Bobbie Molina.
COURTESY OF BOBBIE MOLINA

Bobbie Molina: Yeah, on the black-and-white TV in those days. They came on and everybody saw them there, and from that night on it was like magic. They just presented themselves and those two songs, "I Saw Her Standing There" and "I Want to Hold Your Hand." And then when they put the names on the screen, my favorite one to begin with was Ringo. I just loved the way he flopped his head back and forth and smiled. I know that the other guys were gorgeous, but for some reason, it was Ringo. You know everybody had a favorite Beatle. From there on the next day when I went to school everybody was talking about it. "Did you see The Beatles on TV?" I said, "Yeah, oh my god!" My friend liked Paul and the other one liked John and so on. Then in a couple of days, in the candy store we stopped in on the way home, we saw a pack of gum with The Beatles cards in them. So if you bought gum, you would have pictures they took of The Beatles. And we were buying that bubble gum and collecting the cards. My thing was, "Well, I'm going to go to London and see them one day."

Mary Wilson was one of the legendary Supremes.

Mary Wilson: I was not a Beatles fan at all, to be very honest. The music didn't move me because to me it was kind of square. I was one of those black people who was totally into soul music because that is what I grew up with—soul, the blues, and all that kind of stuff. I became a Beatles fan years later because of their style of writing and the artistry in it as opposed to seeing them perform. Seeing them perform to me was kind of square. We still came from that thing where it was black or white. So they were kind of like "white square." And that's not true of all music because I grew up listening to great radio here in America where you heard all kinds of music—the Brenda Lees and so forth. My best friend from England was Dusty Springfield. I liked her more because she was really singing soulfully. For me, that's more of what it was.

Mary Wilson. COURTESY MARY WILSON

Whoopi Goldberg is an actor, author, comedian, and television personality.

Whoopi Goldberg: I remember the song was "I Want to Hold Your Hand," and they played it on the radio, and I thought, "I like that. I like that. Who is that?"

We used to watch *The Ed Sullivan Show* every Sunday night, my mom, my brother, and I. It wasn't even a question; it was just that's what we do. And man, I'd never seen anybody that looked like that. It was like a revelation. And when you're a little kid, you don't know it's a revelation, but it was like the whole world lit up. Suddenly I felt like I could be friends with them . . . and I'm black! [laughs] . . . I never really thought of them as white guys. They were The Beatles. They were colorless. And they were fucking amazing.

The critics had yet to be convinced. They mostly covered their ears, held their noses, and hoped it would pass.

William F. Buckley Jr., *Boston Globe*, September 13, 1964

The Beatles are not merely awful; I would consider it sacrilegious to say anything less than that they are god awful. They are so unbelievably horribly, so appallingly unmusical, so dogmatically insensitive to the magic of the art that they qualify as crowned heads of anti-music, even as the imposter popes went down in history as "anti-popes."

Newsweek, February 24, 1964

Visually they are a nightmare, tight, dandified Edwardian-Beatnik suits and great pudding bowls of hair. Musically they are a near disaster, guitars and drums slamming out a merciless beat that does away with secondary rhythms, harmony and melody. Their lyrics (punctuated by nutty shouts of "yeah, yeah, yeah") are a catastrophe, a preposterous farrago of Valentine-card romantic sentiments.

Science Newsletter, February 29, 1964

The Beatles follow a line of glamorous figures who aroused passionate cries and deep swoons. Most prominent in the 1940s was Frank Sinatra and in the 1950s Elvis Presley. Their glory passed when they got too old to be teenagers' idols or when teenagers got too old to need them.

The same, it is predicted, will happen to The Beatles.

George McKinnon, *Boston Globe*, February 16, 1964

Don't let The Beatles bother you. If you don't think about them, they will go away, and in a few more years they will probably be bald . . . enjoy your Beatlemania. It won't be fatal and will give you a lot of laughs a few years hence when you find one of their old records.

Bobby Vinton's "There! I Said It Again" held the number-one spot for four weeks in January. After their Sullivan appearance, The Beatles pushed it off the charts with "I Want to Hold Your Hand," which held the spot for seven weeks, toppled only by their next single. "She Loves You" grabs number one for two weeks, followed by "Can't Buy Me Love" for five more weeks. Four weeks later, they do it again with "Love Me Do."

In 1964, the group was certainly successful, but Beatlemania was still gathering steam. In April, they occupied the top five spots on the Billboard Top 100, but they had not yet reached "the toppermost of the poppermost," as Lennon liked to say, a play on the popular UK TV show *Top of the Pops*. The record industry still considered them a passing fad destined to disappear. Decca Records passed on them entirely, allowing Capitol to sign them. With "I Want to Hold Your Hand" and "She Loves You," they had achieved dominant worldwide hits, hits that penetrated all cultures. But they had yet to dominate the public consciousness as icons or heroes.

David Glyde played saxophone in Sounds Incorporated and opened many times for his friends, The Beatles.

> **Dave Glyde**: A lot of people had no idea, didn't think they'd be famous. Why would you? It was the pop industry; it wasn't going to last five minutes. Here we are sixty years later and it's still going.

DAVE GLYDE TELLS HOW SOUNDS INCORPORATED MET THE BEATLES

Sounds Incorporated (later Sounds Inc.) was a British instrumental pop group with a heavy saxophone section made up of Major Griff West (aka Dave Glyde), Barrie Cameron, and Alan Holmes. Rowdy drummer Tony Newman and guitarists John St. John and Wes Hunter completed the group. They enjoyed great popularity in south London but really hit the scene in 1961, when the US chart-topper Gene Vincent arrived to tour and his band was denied work permits. Sounds Incorporated backed Vincent to enormous success. Word got out and "Sounds" was requested by all the American rock and roll and rhythm and blues artists coming to the United Kingdom.

Sounds Incorporated. COURTSEY DAVE GLYDE

Dave Glyde: Little Richard, Sam Cooke, Ben E. King, Brenda Holloway, the Shirelles, Brenda Lee—she and I were in love for a time—we were in the midst of all these fabulous people, it was just one after another, so for us it was just like, "Oh my god!" It was great. Us Pommies [English immigrants] had no idea of the prejudice that was going on in any of the industries. We were just working with these tremendous artists.

The Beatles thought we were an American group because we were playing with all the Americans. Otherwise, we would never have met. The bands from the north of England—Liverpool—and the bands from London in the south of England would never get together because they played totally different music. Liverpool was all black music, rhythm and blues, rock and roll. London was all that poppy sound, Cliff Richard, Elvis, the Ventures. If we hadn't been working with people they idolized, we'd never have become friends.

We were in Hamburg with Little Richard. Billy Preston was with him, too. That was his introduction to The Beatles, too. He was sixteen.

It became friendship. George became my closest friend; we got really close. He told us they had a guy who was going to manage them and wanted to introduce us. We were getting along fine without a manager. I thought it would be awkward. And George said, "He's going to take 15 percent straight off and 25 percent if we make over 2,000 pounds a week," which you couldn't imagine, so it was an exciting thing for them. George said, "If we *ever* earn 2,000 pounds a week, he can have the 25 percent because we'll still be earning all that money. . . . That's impossible, it'll never happen anyway. You should go with him because he's great." So he set it up. We finally drove up to meet Eppy at Nems Enterprises because he was still part of the store then. You know his family had a big store. We went up to meet him and he was lovely.

Brian was a wonderful person, so kind and giving. He was the most wonderful and most honest person in the pop industry at the time. No one was like him.

To be completely honest, when I first saw The Beatles, we were in Hamburg with Gene Vincent. . . . So we finished our gig and . . . as we walked out, I heard the announcer go, "De Beatles Oust Liverpool," and I thought I'll go see these guys and see what this is like. I went back in and listened to a couple of numbers. They did "If You Want to Make a Fool of Somebody" and another regular song they did, and I thought they were dreadful. They didn't have any stage presence; they just stood there. And they had the other drummer at the time. He wasn't very good, didn't have any drive. When they got Ritchie [Ringo], the band became totally different. It had momentum. It had a groove, and to this day when Ritchie plays, he has a groove because he played in other bands playing groove stuff, where[as] the original drummer [Pete Best] was a bit of a star. He was a star in the band, the one all the girls loved. The others didn't look at all groovy. They had ordinary haircuts. He had the Tony Curtis hair with the bunch of grapes in front. He was sittin' there with his collar up. He was the cool guy in the band. When he left, all these girls marched in Liverpool with signs, "Bring Him Back."

And Stuie Sutcliffe, who died, was like the major influence in the band. He couldn't play very well, but he was like the groove master. He was fabulous. He had the image that they all thought was great. And he had the best-looking girlfriend in Hamburg.

Stuart Sutcliffe's girlfriend, Astrid Kirchherr, is credited with giving the lads their new haircuts. She also took provocative, now iconic photos of the group. Stuart quit the band and stayed behind in Hamburg with Astrid. A friend of John's from art school days, he pursued painting but died in 1962 of a brain hemorrhage. Today Sutcliffe's paintings are highly collectible.

Dave Glyde: John was his own man. John could never make out whether he was an intellectual or just a dumb guy from Liverpool. He'd do all that artwork and he'd just do all that.

The only one that was a pop star was Paul. He was the only one interested in being a star, being poppy and up front. Ritchie was a hired hand, the new drummer, and wasn't a Beatle yet, eventually became a full member. He played with other bands. Not like the guys, that's all they'd done.

During The Beatles' 1964 US tour, the Righteous Brothers, then unknown, were signed as an opening act. But after several gigs where the audience shouted, "We want The Beatles!" through their entire performance, they quit.

Dave Glyde: After that, the lads said, "Wherever we go on tour, we want Sounds with us." We had the great pleasure of doing everything with them including all those things behind the scenes [laughs], which was another reason they liked us with them, because they had girlfriends and wives back home, and we would get back to England and we would never tell what happened on the tour. It was all between us. All the sex and drugs was kept between us and of course we never told on them and that was always much appreciated.

Michael Tomasky is an American columnist, commentator, journalist, and author. He is the editor of *The New Republic* and editor in chief of *Democracy*.

In that first wave, in early 1964, most adults mocked the group. Highbrow derision came not just from the *Nation* but the *New Yorker*, the *New Republic* and the *New York Times*. This music was dismissed as a little disease that would pass.

And it's true that all this wasn't seen as subversive yet. That would take another year or two, when the disease hadn't abated but, rather, metastasized and started taking over the culture, becoming dangerous.

Bob Lefsetz: We were becoming adults. This was the beginning of the schism, the youthquake, the separation of children from their parents . . . kids were . . . getting their truth from musicians. Unlike today, parents were not their children's best friends, and soon they would become the enemy.

The reason The Beatles are as big as ever, and everyone knows their music, is because of the baby boomers who were there when it happened all those years ago. They can't stop talking about it.

We've stopped talking about so much more. Dozens of hit acts have been wiped from our memory banks. World events have been shortened to "Where you were when Kennedy was shot." "Where you were when Neil Armstrong walked on the moon." There's no discussion of context, just talk about thinly

LIFE BEFORE SHEA

sliced events. But when it comes to The Beatles, . . . it changed the way you look, the way you thought. You can sing those songs by heart and still do. It was so much more than Ed Sullivan, that was just the beginning.

A line was drawn around the Earth that night, a demarcation line that has never faded with the passage of time. It stands today just as deep as the day it was made: before The Beatles and after The Beatles.

The Rascals.

2

THE WAY TO SHEA

MEET SID BERNSTEIN

Despite The Beatles' remarkable success, many still believed the lads from Liverpool were nothing more than a novelty that would soon fade away. Even legendary rock promoter Bill Graham called them "a passing phase . . . symptoms of the uncertainty of the times and the confusion about us." In the fall of 1964, only one man seemed utterly convinced that The Beatles were the real deal and was willing to bet the farm against Graham and the rest of the naysayers. That man was Sid Bernstein, a hardworking, middle-aged New York music promoter. Quiet with a gentlemanly manner, Sid spoke with the hushed tones of a man who had secret information for you. Short and squat with an enormous appetite for both music and food, Sid always knew where to find the best of both anywhere in New York. In between bites, he made history.

Sid loved music from his earliest memory. Raised in Harlem, the hustling son of Jewish immigrants got hooked on sound and rhythm as a kid. Even as a teenager, he had a marvelous ear for talent when he heard it. He managed his first singer while still in high school. When he returned from World War II, Sid's musical instincts led him to the nightclubs and musical venues. He worked alternately as a promoter, manager, and agent with both new and established talent of the era. In this way, he carved out a decent living for himself, eventually booking class acts like Tony Bennett, Ray Charles, Duke Ellington, and Judy Garland. His appearance was far from the typical suits and ties of the day. Whereas they made deals over martinis, Sid's deals were sealed over corned beef on rye with egg cream chasers. Despite his soft appearance, his reputation was as an innovator, a capable man of ideas—and a mensch in a sea of sharks.

Sid Bernstein.
COURTESY DAWN MICHAELS

> **Bobby Vinton**: He was a wonderful guy, just one of those nice guys. I had nothing but high regard for him. People in his position that have all that power usually have an attitude and they don't really talk to anybody unless you mean a lot financially to them, but he was nice to a lot of the little guys I noticed that didn't make a lot of money, as well as to the big guys. So I have nothing but a lot of respect for him. He was smart and he knew his business.

Felix Cavaliere is a founding member of the Rascals.

> **Felix Cavaliere**: He was a special guy. They don't make them like that anymore. He was unique. He could tell you what was going to happen in terms of music or trends. I don't know if you know this, but he was the first to bring karate to New York City and started the whole craze. He brought tae kwon do to Madison Square Garden and nobody had ever heard of it. So that was his forte, his strong points. I always felt he was like a Mike Todd, that type of a guy; he could *see* what you—the public—were going to like.

Michael Lang is best known as the cocreator of the Woodstock Festival.

> **Michael Lang**: Sid was a sweet man with an irrepressible soul and a storied career.

> **Bob Precht**: Sid, of course, was and is legendary, a pleasure to have known. All the good things said about him ring true . . . a gentleman, talented, innovative, capable at getting things done, and delightfully atypical of the agents/managers of the time. . . . Atypical is a bad choice of words. It infers there's a typical and I dislike generalizations of this sort. A better word is "different"; Sid was different. He had a disarming manner, an avuncular presence. You could not help but like him. He was unlike many, not all, the guys out of MCA and William Morris. One had to smile when he entered a room. Utmost respect.

Seth Zimmerman is a writer, music producer, store owner, and vibes coordinator who was mentored by and partnered with Sid Bernstein, Jimmie Miller, and Ronnie Schneider, among others.

Seth Zimmerman: Sid and I worked on a lot of things together to help the world. Whether it's homeless, hungry, whatever it is, Sid and I used to work on projects that were . . . immensely important causes. The real ones couldn't afford us. So when we found organizations like that that couldn't afford us, we would donate our services. Sid was of that ilk. He was an activist from the time he was a teenager. He would hand out leaflets protesting Father Coughlin in the '30s. Nobody did that! He was investigated by the FBI for that. When the two of us traveled together, Sid and I would share the suite and I'd stay up all night just so I could listen to his stories.

When I was starting out, my business partner for many years was Jimmy Miller—a wild man. When the Stones sang "I was standing in line with Mr. Jimmy," that's who they were talking about. Jimmy's father was part-owner of many Vegas hotels. . . . Did you see *Casino*? That's Bill Miller. Bill Miller was at that time truly the most powerful man in the entertainment industry and nobody knew who the hell he was. . . . He was a very special human being.

At any rate, Sid started booking in New York. And he didn't get permission to book acts in New York. Because these are territories and people have rules about who controls this shit, right? It was Bill Miller who stepped up, "No, Sid's a good guy. Look, he's not a shark. Just leave him alone." It was Bill Miller who allowed and opened the door for Sid to be able to book in New York. Nobody knows that story. I got that from . . . I can't tell you who I got that from.

Vince Calandra, a producer, was an associate producer with *The Ed Sullivan Show* in the 1960s.

Vince Calandra: Sid was one of my all-time favorite people. When he did the thing at Shea Stadium, it was just mind boggling.

You know why I loved him so much? He was a great agent. Look, I was a young kid, you know. And Bernie Gross was nice to me. Jerry Weintraub was nice to me. Sid was a pussycat. . . . You know what? Sid also had a set of balls.

Who would book The Beatles a year ahead of the time, not knowing they were going to be what they were when he called Brian? Brian thought he was crazy. But the guy was brilliant. He had that really great "street sense." Behind that street sense, he had a feeling for people. He was a sweet, lovable man. I mean, I loved him to death. He was one of my top five people in the business, and I've known a lot of people. . . . We got along really, really well. We used to go to the Stage Deli once in a while.

Al Bunetta was a Grammy-winning producer, artist manager, publisher, and label founder.

Al Bunetta: In regard to food, he was a real New Yorker, a sophisticated New Yorker in terms of food places. He loved New York. Once he called me really late and told me to meet him at Rumplemeyer's [a New York City institution famous for its ice cream]. I thought it was some official rock and roll business. He picks me up and we drive over to Rumplemeyer's on Central Park South. And he goes in there—and this is a traditional thing they did for him there—they give him a big bowl of freshly whipped cream. And he goes through the entire bowl of whipped cream, and he gets to the last morsel and he makes a face like it's sour. They come running over, "Mr. Bernstein, is there anything wrong?" "Well, it's a little . . . something's not . . . I don't know, but maybe just . . ." "Get Mr. Bernstein another bowl!" And he eats another bowl! Then he asks me to take him to Papaya's—the Papaya King—for hot dogs, and he has six or seven of them at two o'clock in the morning!

Seth Zimmerman: Sid never drank, smoked, or took drugs. His thing was food. So wherever we were going, I'd say, "Oh Sid, I heard that Ben Cohen's favorite ice cream is in the city. Let's go find it." Or he'd say, "You know, the best hot dog is on this street. Let's go get it." And this is what our adventures were. Sid was adopted. His parents were from Russia, but he was from New York when he was adopted—which was why he ate, by the way. Because nobody told him [that he was adopted]! He discovered it. He found his adoption papers inside a pillow in his house when he was nineteen years old. And in those days, it was like being called a "bastard." Some people drink. Some people do drugs or whatever. He ate.

Ronnie Schneider was the business presence for the Rolling Stones, later The Beatles, including the reorganization of their business arm, Apple Corps, and many other legendary artists.

> **Ronnie Schneider**: We worked with Sid for a little bit. We were getting pizza at Mulberry Street, and across the street was Café Roma, so we'd been eating pizza and we were going to go over to Café Roma to have dinner. Then he also wanted to go over to Nate's to get Danish. That's the way I remember. And I still remember him in his largeness. My God, he was eating so much. We were amazed.

> **Al Bunetta**: He had a habit when you would meet him on the street, he would take his right hand and passionately take you by the nape of your neck and draw you toward him. Then he'd say, "Kiddo, how are you? Good to see you!" and would not let you go.

Ronnie Schneider.
COURTESY RONNIE SCHNEIDER

> **Seth Zimmerman**: He called everybody "kid." I think he just couldn't remember anybody's name. You know, he called me kid for thirty years.

> **Ronnie Schneider**: I used to bump into him all over the world in different hotels and the music business and all that. And whenever I'd see him, no matter who I was with, he'd say, "Oh Ron, how are you and your lovely wife?" [Laughing.] Once, he was even right.

Sid had always worked alone. But when General Artists Corp (GAC)—one of the biggest entertainment agencies in the business—invited him to come on board, he considered it. Working for someone else would give him a little more time to himself. He had a very good reason for wanting that. Sid's great charm won the heart of a gorgeous little California redhead, twenty-one years his junior. After a three-year courtship, Sid found himself a newlywed in his mid-forties when he eloped with Geraldine "Gerry" Gale in July 1963.

"My wife Geraldine was an actress and a singer in *The Sound of Music* [on Broadway] with Mary Martin and played the role of a nun. So, I say I married a nun," he loved to say.

Felix Cavaliere: I remember when they married, and she was a Red Skelton dancer. She was really beautiful, but you know, basically you can tell when somebody's into it, sometimes embarrassingly so, and people like to have the lights on them, and sometimes they don't. And you could tell, basically, she was not that enamored with the so-called glamour life of rock and roll, for what it's worth. She was never at the events. You can tell when somebody doesn't really go after the light, the spotlight.

Gerry had other plans. Almost immediately, she became pregnant. Ten months to the day of their wedding, they had their first child, a son.

* * *

Sid stuck with GAC, which afforded him more free time than when he worked as a promoter. He liked to use that time to keep his mind sharp. This time, Sid decided to take some courses at the New School for Social Research in the Village. At one lecture *New York Post* columnist Dr. Max Lerner explained that if people wanted to learn about democracy in America, they must learn about the great world democracies. To that end, Sid visited Hotaling's, an international newsstand then located in the basement of 41 Park Row, the old *New York Times* building.

Looking over the papers from around the world, Sid quickly realized he could read only English, which limited him to the British papers. He smiled thinking about his wartime experience, the wonderful people he'd met there. He bought several papers, including the *London Times*, every Wednesday for months.

Late in the year, Sid browsed through the *Daily Mirror* back in his office. Naturally, when he turned to the entertainment section, his interest picked up. In the columns of theater and club reviews and the latest films, Sid noticed a five-line entry out of Liverpool. A local singing group called The Beatles was drawing throngs of young people and causing "hysteria." It was that word, Sid later wrote in his autobiography, *Sid Bernstein Calling*, that particularly caught his eye.

The next week there was another article about this group The Beatles drawing huge crowds in other surrounding cities. Again, the word *hysteria* was used and again Sid took note.

The next week, not only the *Daily Mirror*, but several other papers carried stories of sell-out crowds for this band. He bought music trade papers *Melody Maker* and

Musical Express. They had features on The Beatles. One of them predicted that the group was about to explode all over England. Sid called an agent in the London office of his agency to suggest he sign this group, but his idea was met with indifference. The Beatles were a fad. They barely had any radio play in the United Kingdom and none at all in the United States. Sid was told to forget about The Beatles. But as weeks passed and the papers continued to report on the excitement caused by these four young men with their long hair, Sid was sure he was on to something. Even the conservative papers had articles about them. Sid went to the head of the agency to plead his case but got the same response. Forget about The Beatles. But he could not forget; and with every passing day, he worried that someone would beat him to the punch. Sid had to promote The Beatles in the United States.

After several failed attempts, Sid finally got a phone number for Brian Epstein, The Beatles' manager: Childwall 6518 in Liverpool. A woman answered, Brian's mum. The most important phone call of his career was essentially "Hi, Mrs. Epstein, is Brian home?" He was.

BRIAN EPSTEIN MEETS THE BEATLES

The Epstein family business was furniture with several stores in Liverpool. Brian and his brother Clive further developed the business to include radios, appliances, and record players. To complement the latter, Brian introduced a record department called NEMS: North End Music Store. It proved so successful that he opened two more, one at 12-14, Whitechapel, just a short walk from the Cavern, a former fruit cellar and air raid shelter that was now a popular Beat club.

Brian Epstein. BY JOOP VAN BILSEN / ANEFO / WIKIMEDIA COMMONS

In November 1961, a couple of customers at the Whitechapel NEMS requested a record by The Beatles called "My Bonnie," recorded in Hamburg. Brian had seen the band's name in *Mersey Beat* magazine and became curious about them. When he heard they were playing a lunchtime gig at the Cavern on November 9, he decided to check them out with his assistant, Alistair Taylor.

Replica of a NEMS store. BY JENNIFER BOYER / WIKIMEDIA COMMONS

TOP OF THE MOUNTAIN

COURTESY OF JOHN BEZZINI COLLECTION

The place was jam-packed. Brian, in an elegant suit, stuck out in the unkempt crowd. He and Taylor stood in the back, and though they couldn't see much of John, Paul, George, and Pete Best, Brian was impressed with what he heard and with the crowd's enthusiastic response to the music. He later recounted it in his autobiography, *A Cellarful of Noise*.

Brian Epstein: I hadn't had anything to do with management of pop artists before that day that I went down to the Cavern Club and heard The Beatles playing, and this was quite a new world, really, for me.... I was immediately struck by their music, their beat, and their sense of humor on stage—and, even afterwards, when I met them, I was struck again by their personal charm. And it was there that, really, it all started.

Epstein saw them several more times then asked to manage them. They signed a five-year contract at Pete Best's house on January 24, 1962. The first thing Epstein did was clean up their tough appearance—new, matching suits, combed hair, no swearing or smoking onstage. John complained but stopped when the changes started paying off.

Now that they looked more respectable, he set about finding them a record deal. The success of his NEMS stores got him meetings with all the major British labels, every single one of which turned down The Beatles.

Then, in early 1962, Epstein met with George Martin, head of EMI's Parlophone label. In May, Martin agreed to sign them, due in no small part to Epstein's hard-sold belief that they would take the world by storm.

With his boys creating "hysteria" in the United Kingdom, Epstein tried to get America to pay attention, but no one would return his calls. Sid was the only interested party from the States to call. Brian was delighted to hear from him. When Sid told him that he planned to present The Beatles in New York's famed concert venue, Carnegie Hall, he was elated. He made a deal for $6,500 for two shows in one day—the most the group had ever been offered. They had never played such a large hall before—2,830 seats. Epstein was worried about filling them. "My boys don't play to empty seats . . . and with no airplay in the States . . ." Sid assured him the airplay would come. Epstein picked a date far enough in the future that he felt they'd be safe. He wanted to wait until the following year. Sid was disappointed but rolled with it. He opened his calendar to February 1964. The holidays would be over. February 12 was Lincoln's birthday, a Wednesday, so chances were good that Carnegie Hall was not already booked. Plus, it was a holiday, and kids would be out of school. Brian agreed. They had a deal.

THE PIED PIPER OF ROCK AND ROLL

Sid's prediction was, of course, correct. Beatlemania spread to the United States during the eleven months preceding the Carnegie Hall gig. Even better, TV variety-show host Ed Sullivan and his wife experienced Beatlemania firsthand while catching a flight at Heathrow Airport when The Beatles were returning home from a tour. Mobs of frenzied girls were all Sullivan needed to see. He called Brian Epstein, learned of the Carnegie Hall appearance, and booked the group to appear on his show three days before. By then all of New York was mad for the mop tops. Sid's two shows sold out in forty minutes. He could have tripled or quadrupled the ticket prices but wanted the kids to be able to afford to go.

Bernstein's Carnegie Hall shows were the first rock concerts ever at Carnegie Hall. Later, the box office told Sid he could have sold enough tickets to fill a stadium. Bernstein only wished he'd booked a second night, but took great satisfaction in knowing his instincts had been right. The Beatles, three of whom had been playing together for six years by this time, were an overnight sensation in America and stood poised to conquer the world. About that, Sid had no doubts.

> **Seth Zimmerman**: Sid, in his hallway, had this thing from the playbill from Carnegie Hall. That was the first time rock and roll had ever been played in Carnegie Hall. They didn't know The Beatles. They thought they were a folk group. So, if you look, they list the musicians as John McCartney and Paul Lennon. They got it wrong.

Elliott Gordon is a producer, talent agent, and promoter at Elliott Gordon Presents and was one of Sid Bernstein's closest friends.

> **Elliott Gordon**: As often as Sid and I spoke about this, he would always look at me with a smile and say, "El, all I did was make the right phone call. I just happened to dial Brian Epstein's number and I've been taking bows for forty years."

Bill Angelos: In my estimation, that would be my definition of a genius. Guys who make the right phone calls at the right time. . . . It just doesn't happen, and I've been here now eighty years, and you're in the right place at the right time, but you just have to do the right thing. You know? So many doors open to all of us every day. But to see the open door is a whole other art form. Believe me. It requires great attention, and your friend Sid had that aspect: great attention to what was taking place.

Seth Zimmerman: It was Sid. This is why I'm talking to you. Because I'm listening to these things on television and nobody's mentioning Sid's name. According to everybody, Ed Sullivan brought them over. Before Ed Sullivan, it was Sid who did the Carnegie Hall concert. Nobody is writing this stuff down.

Sid had paid attention, alright. He was already reaching out to another British group called the Rolling Stones. There were not as popular as The Beatles, but they were on the rise.

As an agent at GAC, Sid was not allowed to act as a promoter, so for Carnegie, Sid used the name Theater Three Productions, which included his partners and moneylenders, Abe Margolis and Walter Hyman. GAC had no idea Sid was behind it, and before the concert, they went after The Beatles and signed them to the agency. Sid was furious that he was not involved when he was the person who brought The Beatles to their attention in the first place. To placate Sid, GAC offered him a bigger office, a secretary, and a fat raise. Sid wanted a vice president position as well. When the company refused, he walked out.

Sid's partners, Abe and Walter, assured Sid that he didn't need GAC; he could make it on his own, he was big now. Sid Bernstein put himself on the map in 1964 by "discovering" The Beatles and booking them into New York's Carnegie Hall before Ed Sullivan had ever heard of them. As the man who brought The Beatles to America, Sid became the conduit for the British Invasion. His phone rang off the hook. His life was wonderful: a beautiful wife, a baby boy, and his business as a promoter was booming. All the bands were calling him to bring them to the United States: Manfred Mann, the Kinks, the Moody Blues, the Dave Clark Five, Herman's Hermits, and the Animals. Kids followed Sid wherever he went and camped in front of his building. He became "the Pied Piper of Rock and Roll," as Elliott Gordon called him, the ambassador for the British Invasion.

Steve Van Zandt is an American singer, songwriter, musician, producer, actor, activist, and author.

Steve Van Zandt: The British Invasion was the most important event of my life. The British Invasion is the reason I play music.

THE CONCEPT

Although Sid Bernstein had great success heralding the British Invasion, he did have stories of the ones that got away. He let an unknown Barbra Streisand and Simon and Garfunkel slip through his fingers by simply not taking the time to hear them. He did allow the great Laura Nyro a chance to audition for him, but he fell asleep while she played. Nyro was furious and never forgave him.

Elliott Gordon: It wasn't really Sid's fault. He suffered from narcolepsy, the sleeping disease. But Sid rarely shared that information, so those who experienced it simply thought he was rude.

When he booked The Beatles and the Stones in New York, Sid easily could have sold more nights. So in a terrible miscalculation, he thought he should book other British bands for three or four nights instead of one or two. Problem was that none of these other bands were The Beatles or the Stones. Sid lost his partners' money on every booking. The last was the Animals. They had a monster hit at the time called "House of the Rising Sun." So Sid booked them for five and lost his shirt—or rather Abe's shirt.

Abe had no money problems. He was in this for the fun and because he liked Sid. The deal he made with him was more than generous. Abe put up all the money. If Sid made a profit, Abe was repaid exactly what he put out and nothing more. If Sid's bookings bombed, Abe took the entire loss.

Abe's wife, Gert, was not nearly as fond of Sid as her husband. After the debacle with the Animals, unbeknownst to her husband, she paid Sid a visit. She let him know in no uncertain terms that he was to stay away from Abe in all ways financial. Walter Hyman folded his tent and left too. Sid found himself at forty-six with no job, no money, no financiers. He was behind in his rent at West Thirteenth Street and Sixth Avenue in the Village, he owed the grocer, and his wife had just given birth to their second child, a daughter. October 1964 blew cold and penetrating for Sid.

"Most guys would have gotten a job," Sid told Elliott Gordon, "but 50 years later, nobody would be taking their picture like they do mine."

The pressure was on to come up with something big, really big. His marriage and his reputation depended on it. Gerry was threatening to go live with her mother. Sick with worry, Sid couldn't sleep. He fed his nerves and fears with some of the best food in New York. *Something really big.* He had a direct line to the biggest act in show business. There was no one bigger anywhere in the world than The Beatles, and Sid's relationship with their manager, Brian Epstein, was strong. But where to book them? Even Madison Square Garden wasn't big enough for what Sid envisioned. Then he remembered what the Carnegie Hall box office told him: he could have sold three times the tickets—"enough to fill a stadium." That's when he got the idea. He would book the biggest act in the biggest venue—a sports stadium. With that thought, the concert business would forever change.

A rock concert in a baseball stadium was unheard of. Even Elvis "the Pelvis" Presley had played only a handful of smaller sports stadium shows back in 1956 and '57 before going into the army, but none of those held more than twenty-six thousand. The Beatles would have to sell more than twice that. No question, their concerts were sellouts, but those were mostly in smaller indoor arenas for ten to fifteen thousand fans. In England they were still playing large theaters. Nothing on this scale had ever been attempted in rock and roll.

> **Bobby Vinton:** I had played large venues, but nothing like that. Nobody worked in a stadium like that, with all of those people.

Friends worried that Sid had lost all rational thought. Family tried desperately to change his mind, but he remained steadfast. There was no doubt in his mind that The Beatles could fill a stadium—but which one? Sid went to his favorite Italian restaurant to think it through. The food was excellent, and they always had a plate for him on the house. Sid weighed the facts over spaghetti smothered in meat sauce. There was Yankee Stadium in the Bronx. It was well-known but also well-worn and in need of repair. No, the immaculate Brian Epstein would hate it. He waved to the waitress for more bread. "More bread for Mr. Bernstein," said the owner's wife.

The Mets had a new stadium in Queens with fifty-five thousand seats. William A. Shea Municipal Stadium was shiny new, and the neighborhood was better. That's it—the perfect place. Shea Stadium it would be. He mopped up the sauce with another piece of bread. Sid Bernstein Presents The Beatles at Shea Stadium. Deaf to the desperate pleas of friends and family, he put his idea in motion.

THE CONDITION

Sid reached for the phone and called his colleague, Jim Thompson, Shea Stadium's general manager. Without revealing his idea, he checked on the possibility of renting the stadium. Thompson told him that the fee for a day was $25,000—close to $200,000 today. Without a pause, Sid said he'd get back to him.

Next, Sid called Brian Epstein. Through their dealings together, Sid had come to know his family and looked on Brian with great fondness. Sid held a special place with Brian and the boys, too, as the first American to show any interest in them, the first to bring them to the States. Their relationship went beyond business. Brian was always happy to hear from him. After the usual inquiries about each other's families, Sid moved on to business. He wanted to bring the boys to New York again.

"I'm planning a US tour late in the summer. I think the first stop in New York fits great. What have you got in mind?" Brian asked.

Sid, his full weight leaning back in his chair, began the big buildup: the boys are breaking all previous rules, setting new records. They are ready for this. Let's book them at a sports stadium called Shea.

"How many does it seat?" asked Brian.

"Fifty-six thousand," Sid replied.

"No," said Brian without a moment's hesitation.

He told Sid they'd been playing 3,500-seat houses with lines down the block, and Brian liked it that way. A concert this size was an enormous risk. If it wasn't a sellout, the naysayers would celebrate it as a failure, confirming their earlier predictions about the group as only a fleeting curiosity. He would never let that happen. *Maybe* he'd take a chance on Madison Square Garden at twenty thousand seats but fifty-six thousand? Absolutely not. The Beatles did not play to empty seats.

Sid would not back down. He could not take no for an answer. He had to get this booking. He sat up in his chair and, in a completely uncharacteristic move, he became aggressive. It was not his usual demeanor; in fact, it may have been the only time in his career he behaved this way. He pushed back hard, backing Brian into a corner with an offer he simply could not refuse.

"I am so convinced that the show will be a sellout," Sid blurted out, "I guarantee you $10 for every empty seat."

Ten dollars was almost twice the price of the most expensive ticket. Mind you, Sid could not buy himself lunch, but this was do-or-die. The offer tumbled out before he could stop himself. It was met with silence. Brian ran the numbers and considered it carefully.

"Well . . . you do know New York better than I do . . . and with these boys, I'm beginning to believe anything is possible."

Sid leaned forward in his chair, "Then we have a deal?"

"Almost . . . I just have a few conditions." The date would be August 15, 1965. For Carnegie Hall, he'd agreed to $6,500 for two shows, but a lot had happened in a year. Now Brian wanted $100,000 against 60 percent of the gross for one twenty-eight-minute show. And he would need a 50 percent deposit to lock the deal.

"Brian, my money is all tied up at the moment."

"I'll hold the date for four months. I'll be in New York in January. If you don't have the money then, the show is off."

"That won't be a problem."

"There's one more condition, Sid. Until I have the 50 percent, you cannot advertise the concert, no announcements, no publicity."

"But Brian, how can I raise the money if I can't advertise?"

"I didn't say you couldn't talk about it."

🥾🥾🥾🥾

It was a tough condition, but Sid, ever the optimist, felt he'd cleared the first hurdle. He'd gotten Brian to say yes. He took a bite of a jelly doughnut. Then he called Jim Thompson at Shea Stadium. He was the first person he told.

"Jim, I want to hold August 15th. I'm bringing The Beatles to Shea."

"Sid, that's amazing. You got it. It's on the calendar."

Bernstein's reputation was all that was needed. Thompson knew Sid was as good as his word. The money would come.

> **Elliott Gordon**: He arranged to rent a stadium when he couldn't pay his own rent. If that's not guts, I don't know what is.

The second person Sid told was his wife, Gerry. She responded differently.

"But where will you get $50,000 without advertising?" she cried. "You offered him $10 for every empty seat when the highest ticket price is $5.65? Oh Sid, what have you done to us?"

ALL CIRCUITS ARE BUSY

A despondent Sid chomped down on the last of a slice of his favorite pizza as he pushed his son in a stroller for their daily constitutional in Washington Square Park. His wife's words from the night before rang in his ears. What was he going to do? How can he sell tickets to a concert without advertising? Gerry was even more furious with him now. Lost in thought, he didn't notice the teenagers who had gathered around him. All the kids knew Sid.

"What's your next show, Mr. Bernstein? Who are you bringing to New York next?"

Sid wiped his mouth with a paper napkin while contemplating how to respond. Brian had said no advertising, but he did tell Sid he could *talk* about the show, so he talked. "Next August, I'm bringing The Beatles to Shea Stadium."

The reaction was instantaneous. The kids shouted and screamed all at once. Some shoved money at him right there. One even fainted. All of them wanted to know how they could get tickets. Sid told them to wait there.

Bernstein pushed his gleeful child at lightning speed—or at least as fast as Sid could go—down the street and straight into his local post office. He put a few dollars down for a mailbox—box 21. Then he returned to the park.

Word had already spread, and a large, eager crowd waited for him. He gave everyone the ticket prices—$4.50, $5.00, and $5.65—and the post office box to mail in their orders. Every day thereafter during his walks with his son, he told kids gathered in the park how to see The Beatles at Shea Stadium next summer.

Three weeks passed this way before Sid had the courage to check box 21. He and Gerry were barely speaking. His entire future was dependent on what was inside that box. He was so nervous he forgot the key and had to ask the clerk for help.

"You're box 21? Hey, Joe, look who's here—Mr. Box 21." Joe came out from the back room to look at Sid, who was puzzled by the reception.

"I gotta see this guy! Wait here a minute," he told Sid, disappearing in the back. He reappeared hauling a giant sack crammed with letters. Sid was astonished. "And there's two more bags just like it in the back." Sid held the counter for support. Never in his wildest dreams did he imagine this. He stumbled for the door.

"Hey, 21! Where you goin'?"

"I'm going to get my car."

At home, Sid and Gerry stared silently at the three bags. Finally, Gerry reached into the bag closest to her and ripped open an envelope. A $20 bill fell out. She opened another: dollar bills and coins dropped out. In a third envelope, she found 30 yen!

"Sid! They're all filled with money!"

Strictly by word-of-mouth through some vast teenagers' international network, news of The Beatles' appearance at Shea Stadium had flown from Washington Square Park around the world. Ticket orders came from Europe, Japan, even from behind the Iron Curtain. Sid was astounded. This was really going to happen. Relief inundated them both. The cold war at the Bernstein home was officially over. Gerry put dinner on. All was right again in his world.

To count these massive piles of mail, Sid once again turned to young people for help. He began with his babysitter, Kathleen, a student nurse. The Bernsteins were popular with the student nurses, who all dreamed of being there when Paul McCartney or Mick Jagger called. Sid asked if she could get eight or ten friends for a temporary job opening mail. Could she!

The following week, eight girls reported for work. Sid and Gerry created an efficient system to process the payments and orders. Every weeknight, the girls came over and repeated this process until all the tickets had been sold. It took three months, and at least three thousand envelopes still remained unopened. The girls were instructed to write "Return to Sender" across them, and Sid mailed them back.

The take was $304,000. Shea Stadium was a sellout. There would be no payments to Brian Epstein for empty seats. So far, Sid's only expense had been for the post office box.

THE HOLIDAZE

Brian Epstein created a whirlwind of activity for the group in 1964. The Beatles embarked on their first US tour in August and September—twenty-five performances in thirty-three days. Then back home for endless TV and press booked around recording studio time. They kept up the pace, leaving for their UK tour in October—twenty-seven performances in thirty-two days. By the time the holidays rolled around, all they wanted and needed to do was be at home with their families. Instead, they found themselves the headliners of a Christmas variety show just like the year before.

Granted, the '63–'64 *Beatles' Christmas Show* had been a blast. The show featured a corny vaudeville-style comedy sketch that offered lots of laughs, with John as the villain who menaces the helpless damsel, George, until Paul, the clean-cut hero, rescues "her" with the help of an elf, Ringo. In fact, the silliness reflected the irreverent humor that made them so appealing. For the boys, it served as a kind of release. Yet at the end of 1964—this surreal year in which The Beatles surpassed every dream they ever had—Brian committed them to a show that dragged them right back to where they were a year ago, doing this meaningless froth.

The Beatles' Christmas Show ran from Christmas Eve until January 16, 1965, at the Hammersmith Odeon, an art deco theater in London that held thirty-five hundred people. The Beatles did two performances a night—6:15 and 8:45—to meet the demand for tickets. Appearing with them were Freddie and the Dreamers, Sounds Incorporated, Michael Haslam—the latter also managed by Brian Epstein—and the Yardbirds, among others.

> **Dave Glyde**: It was weird. Because the tradition of Christmas shows was . . . a show. The producer had this idea they would have The Beatles in this winter scene dressed like Eskimos, right? And they would drag these live donkeys out on stage. You have to wonder why someone needed them to do that and dress

up. . . . "It's got to be entertaining. You can't just have a pop group singing. There's got to be entertainment!" And we'd sit in the dressing room with them and the complaining that would go on: "What the hell is this? Why are we doing this?" Ringo hated it. He couldn't stand it. They all hated it.

The Beatles appeared in two sketches, one with Freddie Garrity of Freddie and the Dreamers and another with emcee Jimmy Savile, host of TV's *Top of the Pops*. They closed the shows with an eleven-song set: "Twist and Shout," "I'm a Loser," "Baby's in Black," "Everybody's Trying to Be My Baby," "Can't Buy Me Love," "Honey Don't," "I Feel Fine," "She's a Woman," "A Hard Day's Night," "Rock and Roll Music," and "Long Tall Sally."

Jim McCarty is the drummer and founding member of the Yardbirds.

Jim McCarty of the Yardbirds.
COURTESY MARY CELESTINA

Jim McCarty: The Hammersmith hired us because we were locals, right down the road in Richmond; that's why we were there. [Laughs.] They worked us hard with two shows a day, but we only played for twenty minutes; so . . . it was easy, and we got to know the boys. We watched The Beatles' set every day, but I don't think they heard us.

On the contrary, George Harrison was intrigued by the Yardbirds' lead guitarist, Jimmy Page. Paul must have been listening too—and liked what he heard—because he sought out the band's opinion on a song he was working on.

Jim McCarty: One day Paul came in and asked us to listen to a song he was working on. He called it "Scrambled Eggs." Of course, that became "Yesterday." For the record, we thought it was great. [Laughs.]

The four lads toiled through four weeks of *Another Beatles Christmas Show*. John particularly hated it. He felt trapped in The Beatles—the act, not the group. He longed to explore the music, but in the studio, not on stage. The constant screaming during their performances made it impossible for them to even hear themselves. The audiences sure weren't listening. And ever since George told a reporter that they loved jelly babies (aka jelly beans), fans threw them relentlessly, unaware of how much they stung when they hit their mark. The Beatles spent half their shows dodging them. Brian apologized, vowed never to book the holidays again, and promised vacation time when it was over, but John remained unforgiving throughout the run.

The Beatles had little time to process their success. The side effects of their unprecedented fame went beyond anything they could have imagined.

Derek Taylor was a respected British journalist and writer who became The Beatles' press secretary and a close friend.

> **Derek Taylor**: In the heyday, the mad days, the presence of the fans in vast swarming buzzing numbers made the living of normal lives impossible. As George has said, by 1965, the novelty of being famous had worn off. He was not to enjoy the fame in the same way again. Everywhere The Beatles lived in the 1960s, everywhere their parents lived, everywhere they had offices or their officers had offices, everywhere they made films or records, wherever they spent their leisure or were rumored to spend it, was surrounded, attended, placed under twenty-four-hour surveillance by fans. They were mainly, but not all, young people; the hard core were the people who were buying the records, but there were a lot of loonies in there too, attending the concerts, screaming in their tens of thousands at the airports.

> **George**: The first big American trip, when we arrived in San Francisco in 1964, they wanted to do a ticker tape parade and I remember saying "No, no, no." That imagery of people being shot, Kennedy, Beatlemania, madness . . . Talk about pressures!

In Montreal, demonstrators burned British flags, and Ringo received a death threat. Later, there was a kidnapping threat for John's son, Julian. A seedy fringe group developed—parasites who wished to profit by selling drugs or by just being in the presence of The Beatles. These hangers-on shadowed the "in crowd," but their threat was not always obvious.

Film director Richard Lester directed The Beatles in *A Hard Day's Night* and *Help!*

Richard Lester: I saw it happen to Paul McCartney once, the most beautiful girl I've ever seen trying to persuade him to take heroin. It was an absolutely chilling exercise in controlled evil.

George: There was more good than evil in being a Beatle, but it was awful being on the front page of everyone's life, every day. What an intrusion into our lives. Even the best thrill soon got tiring. You don't really laugh twice at the same joke, do you, unless you really get silly.

They'd been offered women of every shape, size, and color. They were revered like gods by some. The sick begged to meet them, and handicapped people were brought backstage to be touched by one of The Fab Four. They were brought in wheelchairs and even in oxygen tents. The lads were young, small-town guys without much life experience. Even senior members Ringo and John were only twenty-four. They were simply gobsmacked. The belief that they could heal the afflicted was incomprehensible to them.

George: We were only trying to play rock 'n' roll. What did they think we'd be able to do?

John: . . . We were . . . surrounded . . . all the time, and . . . they would all be touching us. It was horrifying.

Beatlemania was not just a phenomenon. It was the catalyst for a cultural shift that would alter the way people around the world viewed and consumed popular culture . . . the incomparable electricity between performer and audience that turned the music into a movement, a common experience into something sublime.—press release for *The Beatles: Eight Days a Week—The Touring Years*, directed by Ron Howard

3

GOING FOR BROKE

THE COUNTDOWN BEGINS

The year 1965 was a whole other animal for just about everyone. Television went from black and white to color and, in a flash, brought a vivid, often shocking kaleidoscope of events into the nation's living rooms: the bloody jungles of Vietnam, attacks on Martin Luther King Jr. and his Freedom Marchers, flower power and the hippie movement, the birth control pill, the Peace Corps, Timothy Leary and the advent of LSD, the Watts riots, the miniskirt, James Bond, the space race, Elizabeth Taylor and Richard Burton's brazen affair—while both were married to other people. "Yeah! Yeah! Yeah!"—1965 was a new dawn. Young people filled with hope and curiosity were ready and willing to explore the new territory before them. The generation that would become known as the baby boomers had not yet considered themselves a powerful, united force. But against the backdrop of a remarkably volatile year in our nation's history, a spirited, curious new generation would soon claim the decade for their own. And Shea would become ground zero.

Sid Bernstein: It was beyond amazing.

SEALING THE DEAL

January 1965

    Ringo proposes to Maureen Cox at the Ad Lib Club. She says yes.
    Alan Freed, the "Father of Rock 'n' Roll," dies in Palm Springs.
    "I Feel Fine" holds the number-one spot for two weeks, toppled by the Supremes' "Come See about Me."
    Beatles '65 goes number-one and stays there for nine weeks.
    The New York Jets sign quarterback Joe Namath.
    Hullabaloo, a weekly pop music variety show, premieres on NBC.

Sid Bernstein, wiping the remnants of an éclair from his mouth, arrived at the fabled Plaza Hotel for his appointed meeting with Brian in his suite. They had spoken by phone, but this was the first time they had seen each other in nearly a year, and Sid was caught off guard. Brian seemed different—anxious, uptight, with deep circles under his eyes. Sid surmised that Beatlemania was taking quite a toll on his friend. He asked about Queenie, Brian's mum, and about his brother, Clive. Brian filled him in about family and the boys. Then the two men got down to the business of Shea. Sid had offered a guarantee of $100,000. On this day he was to present Brian with a check for half the amount.

    "Have you got the retainer?" Brian asked.

    "I've done better than that," he said, handing him a check for the entire amount.

    "I must say, Sid, I wasn't sure you'd have the retainer, but I never dreamed you'd raise the whole amount with the no-advertising restriction I placed on you."

    "Brian, I wish we'd agreed to three shows. I could have sold out all of them." Sid never told how he had done it. He was still in awe himself. The youthquake knew no borders.

    "Well, this is stupendous, Sid. I can't wait to tell the boys."

    "Take care, Brian," Sid said, and he meant it. He was worried about his friend.

    Bernstein made his way slowly back to his office, gnawing a warm pretzel. Just as he eased his wide girth onto his leather chair, the phone rang. Andrew Loog Oldham, manager of the Rolling Stones, wanted Sid to bring the Stones back to New York. Sid had just the venue in mind. Within minutes, he'd set up a date for the Stones at the Academy of Music. May 1 for one afternoon show—$10,000.

Oldham was delighted. Sid stopped to drink in the moment: the Stones in May and The Beatles in August. Not a bad day's work. He reached for the rest of the pretzel and finished it off.

Though Sid couldn't know, he had good reason to worry about Brian. Epstein's schedule had grown threefold. He had taken on more clients, which meant more pressure. And, yes, Beatlemania was certainly part of the cause of his weary look. "Eppy" saw 1965 as a peak year for Beatlemania, a time to cash in as aggressively as possible on what he predicted would be their biggest concert tour. But that source of income would not last forever, so he was also researching sources of long-term income. In 1963, he formed Northern Songs Ltd., a publishing company, with Dick James, John, and Paul. Now he toyed with the idea of going public, trading shares on the London Stock Exchange to save on capital gains tax. At the time, John and Paul were paying 83 percent tax, providing much-needed revenue to the British treasury. There was much to consider, but the added pressure seemed to bring out the worst in Brian. His drug use increased. He had always dabbled with uppers and downers, but recently he'd stepped up his regime. Along with his morning amphetamines, he'd added something to relax him at night, and washed it all down with cocktails. Brian harbored a secret life on the edge. Unlike the boys, who spent their recreational hours at clubs like the Ad Lib with friends and good music, Brian was gambling at private establishments like the Renaissance or the Curzon Club and losing large sums on a single roll of the dice without blinking an eye. When he did win, he rarely picked up the money. There was no pleasure in it. When not gambling, Epstein sought the companionship of paid male lovers: young, tough, often crude. Not even The Beatles knew the extent of his private life.

Meanwhile, Sid was hired as the talent coordinator of the new NBC prime-time hit *Hullabaloo*, a pop music variety series that showcased the leading pop/rock acts of the day and featured the *Hullabaloo* dancers, a team of four men and six women. The show shot mostly in New York at 30 Rock, and Sid booked many of the British Invasion groups including the Stones, the Animals, and Freddie and the Dreamers, who were managed by Brian Epstein. Even Brian made a few appearances on the show.

Epstein on *Hullabaloo*. BY NBC TELEVISION / WIKIMEDIA COMMONS

TOP OF THE MOUNTAIN

Dawn Michaels was a dancer who grew up in western New York and New Jersey.

Dawn Michaels. COURTESY DAWN MICHAELS

Dawn Michaels: I was raised by my father and my grandfather. My father loved me; I know he did. He was just a very angry sort, very militaristic, very German, . . . always yelling and screaming. Dancing was always my—I think that's just what I was born to do. I think my father probably put me in ballet classes initially in conjunction with his father, who was a wonderful, kind man. . . . That's where it started. . . .

My first jazz class—at thirteen—was phenomenal. I studied with Luigi. He was brilliant, absolutely the master of jazz—"and a five, six, seven, eight!" I spent all my time there. I told my father I didn't want to live with him anymore. I didn't want to go to school. I hated school. All I wanted to do was dance. I left home very young. I was very unhappy. I was on my own in Manhattan at thirteen. I lived with a girl, about twenty-two. . . . I was a baby. That's when I started getting my first shows.

In 1965, I got back from eight months in Japan in *West Side Story* and immediately did *Hullabaloo* with Donna McKechnie, Suzanne Charney, Lada Edmund Jr., Michael Bennett, and Patrick Adiarte. He was always my partner in any shows we did because he was so short. I was only five feet two. I did the first six or seven episodes with choreographer David Winters, who was amazing.

Susan Silva, another *Hullaballoo* dancer, also discovered dance at a young age.

Susan Silva: One day when I was three, my mother took me to the movies to see *The Red Shoes*, and from that day on I wanted to dance. We were very poor. My father was sick from the time I was one. He died when I was nine. They came out of the Holocaust. I am first-born American, so we didn't have any money, on welfare. I was able to get scholarships all the time. We lived in Washington Heights, and I was able to get into a school downtown. When I was a couple of years older, maybe six, I got a scholarship to the Metropolitan Opera Ballet School, and they had very famous tutors back then: Anthony Tudor, Mark Kraft, all the big names in ballet. That's really what I wanted to do, but my back was never strong enough for pointe. I wound up switching into jazz, modern, that kind of stuff, and I was on scholarship at another

GOING FOR BROKE

Hullabalo Dancers front: Donna McKechnie and Suzanne Charney. Second row center: Dawn Michaels with Lada Edmund, Jr., seated atop the "B."

school—the New Dance Group, Forty-Seventh Street, downtown Manhattan on the West Side.

I did *Hullabaloo* and some TV. Dawn and I did the *Soupy Sales Show* together. We did five shows a day at the Paramount. We'd do a show, then they'd screen *Operation Petticoat*, then we'd do another show. I did some off Broadway, but dancers don't make a lot of money. I schlepped makeup for some private makeup company along with my dance bag. In between auditions, I would sell makeup in office buildings for extra money.

Alan Freed. BY TGC-TOPPS GUM CARDS / WIKIMEDIA COMMONS

Alan Freed wasn't just the King of Rock and Roll, he coined the term. . . . As a disc jockey, he conquered Cleveland, then New York. . . . He brought the music he loved directly to fans by organizing live shows. One show in Cleveland in 1952 sold 10,000 tickets and turned 20,000 more away. Police . . . shut down the show before a riot ensued. Historians call this the first rock and roll concert. Freed's popularity soared. . . . Fans saw him as a . . . champion of the music and the new way of life that came with it. But many disapproved of Freed's influence on the youth. Freed's stage shows . . . drew a racially mixed crowd . . . popular . . . with kids. . . . To the rest, Freed became the enemy. . . . In late 1959, a House subcommittee turned its attention to payola—the practice of disc jockeys taking money or gifts from record companies in exchange for playing their artists. Freed and six others were indicted for misdemeanor commercial bribery charges which dated back ten years. Freed pleaded guilty to 2 of 99 counts and paid a $300 fine. . . . [W]eeks later came Federal charges of tax evasion on the payola money. Freed, defeated and drinking heavily, could no longer fight back. He died January 20, 1965, of kidney failure brought on by cirrhosis of the liver. He was 43. His ashes rest where it all began for him—in Cleveland. American youth was safe again.

Mr. Rock and Roll. COURTESY DONDI BASTONE COLLECTION

Originally published in *The Plain Dealer*, January 21, 1965.

NEW DAWN IN THE UNITED KINGDOM

The Beatles looked forward to 1965 with anticipation. They had conquered America and were bursting with confidence—and money. As they struggled to live with their fame, they adjusted quickly to the fortune that accompanied it. John, Cynthia, and Julian moved to a twenty-seven-room estate in exclusive Weybridge. Ringo and Maureen would soon be their neighbors. George and Pattie bought a bungalow in exclusive Claremont Estate and an Aston Martin DB5. For the time being, Paul was happy, living comfortably with Jane Asher and her family in London. When the Christmas show finally ended, they planned their promised getaways. Paul and Jane took off on February 4 for Hammamet, Tunisia, as far from the screaming fans as they could get. Once there, Paul finally began to relax. Wandering the grounds of his vacation villa, he discovered a small amphitheater with amazing sound. Inspired, he started working on a new song. He finished it in the villa in a lavish bathroom complete with a sunken bath that provided the perfect acoustics. McCartney called it "Another Girl."

John and Cynthia left on February 25 to join producer George Martin and girlfriend Judy Lockhart-Smith for twelve days in St. Moritz in the Swiss Alps. The trip was a much-needed break from the stress that plagued the couple. Beatlemania had not been kind to their young marriage. While John dealt with the chaos and intrusion of fame, Cyn tried desperately to hold on to some kind of normality for the sake of her child and family. But this trip was about letting go of all that. They adored George and Judy and were determined to have fun.

"A delightful couple and perfectly matched," Cynthia later wrote in her autobiography, *A Twist of Lennon*. "He was elegant with a sly humor."

On the first day, after a ski lesson, Cyn and John heard Judy screaming with laughter from their connecting room, yelling for them to come in. There was George in black tights and his long underwear, posing daintily like a ballerina. He made a move, tripped, and promptly broke his foot. During the next eleven days while the others hit the slopes, Martin sat glumly in the lodge, his foot in a plaster cast as all passersby asked on which mountain it happened.

"Yes, George," John would chide him. "Which mountain were you on?"

George Martin: It was during this time that John was writing songs for *Rubber Soul* and one of the songs he composed in the hotel bedroom, while we were all gathered around nursing my broken foot, was a little ditty he would play to me on his acoustic guitar. The song had the provisional title "This Bird Has Flown." It became "Norwegian Wood."

John: "Norwegian Wood" is my song completely. It was about an affair I was having. I was very careful and paranoid because I didn't want my wife, Cyn, to know that there really was something going on outside of the household. I'd always had some kind of affairs going, so I was trying to be sophisticated in writing about an affair, but in such a smoke-screen way that you couldn't tell. But I can't remember any specific woman it had to do with.

Meanwhile back at home, Ringo and Mo got news that changed everything. She was pregnant. Ringo, over the moon, could barely keep the secret, but first things first. On January 20, Ringo picked the most public place for the Swinging London set to propose to Mo—the Ad Lib Club. Hidden away on the top floor above the Prince Charles Cinema in Chinatown, pop stars like the Stones and the Kinks, Long John Baldry, the Animals, Eric Clapton, fashion designers Mary Quant and Jean Muir, and actresses Hayley Mills and Julie Christie table-hopped and carried on above the traffic in Leicester Square. Even Princess Margaret stopped in occasionally. The crowd loved the music policy: exclusively black American soul and blues records—Motown and Stax. The Ad Lib was where it was happening, the center of the scene.

Alfred "Alf" Bicknell was The Beatles' private chauffeur from 1964 to 1966.

Alf Bicknell: The Ad Lib Club was . . . the first place I started taking them after the Christmas Shows. . . . We would turn up and they would be whisked in. . . . They were The Beatles and that was that.

Paul: Alf was special . . . loyal . . . someone you can trust, and . . . a likeable person. I was always glad to have had him on our side.

The Ad Lib was the perfect spot. Ringo popped the question. Maureen was ecstatic. Champagne flowed and friends cheered.

Cynthia Lennon: I loved Maureen, she was down to earth, honest . . . madly in love. . . . [T]heir future seemed very secure; and it was a very happy occasion for all.

The couple had met in the early days at the Cavern Club. Mo was in the audience and Ringo walked her and her girlfriend home one night. That was it for them both. The attraction was immediate. They were soon going steady.

Tony Barrow, press agent for The Beatles from 1962 to 1968, coined the phrase "The Fab Four."

> **Tony Barrow:** We were not at all surprised by the fact that Ringo and Maureen were marrying. In the privacy of The Beatles inner circle, they had acted like a pair of lovebirds, cuddling . . . at clubs and parties for as long as we could remember. The only thing that shocked us was how quickly the wedding plans were put together.

February 1965

Ringo marries Maureen Cox.

The Beatles record the soundtrack for their new film, *Help!* They complete the album in six days.

Petula Clark has a monster hit with "Downtown."

John passes his driving test.

George has his tonsils out.

A Hard Day's Night album is released in the United Kingdom.

The Beatles fly to the Bahamas to shoot their second film, *Eight Arms to Hold You*, eventually retitled *Help!*

Cannibal and the Headhunters release "Land of 1,000 Dances," which climbs to number thirty on the Billboard Top 100 chart.

Malcolm X is assassinated in New York.

President Johnson orders more bombing in North Vietnam.

Petula Clark. COURTESY DONDI BASTONE COLLECTION

Cannibal and the Headhunters. COURTESY DONDI BASTONE COLLECTION

The wedding plans involved a top-secret ceremony at the register office in Caxton Hall; there would be hell to pay if word leaked out. Brian, like 007 on a mission, handled every last detail, his duty as both Ringo's best man and his manager. Even the other Beatles were told only a day or two beforehand. The reason for the secrecy went beyond Mo's delicate condition. Disruptive fans followed the happy couple wherever they went. And if Mo was alone without her Ritchie, female fans actually scratched and spit at her. She dared not even go alone to the bathroom at the Ad

Lib. The eighteen-year-old hated the spotlight and was adamant that her nuptials not be spoiled.

Things happened so quickly that Paul was not able to make it back from Tunisia. "It was just a drag I wasn't there because I would have enjoyed it." He would have been among a group of ten or fewer. Beyond the couple's parents, John, George, and Brian, few were included that early Thursday morning, February 11. The bride got her wish. Her special day was not marred by fans or the press.

John later joked to a reporter that Ringo had forgotten to get appropriate boutonnieres for George and himself. "We were going to wear radishes, actually." George, who arrived by bicycle, wryly announced the score: "Two down . . . two to go."

It was the perfect private moment during a year in which privacy was at a premium for all of The Beatles.

Cynthia Lennon: Every single thing they did or said was repeated, reported and analyzed. Individual freedom had become a luxury of the past. The inevitable step they took out of their dilemma was a step in the direction of drugs and the resultant freedom of the mind. I felt the acceleration of our circumstances grasping us all . . . and I was frightened. John was too involved to be objective; and it was always his nature to take the plunge whatever.

Mary Wilson: It was not overwhelming for us as teenage girls to grab the number-one spot from The Beatles over and over. What was overwhelming for me in terms of being good is that we three little black girls had grown up in the civil rights era right there. And our parents were always telling us, "When you go out, you represent the black community. You've got to be your very best. Whatever you do, you have to be your very best." My mother couldn't read or write. The one thing she wanted to see was her children go to college. This was a great thing for her. Our parents didn't really want us to be singers. They wanted us to become doctors and lawyers and schoolteachers and nurses and those kinds of things. That's the kind of household we grew up in. So the singing was something that totally destroyed our family's hopes of us ever becoming anything . . . until we got the hit record.

I remember saying to Eddie Holland, one of the members of the Dozier Holland group, . . . "Eddie, we need to have a hit record, because if we don't, our parents are going to make us go to college." We were still the underlings, you know, who weren't on top. We were opening the shows and things like that. So that hit record in August 1964 changed our lives; I mean totally changed our lives. "Where Did Our Love Go" became number one. And it moved us further than what any of us, our parents, thought about. It was amazing.

GOING FOR BROKE

Pot smoking was an accepted and relatively harmless pastime of members of the pop world. . . . If they hadn't taken something to relax they would have gone completely crazy. . . . [T]hey smoked it whenever they could.

The nearer John travelled to the center of the whirlpool, the farther away I pulled. . . . I wanted desperately to hang onto sanity; John needed to escape from his reality. I understood completely, but couldn't go along with him.

Where Did Our Love Go? COURTESY DONDI BASTONE COLLECTION

The Beatles' song publishing company, Northern Songs Ltd., was floated on the stock exchange February 18, 1965. Previously co-owned by John Lennon, Paul McCartney, Brian Epstein, and Dick James, it was restructured, with 1,170,000 of the company's five million shares made available to the public. The bulk of the shares remained within The Beatles' circle. Lennon and McCartney retained 750,000 each; NEMS Enterprises controlled 375,000; Harrison and Starr each held 40,000; and Dick James and his business partner Charles Silver each retained 937,500. Initial investors were required to purchase a minimum of 200 shares at a value of £39 ($875 today), putting them well beyond the reach of most fans. When trading opened, the price dropped sharply but soon recovered to double the opening value. At the time of floatation, Northern Songs was valued at £2.7 million (more than $6 million). The company's previous owners each sold a quarter of their holdings, netting Lennon and McCartney a tax-free windfall of £94,270 ($2,171,119 today) each. However, the company was now vulnerable to future takeover attempts, and the floatation eventually led to the songwriters losing the rights to their songs.

EIGHT ARMS TO HOLD YOU

On February 22, The Beatles left for New Providence Island in the Bahamas to shoot their second film titled *Eight Arms to Hold You*, Ringo's idea. The boys couldn't wait to trade cold, dreary London for a tropical island. Wives and girlfriends were not invited.

The production charted a Boeing 707 to fly seventy-eight cast and crew members. Costars Eleanor Bron and Victor Spinetti were already onboard when the boys arrived, along with director Richard Lester, producer Walter Shenson, Brian, Neil Aspinall, their tour manager and an old school friend of Paul's, and Mal Evans, road manager and the six-foot-six former bouncer at the Cavern. More than fourteen hundred enthusiastic fans came to see The Beatles off, a sight that always moved them. They waved back enthusiastically then boarded the flight.

> **George**: We smoked . . . all the way to the Bahamas. Mal smoked cigars to drown out the smell.

John spent a good deal of the flight chatting up Eleanor Bron. An accomplished stage and television comedian and writer, she would make her film debut in *Eight Arms to Hold You*.

The flight stopped in New York to refuel. Much to the disappointment of US Customs and Immigration, neither The Beatles nor anyone in their party left the plane. None of them was in any shape to do that.

Upon arrival in the Bahamas, a rather disheveled Fab Four held a swiftly organized press conference at the airport. Then they were whisked to their suites at the Balmoral Club near Cable Beach, Nassau, where they relaxed and later enjoyed a midnight swim in the ocean.

Shooting began a few days later.

HIGH TIMES

March 1965

Motown releases Brenda Holloway's "(What Are You Gonna Do) When I'm Gone" and it rises to number twenty-five.

Early Beatles is released in the United States.

"Eight Days a Week" shoots to number one followed by "Stop! In the Name of Love" by the Supremes.

Martin Luther King leads 3,200 marchers from Selma to Montgomery. State troopers attack with clubs and tear gas. The violent response is broadcast on television.

Klansmen shoot and kill Viola Liuzzo, a mother of five from Michigan, as she drives marchers from Montgomery back to Selma.

Brenda Holloway. COURTESY DONDI BASTONE COLLECTION

In their first film, *A Hard Day's Night*, all the boys shared center stage. Richard Lester shot it in black and white, which lent a documentary air to it, presenting an exaggerated version of the boys. Each of them had their "moment" in the film, but Ringo emerged as the standout with some real acting ability.

This time, Lester shot in color, and the boys shared the screen with a stellar team of British actors including Eleanor Bron, Victor Spinetti, Leo McKern, and Roy Kinnear. For once, Ringo was at the center of the story, a position that he greatly enjoyed. The others had less to do. John was overheard to say that he felt like a bit player. Furthermore, the story seemed a bit silly: a mad scientist and his klutzy assistant fiendishly plotting against Ringo and the boys, who are also being chased by an Eastern cult.

Eight Days a Week.

John: I realize, looking back, how advanced it was . . . a precursor for the *Batman* Pow! Wow! on TV. . . . But he never explained it to us . . . partly because we were smoking marijuana for breakfast during that period. Nobody could communicate with us.

Paul: We were pretty disinterested. . . . In all truthfulness, we spent a lot of that film slightly stoned.

Richard Lester: They were high all the time we were shooting. But there was no harm in it then. It was a happy high.

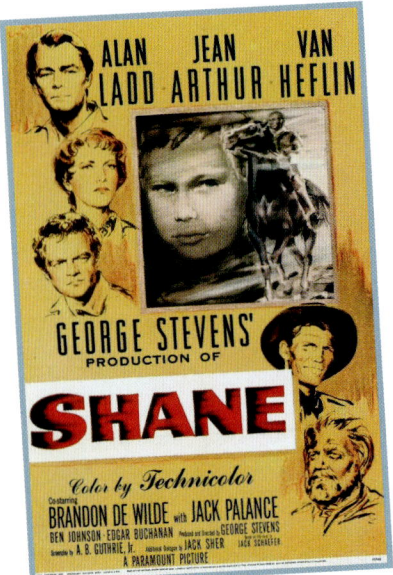

Shane earned deWilde an Oscar nod. COURTESY OF BEVERLY WASHBURN

Spectators barely noticed, if at all. Mesmerized by the group's presence, crowds gathered on the beach to watch the filming. Many forgot themselves completely and walked straight through a shot to ask for autographs.

The arrival of an American movie star was a welcome distraction, especially one with his own stash. Brandon deWilde was a sensation on Broadway at the age of seven and an Oscar nominee at ten—the youngest to date. His youthful good looks and small build that helped propel him to child stardom worked against him as an adult. At twenty-two, he wanted to take time off from acting and do something else. He could sing, and like most people his age, music was a huge influence. He convinced close friend Gram Parsons and his band to make a recording with him. After that, Brandon was hooked. He longed to make an album and could barely believe his luck that he and his wife would vacation in the same place as the most famous rock and roll band in the world. Others say he knew The Beatles were going to be there and the meeting was no accident. Regardless, introductions were made, and Brandon and his wife were invited to their suite.

Inside, Brandon lit a joint. George thought him a James Dean type. Paul remembers deWilde as "a nice guy who was fascinated by what we did. A sort of Brat Pack actor. We chatted endlessly, and I seem to remember writing 'Wait' in front of him and him being interested to see it written."

The most significant occurrence during the filming happened to George, who celebrated his twenty-second birthday a few days after he arrived. Though unaware at the time, he received a special gift that day. The boys were standing by with bicycles off camera waiting for the call for action when a small man in orange robes walked toward them. Swami Vishnu Devananda handed them each his book on hatha yoga. Two years later, it was the very book George needed as his spiritual journey unfolded.

The shoot in the Bahamas wrapped on March 10. The boys returned home but were off again two days later, this time to Austria for more shooting. None of them had ever been there before and only John had any experience on skis. Despite this and without any instruction, producers recklessly put their four stars in a very dangerous situation.

George: They took us up a mountain, gave us our boots, gave us our skis, and gave us a push.

Fortunately for all, the boys survived and managed to avoid serious injuries. But, except for Ringo, the shoot held little interest for them. John was bored stiff. He hadn't been home in more than a month. He wanted to see his family and, even more, he wanted to write songs. Instead, he was playing second fiddle in an inconsequential movie. Already struggling with his role as a Beatle, he now felt completely lost.

When the shoot wrapped on March 22, The Fab Four happily headed home.

ROLLING STONES ARE ROCK AND ROLL'S BAD BOYS

When you know the kind of troubles the Stones got into later on, this one is laughable. But for a group coming up in 1965, public urination did not go down in the plus column.

On March 18, the Stones were driving home from a gig in London when bassist Bill Wyman broadcast his need for a bathroom. They pulled into the next gas station, but when Bill asked the forty-one-year-old attendant, Charles Keeley, where he could "have a leak," he was told there was no bathroom. Keeley later described twenty-nine-year-old Wyman as "a shaggy-haired monster wearing dark glasses."

"Absolutely bursting to go," Wyman later wrote, "I returned to the car, where I explained what had happened. [Mick Jagger] took my hand and said, 'Come on, Bill, we'll find you a toilet.' Then Mick, myself, Joey Page and [Brian Jones] returned to the attendant and asked him once more if we could use the toilet. He started screaming at us."

That was when twenty-one-year-old Mick reportedly announced, "We'll piss anywhere, man." The other three began chanting the phrase. They marched outside and all relieved themselves on the wall of the station, with Keith joining in. The police arrived almost immediately, and the incident made all the papers the following day.

ONE STEP FORWARD, TWO STEPS BACK

Back in the States, Sid Bernstein moved forward with the concert plans. The simple, wooden stage he'd commissioned cost twice the original estimate. And the insurance estimate had come in low by 50 percent. Bernstein's profits were taking a big hit.

Then came the call from Mayor Wagner's office: "Sid, we have a problem. This Beatles concert isn't going to work after all. We're going to have to call it off."

Bernstein fell back in his chair. The City of New York had presented the mayor's office with a long list of security issues it feared could result from the concert—everything from a traffic jam in the Holland Tunnel to the safety of the fans on city property at the ballpark.

It seemed that the prospect of fifty-five thousand highly excited, screaming youngsters could be dangerous. The mayor expressed concern. His representative suggested that someone from the mayor's office sit in on all the meetings with the police department, traffic control, and security.

The biggest logistical problem the city faced was how to get the band in and out of the stadium. Sid held many meetings about it, consulted with Brian, then met again with staff from the various departments. Eventually they came up with a solution. The Beatles would leave the Warwick Hotel in a limo and head to a Wall Street heliport where a waiting helicopter would fly them directly into the stadium. The mayor's office rejected that immediately. Should excited fans rush the field, it would be a catastrophe. No, the helicopter would land across from the stadium on the grounds of the New York World's Fair. A waiting car would then drive them through the outfield gates, across the field, and under the stands.

The police, Mayor Wagner's reps, Sid, and Brian all felt that this was a good plan. They reversed it for The Beatles' exit. When the boys finished their last song, the outfield gates would open. As they took their bows, the car would drive up to the back of the stage. The Beatles would hop in the car and go out the back gates before the fans realized what was happening. Sid assured Brian that they would use the same plan for President Lyndon B. Johnson.

That covered the entrance and exit, but what about security in between? This was unchartered territory, unprecedented in rock and roll. And just who was the guinea pig for this maiden attempt? Only the most popular band in the world! Beatle fans were a new animal and wildly unpredictable. If enough of them broke loose, they could hurt the boys or themselves. Every effort must be made to curtail what could become a dangerous situation.

It eventually was decided that the first layer of defense between the crowd and the stage would be three rows of metal barricades surrounding the entire infield and spaced so that they would have to be vaulted one at a time—if any errant fans managed to get past the stadium ushers and security patrol. Beyond the stadium staff, fans would have to contend with a large contingent of New York City cops, three hundred moonlighting cops, and forty karate black belts—Sid's idea. If anyone could make it past all that to the stage, Mal Evans and Neil Aspinall would be waiting for them. On top of that, even more cops and mounted police were at the ready outside the stadium: an estimated two thousand security personnel in all. At last, everyone seemed satisfied.

With Brian Epstein paid in full, Sid finally had free rein to promote the concert. He had the biggest event in the history of show business, and no one knew about it.

Obviously, Sid couldn't sell more tickets, but—always a showman—he wanted to whip people into a frenzy, get the press writing about it. Today we call it "creating buzz." He handed out more than a thousand press passes and supplied several radio stations with tickets for giveaways.

As far as Cousin Brucie's listeners were concerned, no one communicated joy and excitement better than he did. When The Beatles first arrived, the Radio Hall of Famer was instrumental in launching them in the United States, heralding their records and broadcasting live interviews from their hotel suite in 1964.

> **Cousin Brucie:** As we were getting closer to Shea Stadium, Beatlemania was getting crazy. It was reaching a fever pitch. You couldn't go to the bathroom and flush a toilet without seeing a picture of John or Paul. I mean, it was there, everywhere you went. Sid used to like to paste things up. He loved to stick up stickers. Jesus Christ . . . I swear every time I went to a toilet or a men's room—"Sid Bernstein Presents!"

In selfless Bernstein fashion, Sid invited Ed Sullivan to introduce The Beatles onstage. Though it was Sid who first discovered and booked them in the United States and though it was Sid pulling off this incredible event, he knew Sullivan was best for the show. The number-one man on US television had a relationship with the band. The public responded to that relationship. Of course, Sullivan responded too. He loved the idea and immediately agreed to introduce them at Shea Stadium. What's more, he wanted to film it and began talks with Brian Epstein. A deal was struck—sans Bernstein.

Epstein announced to the press: "I am arranging to have the whole fantastic performance filmed, and, if it is suitable, I will arrange worldwide release for it almost immediately afterwards."

The anticipation on the East Coast was already in fourth gear. Fans, desperate for tickets, followed Sid wherever he went and even camped in front of his apartment building. Neither Sid nor The Beatles ever really considered that during that year, from concept to concert, thousands of stories were set in motion for thousands of American youths who dreamed and schemed to see The Beatles at Shea Stadium.

DREAMERS AND SCHEMERS

Bobbie Molina was born in Texas, but her father's military career brought the family to New York, specifically the Bronx, in 1962. The adjustment was difficult for the eleven-year-old. She struggled to find things in common with her new classmates—until February 9, 1964.

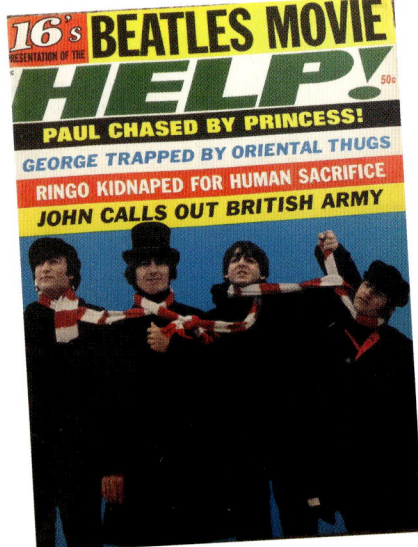

16 Magazine.

Bobbie Molina: From the moment I first saw them on *Ed Sullivan*, . . . it was like magic. I started buying *16* magazine to keep up with the latest news, to keep up with them and their girlfriends. It was so wonderful, every month a new issue would come out.

One time I was reading dreams that fans had and of everybody else getting things they wished for. And I thought, "What if I wanted to wish to see The Beatles? I'd really like to see them. . . . I'm going to write to them and tell them that I want four tickets to go see The Beatles in concert when they come to New York." With that, I sent it out with a stamp and everything, like the old days.

Eric J. Adams, eight, spied on his sister, fourteen, and her friends playing Beatle records and mooning over them. He was intrigued.

Eric J. Adams. COURTESY ERIC J. ADAMS

Eric J. Adams: My sister Denise was a perfect teenager and was already a massive Beatle fan and had collected all sorts of memorabilia. I absolutely knew who The Beatles were, and I knew their songs. I loved them and I was just starting to understand music and pop music. . . . I remember watching The Beatles on *Ed Sullivan* for the first time. That was a big event in our house.

Fifteen-year-old Mary Louise Streep—Meryl—kissed her Paul McCartney poster goodbye then dashed out the door for high school in Bernardsville, New Jersey. She had yet to hear about the Shea Stadium concert, but when she did, she would give one of her greatest performances in hopes of going.

Buddy Perst, a bartender at New York's tony Delmonico's, served a new customer, an obvious wiseguy who called himself Blackie. It was slow and the two men conversed casually, easily. Blackie liked Buddy and returned frequently.

Linda Eastman had suffered a few rough years. She left college after she lost her mother in a 1962 plane crash then rebounded with marriage and a baby. The marriage came to an amicable end in 1965. Linda and her daughter, Heather, left Arizona and returned to Manhattan for a fresh start.

While working as a receptionist at *Town & Country* magazine, she dated photographer David Dalton. She scrutinized his technique, fascinated with his style: how he used light, the way he worked with his subjects. She loved everything about photography. Linda invested in some cameras and began shooting what interested her—rock and roll musicians. *Town & Country* was impressed enough with her work to let her shoot the Rolling Stones at a public relations party on a yacht. The shoot became a defining moment for her and set her on a trajectory to become Mrs. Paul McCartney four years later.

Linda Eastman: It was an incredible time for all of us. There was a lot of hope in the air. We were all young and away from home for the first time in our lives. We were also working for ourselves. It felt like being in Hollywood at the time when Hollywood was relatively innocent. We all knew something was happening, but it hadn't been discovered yet.

BODY AND SOUL

April 1965

NEMS Enterprises, The Beatles' management company run by Brian Epstein, announces that Ringo and his wife Maureen are expecting their first child in September.

The Beatles attend the launch night of Downstairs at the Pickwick, a London nightclub.

The New York World's Fair opens, running for two six-month seasons: April 22 to October 18, 1964, and April 21 to October 17, 1965, playing host to more than fifty-one million people.

The lads appear on five TV shows in a week: *Thank Your Lucky Stars*, *Top of the Pops*, *New Musical Express Music Awards Live*, *Eamonn Andrews Show*, and *Ready, Steady, Go!*

The Beatles win two Grammys: Best New Artist and Best Performance by a Vocal Group for "A Hard Day's Night."

Students for a Democratic Society (SDS) leads its first march against the Vietnam War.

Florida State University students protest.
STATE ARCHIVES OF FLORIDA, *FLORIDA MEMORY*

Filming continued on *Help!* in and around London and at Twickenham Studios. George had a seminal moment on the set. Director Richard Lester was shooting the interior kitchen and dining scenes at the Rajahama Indian restaurant when something positively life-altering occurred.

> **George**: We were waiting to shoot the scene in the restaurant when the guy gets thrown in the soup and there were a few Indian musicians playing in the background. I remember picking up the sitar and trying to hold it and thinking, "This is a funny sound."
>
> I felt as though I knew it. It was everything, everything I could think of. It was like every music I had ever heard, but twenty times better than everything all put together. It was just so strong, so overwhelmingly positive, it buzzed me right out of my brain.

The discovery of the sitar and Indian music was the first step on George's path to spiritual enlightenment; it also gave him a new status within The Beatles. George's talent was never in question, but he was the baby of the group, still just a teenager when John was married with a child on the way. No question he was a bit daunted by his older mates, the writing team of Lennon and McCartney. He became "the quiet Beatle," not because he was more subdued than the others, but because he was still struggling to find his place. But as he grew to love this new music and the spirituality it brought with it, he took the lead, influencing the group's music and later their minds by bringing them all to India to study transcendental meditation.

Around this time, George and Pattie and John and Cyn attended a dinner party at the home of a prominent dentist, John Riley. They'd dined together a few times, seen him at the clubs. The London club scene was a small world. As George said, "Everybody knew each other."

John and George and their wives had after-dinner plans to see their friend Klaus Voormann performing in a trio at the Pickwick Club, a small restaurant with a stage. They were preparing to go when their host said, "At least finish your coffee." They politely did so but felt pressured to stay. George recalled that Riley's girlfriend, Cyndy Bury, had "enormous breasts" and sensed that the couple was hoping for some kind of sexual orgy. John got the same feeling. They were both wrong. Riley crouched in a corner with John and confessed that he'd dosed the four of them with

LSD. He said it was very pure, having originated with Michael Hollingshead, the man who first "turned on" psychologist Timothy Leary. Leary was famously—or infamously—associated with the drug. Fired from Harvard for experimenting with it, he became its leading proponent, encouraging people to "turn on, tune in and drop out."

Lennon was furious. "How dare you fucking do this to us?" He grabbed George and whispered to him, "We've had LSD." The dentist had put it on the sugar cubes they'd dropped in their coffee. George had never heard of the stuff and didn't know what John was talking about. He soon found out.

The two couples grabbed their coats and left.

> **Alf Bicknell**: There are various stories surrounding this incident: that they went on to a club or that George was driving . . . not true. I can swear to that.

According to Alf, they explained to him what had happened and were panicky. None of them knew what to do. Alf made the decision for them. He'd take them back to George's house. Once in familiar surroundings, they were able to relax a bit. Alf said they were hallucinating a great deal, but after a short time, he felt it was safe to leave them.

> **John**: It was terrifying, but it was fantastic.

Terrifying, John felt, because it caused the boys to look deep within themselves. George felt it immediately, like a "light bulb" went on in his head. He'd found the perfect means with which to explore his spirituality.

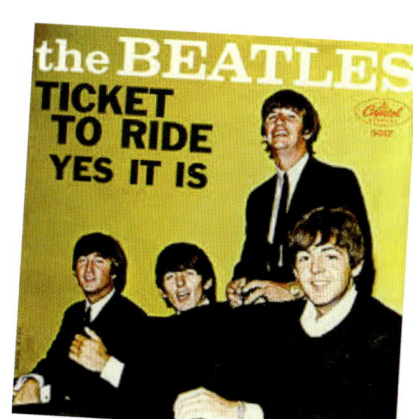
Ticket to Ride.

> **George**: John and I spent a lot of time together from then on and I felt closer to him than all the others, right through until his death.

"Ticket to Ride" topped the UK chart for a full month. Critics praised their new sound, noting a new and different approach to the music. It hit number one in the United States for a week but was knocked off once again by the Supremes, this time with their hit "Back in My Arms Again."

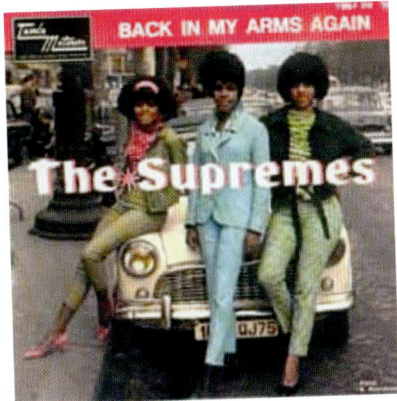
Back in My Arms Again. COURTESY DONDI BASTONE COLLECTION

Mary Wilson: We had five consecutive number ones between '64 and '65. And you know, five consecutive number ones for anybody was great. We kind of helped keep America up there on that high level with the English people.

We traveled around the world in '65. We did the Motown Review tour over in England. And then we went to Paris and recorded. We were starting to do TV shows with say, Lena Horne. A lot of the actors and actresses came to see our shows in London at the Talk of the Town, all kinds of people. We hung out with Princess Christina in Sweden. She would drag her brother to our shows. He's now the king of Sweden. We were doing all those things in 1965. . . . And we were girls, which was something different—especially being black. When we would go to radio stations and TV shows, you didn't see women who were CEOs. They were bringing the tea and the coffee.

So here we were at the top of the heap. This is the time when we were up there. And we became really major stars . . . competing with these male people—the Elvis Presleys, The Beatles. As far as we were concerned, The Beatles were on the same level as we were. But Marvin Gaye, Stevie Wonder, the Miracles, the Temptations, the Marvelettes, Martha and the Vandellas—for us, it was all the Motown artists who were big stars. We were happy because now we were on the same level as these people we had admired from earlier on. The Beatles were not in our mind. But, you know, America was kind of besotted by The Beatles.

HELP!

May 1965

The Rolling Stones play the Academy of Music in New York City.

Draft card burnings in the United States increase.

Muhammad Ali knocks out Sonny Liston for the world heavyweight title.

Paul McCartney and Jane Asher saw Gene Barry perform at London nightclub Talk of the Town and spoke to him after the show, ending the night at Downstairs at the Pickwick.

John and Cynthia explore the Cannes Film Festival. John is interviewed by reporter Martin Agronsky for CBS's *The Merv Griffin Show*.

Paul and Jane visit Portugal.

"The Beatles (Invite You to Take a Ticket to Ride)"—the final BBC radio session.

Early May saw The Beatles again packing their bags, this time for a three-day *Help!* shoot on nearby Salisbury Plain. A wide-open space of three hundred square miles, the plain was teeming with prehistoric monuments like Stonehenge. And though it was spring, a bitter cold wind swept the unprotected land all week.

Each day Alf drove the boys from the Antrobus Arms in Amesbury, Wiltshire, to the filming location, Knighton Down in Larkhill, in a black Austin Princess limousine. The reliable driver was prepared for anything, loading the car with whatever the boys might need: aspirin, hot tea, sandwiches, cigarettes, magazines, a change of clothes.

The car was left unlocked in the hotel garage during the day, and items of clothing, cigarette butts, and other "souvenirs" were taken by fans.

The film shoot shared the plain with troops from 3 Division, Royal Artillery, who were on exercises there. The army generously allowed their tanks and other equipment to appear in the film. They were long, difficult days, and all were happy to get back to the hotel.

> **Alf Bicknell**: All of us . . . were staying together in the hotel. . . . [After] dinner . . . a couple of tables would be pushed together and this wonderful ensemble of artists would hold court regaling each other with stories till the wee small hours. Eleanor Bron was an expert at telling tales, acting everything out; she had everyone in stitches.

Eleanor made an impression on The Beatles, too. Paul thought of her later when he wrote "Eleanor Rigby," and rumors flew that she and John had a fling during filming. A bit older, cultured, charming, and Jewish, Eleanor fascinated John.

After dinner, some of the gang played poker, primarily Alf, Leo McKern, and Ringo as the core group. Apparently, McKern was the shrewdest player. Alf lost a small fortune to him.

One morning on the way to the set, Alf noticed in the rearview mirror that John was staring at him. Without warning, he grabbed Alf's chauffeur's cap and tossed it out the window. Alf panicked, fearing he'd been fired. "Don't worry, Alf," said John, "you don't need that. You're one of us now." All four boys were grinning ear to ear.

A few days later, Alf again caught John watching him. Lennon leaned forward, "Do you want to come on tour with us to America?"

Alf Bicknell: With John you only got one chance and then the matter would be forgotten, never to be repeated. I said "Yes!" immediately. . . . I was exploding inside with excitement.

The three-day shoot on Salisbury Plain mercifully came to an end on May 6, and The Beatles returned to Twickenham Film Studios.

Close to this time, Brian showed up on the set, keyed up and behaving "rather secretively" Paul remembered. He collected the boys and huddled with them in a dressing room. He had special news: the prime minister and the queen were awarding them each an MBE. They would be Members of the Order of the British Empire. Epstein expected a big reaction, but all he got was puzzled looks. One of the boys asked what that was. He patiently explained that it was an honor given in exchange for service; in this case, all the revenue they'd brought to England. They would receive their medals from the queen at Buckingham Palace in a special ceremony.

None of them had a problem with it in the beginning. Ringo thought it was cool. But when the group began asking around about what it all really meant, "then the cynicism started to creep in a little," Paul recalled. John was flat-out embarrassed.

John: We all agreed it was daft. . . . Then it all just seemed part of the game we'd agreed to play. . . . We'd nothing to lose, except that bit in you that said you didn't believe in it.

They told Brian they were not going to accept, but Epstein convinced them otherwise.

John: We had to do a lot of selling out then.

On May 9, after filming in London and Twickenham all day, The Beatles headed to London's Royal Albert Hall to see Bob Dylan. After the show, they dropped by his suite at the Savoy with singer Alma Cogan. Beat poet Allen Ginsberg slipped off the arm of a couch into John's lap as an icebreaker. The lads stayed a bit longer, then spent the rest of the evening nightclubbing in London.

Alma Cogan, called the "Girl with a Giggle in her Voice," was already a star when she met The Beatles in early 1964. In fact, she was the highest paid British female entertainer in the 1950s and '60s. During rehearsals for *Sunday Night at the Palladium*, the guys flipped for her sense of humor, and she adored them. As she did with all her showbiz friends, after rehearsal, she invited the boys back to her home in Kensington, where she lived with her mum and sister.

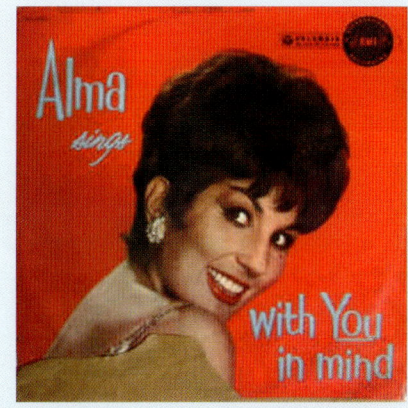

Alma Cogan. COURTESY DONDI BASTONE COLLECTION

The boys had to be smuggled out of the theater before the show ended. They got to Alma's before she did—and before she had a chance to tell her mum they were coming. No matter, they were warmly welcomed. It almost felt like home with Alma's mum making tea and sandwiches. Alma finally arrived with a few other performers. They talked easily, played parlor games, socialized. The Beatles felt so relaxed that they returned many times to see "Mrs. Macogie," as they called Alma's mum.

Paul: They were very nice, Alma and her sister Sandra. . . . I saw a documentary about John Betjeman who said that when he got out of college there was a country house to which he was invited. And he said, "There I learned to be a guest," and that's what was happening to us at Alma's flat. There we learned to play charades, and we started to do it at our own parties. It was just a little learning curve. We'd never seen anything like this, but we liked a laugh; so we played charades with Stanley Baker and with Bruce Forsyth; he was always at those things, Bruce was absolutely great. . . . They were all a little older than us, probably ten, twelve years older than us, but they were great fun, very confident showbiz people who welcomed us into their circle. It was exciting for us, we would hear all the showbizzy gossip and meet people there that we hadn't met before; Lionel Bart would sometimes be there, Tommy Steele, Lionel Blair would nearly always be there.

And in Alma's heyday, Princess Margaret, Audrey Hepburn, Cary Grant, Sir Noel Coward, Ethel Merman, Danny Kaye, and Sammy Davis Jr. were all regulars.

Paul once awoke with such a complete melody in his head that he was afraid he might have subconsciously "lifted" a song he'd heard somewhere.

Paul: I took it round to Alma Cogan at her flat in Kensington and asked, "What's this song?" because Alma was a bit of a song buff; there are a lot of people around like that and I admire them a lot. Alma was very songy, knew a lot of Jerome Kern and Cole Porter and that kind of thing, and she said, "I don't know what it is, but it's beautiful."

The beautiful melody would eventually be called "Yesterday."

Alma's friendship with Brian Epstein was even closer. Both were more ensconced in old-fashioned showbiz. They were closer in age and both from Jewish homes. Eppy brought her gifts from his travels and even took her home to meet his mum. Brian published a song she wrote, "I Knew Right Away," and Paul played tambourine on the recording and the flip side, "It's You." Friends thought they would marry despite Brian's sexual preference.

But many believed she was most fond of John. He'd nicknamed her "Sara Sequin" and spent hours with her and her family, although he preferred to visit when no one else was around. Sandra said her sister was dating Brian Morris, manager of the Ad Lib, who was mad about her.

Cynthia recounted that she and John used to look on Alma as "out of date, unhip." In fact, back in art school days, John ridiculed her with a ruthless imitation. There's no question that a close friendship grew between the two artists, but just how close? After Cynthia's death in 2015, John Lennon's biographer published her previously unreleased quotes regarding Cogan.

> **Cynthia Lennon**: In the flesh she was beautiful, intelligent and funny, oozing sex appeal. . . . John thought I didn't know anything about him and Alma, and I never let on. Now that I think about it, with all the emotion gone out of it, I can see the attraction. Alma was about eight years older than John . . . Don't forget that Yoko was also older than John by about seven years. Like Yoko . . . Alma was a very compelling woman.

> **Sandra Cogan**: I knew about Alma and John, of course, but it was something no one admitted because John was married. We had a very strict Jewish upbringing and my mother would never have approved of a relationship between Alma and a married man.

Alma remained close to the group, but sadly, less than a year later, she was diagnosed with ovarian cancer. She died in October 1966, just thirty-four years old. John was bereft.

> **George**: John was potty about her. He thought her really sexy and was gutted when she died.

In 1986, EMI released a special double album celebrating Alma's career. Paul wrote liner notes.

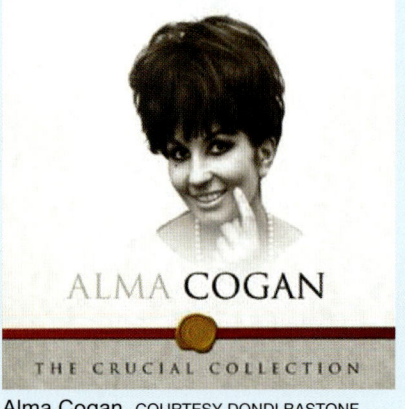

Alma Cogan. COURTESY DONDI BASTONE COLLECTION

May 10 and 11 marked the final two days of filming for the boys. It was a location shoot at Cliveden House in Berkshire, home of Lord and Lady Astor. Their magnificent estate stood in for Buckingham Palace. The mood was upbeat. The crew and the lads were, by this point, very chummy, friendly enough for some good-natured ribbing. One of the crew made a remark about the boys being a bit out of shape. The jibes continued over lunch until one group challenged the other to a relay race.

The Astors had an enormous front lawn, close to 150 yards. Teams consisted of six—The Beatles, Neil, and Alf against four or five other teams: the electricians, transportation, cameramen, and the like, with each runner covering seventy or eighty yards. The Beatles ran the first four legs, then Neil.

> **Alf Bicknell**: The five of them had given me a tremendous start. . . . Towards the end of my sprint . . . I could hear this guy behind me—he'd made up all this lead the boys had given me.

Alf, thirty-five, was determined not to let the boys down. Besides, he knew he'd never hear the end of it if he lost. As he approached the finish, he flung himself over just seconds before his opponent. The boys gathered around him amid cheers and backslapping. Even the Astors got in on the fun, presenting The Beatles with a crystal vase. "I think Paul took that," recalled Alf. And somewhere there is an 8-millimeter home movie of the entire event shot by a crew member—if it survived. With that, fifty-four days of shooting came to an end.

Soon after, the Shadows guitarist Bruce Welch hosted Paul and Jane at his villa on the southeast coast of Portugal. For the entire five-hour drive from the Lisbon airport, Paul worked on the lyrics for his "dream" melody. The moment he arrived, he wanted to sing "Yesterday" for Bruce. "I knew it was magic," said Welch.

BEATLES VERSUS STONES

Amid his ongoing meetings and arrangements for Shea, Sid Bernstein welcomed the Rolling Stones to New York on May 29—but not with open arms. The Stones were always great to him, but their fans were a rougher bunch, rowdier than Beatle People. After he booked The Beatles at Carnegie Hall in February 1964, he followed with the Stones. But raucous Stones fans broke seats and did other damage. Sid was persona non grata at Carnegie Hall for some time after that. He was careful about where he booked the Stones from then on. For their next appearance, he decided on the Academy of Music. It was bigger than Carnegie and cost less to rent so it was a win for them both.

Bill Angelos: The Stones had a reputation as the bad boys of rock and roll. . . . Well, that's true, and there was a manufactured animosity between the two groups that really didn't exist, but someone managed to conjure it up.

Ronnie Schneider: There was always a competition between The Beatles and the Stones. They showed respect. Everybody loved each other but there was always a competition. . . . The similarity between The Beatles and the Stones was that the sum was greater than the parts. It would be amazing the things they'd create. I would watch each group get together; there would be a magic that each one added to the things they were doing. I was in sessions with them all. That was the magic. Watching how somebody would come in with an idea and how it would expand and grow and become something fantastic at the end. That was just one little thing from working with them.

Mick Jagger: We had sort of a lot of rivalry in those early years and a little bit of friction, but we always ended up friends and . . . still are. Those were some of the greatest times of our lives.

COME TOGETHER

June 1965
John, George, and Ringo attend the premiere of Richard Lester's *The Knack (and How to Get It)*.
Paul and Jane return from Portugal June 11. "Yesterday" is finally finished.
UK EP release of *Beatles for Sale*.
A press conference follows the announcement that The Beatles are to be awarded MBEs. Nine former recipients return their medals.

US album release of *Beatles VI* will hit number one on the charts and stay there for six weeks.

Mary Louise Streep turns sixteen.

Paul records "Yesterday" with a string quartet.

The Beatles leave for a fifteen-date concert tour of France, Italy, and Spain on June 19. It's their first concert in six months and their first time in Italy.

On June 24, John Lennon's second book, *A Spaniard in the Works*, is published. He will sell more than one hundred thousand copies.

Lyndon Johnson authorizes first US ground combat forces in Vietnam.

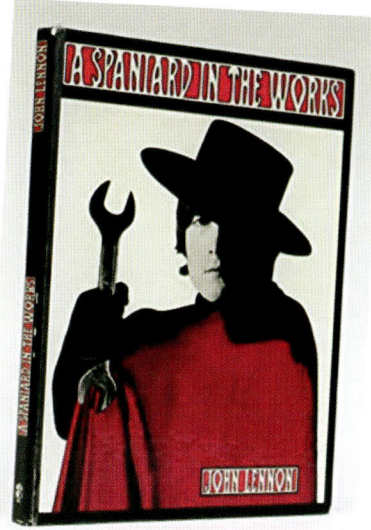

BARBARA REW COLLECTION

A hand-drawn invitation for The Beatles to attend Allen Ginsberg's thirty-ninth birthday in London arrived at NEMS. The party was June 3 at filmmaker David Larcher's basement flat in Chester Square.

Birthday boy Allen got smashed and removed all his clothes except for his underwear, which he wore as a hat. A "Do Not Disturb" sign around his penis completed the ensemble. Just then John and George arrived with Cynthia and Pattie. The boys caught sight of Ginsberg and scanned the room for photographers. Relieved to find none, the couples entered and got drinks. Allen kissed John's cheek and the two chatted. John told him that the magazine he drew in art school was called *The Daily Howl* in tribute to Ginsberg's poem. John was in no way offended by Ginsberg's lack of attire, but the boys didn't stay long. Barry Miles, owner of Indica Gallery, where John would meet Yoko Ono the following year, asked John why he was leaving so soon. He whispered, "You don't do that in front of the birds!"

Ronnie Schneider graduated from the University of Miami, where he majored in accounting. Some of his friends planned to take some time for themselves, backpacking through Europe or climbing mountains, but not Ronnie. He had a job, and he couldn't wait to get to it. He was on his way to New York for what would be the rock and roll adventure of a lifetime.

Ronnie Schneider: I left Miami a week after graduation in June ([I] didn't go to the ceremonies even though I was supposed to be onstage with the dean's list graduates—my mother was pissed). Same thing I did the two years prior. Moved to New York for good in '65.

TOP OF THE MOUNTAIN

Seventeen-year-old Denise Mourges graduated from high school with big dreams of dancing professionally. She didn't know it, but she was about to land the job of a lifetime.

Denise Mourges: I was living on the West Side of New York in the theater district. I was working with Murray the K as a dancer. My sister, our friends, we were all part of this little group that was in the right place at the right time. We had the right look because it was honestly us. We were young American girls that were taken with the music and the energy of the time.

I had just gotten an audition for a group called the Pussycats. United Artists was putting it together. They had the movie out, *What's New, Pussycat?* and they wanted to send this girl group around the country singing "What's New Pussycat?" I was waiting for contracts.

Dawn Michaels: I was in rehearsal for a road show of *Kismet*, which was suddenly cancelled. The choreographer was Hal Loman. Hal invited me to be part of a group that was being put together to back up rock and roll stars called the Discotheque Dancers. It was not my usual sort of gig, but I had nothing else lined up and Hal was great, so I said yes.

Denise Mourges: We read about this call at a small studio up on Eighth Avenue . . . and my sister and my friend and I went. We'd go for every audition. Open call, we went.

I walked in the door and the choreographer said, "You. Get on the floor." I just did a couple of turns and no big shakes, you know. And they said, "You got the job."

I was like, "Oh, my gosh!" Because I already had a job. I was playing it cool because I didn't want to say no. You went on a lot of auditions, but it's not like you got a lot of jobs. The singing thing sounded more exciting, so I was holding out for that. But the gig for United Artists fell through at the last minute. . . . That's how I got it—by default.

Dawn Michaels.
COURTESY DAWN MICHAELS

Susan Silva: I was eighteen and already working in New York as a dancer early in my career. Back in the day, they used to have open calls, and hundreds of dancers would show up and it would go on for a whole day until they pared it down to eight girls. I heard about a closed audition for the Hal Loman dancers and got in through Judy, a friend of a friend. We did not know it was for The Beatles. The girls had to have longer hair. It was an act that a very big management team—Management Three—was putting together not only for this, but for other shows. We did the Latin Casino with Robert Goulet, Norm Crosby. We did Tony Martin, Marvin Gaye. But looking back, this audition was really mainly for The Beatles. I really could have cared less about them [The Beatles]. I was not into them. I was into my career, not into the hundreds of screaming girls. . . . To me, this was a job, a kind of an unusual job.

Tony Martin program.
COURTESY DAWN MICHAELS

Dawn Michaels: We were at rehearsal for a job with Tony Martin and Nancy Aames. We were downstairs having lunch in this little lunchroom off the rehearsal space and the choreographer came in and said, "You're opening for The Beatles."

The other girls started screaming, and I said, "Who are The Beatles?" I really didn't know. Then I called my cousin and told her; and she said, "You're *what*?"

Denise Mourges: Oh my God, I mean, can you imagine? We were over the moon! I mean, it was unbelievable. Of all the people in the United States and in the world who would have died to go and it was us—five girls and a boy. It was really extraordinary.

Discotheque Dancers from left to right: Denise, Ronnie, Steve, Dawn, Judy, Susan. JAMES J. KRIEGSMANN

I went home, and my little group of four or five girlfriends were there hanging out with my mom. I came in and said, "I'm going on tour with The Beatles!" and the next thing I knew, I had hands around my throat! It was like they wanted to kill me. I mean, not really . . . but yeah! It was crazy. I couldn't believe it.

Other members of the Discotheque Dancers included Judy, a teacher on summer vacation, Ronnie Schwartz, and Steve Levitt.

Dawn Michaels: Ronnie toured with us, but she was not a good dancer at all. [Laughs.]

Susan Silva: I have no clue why Judy was there. Ronnie couldn't dance much, but Judy was worse.

Dawn Michaels: They were go-go dancers but weren't formally trained. Ronnie and I roomed together and became best buddies on the tour. Jerry Weintraub was our manager. Steve and I appeared on *The Dick Cavett Show* saying we'd be touring with The Beatles. We backed Marvin Gaye at a show in New Jersey. By this time, I had already worked with some of the biggest names on Broadway and in music, so this was not a heady experience for me . . . but by the time this came to be, I realized the importance of it, of touring with The Beatles and I was thrilled. This was the first time I'd been involved with so much drama, with people being hysterical over you.

COURTESY DAWN MICHAELS

Denise Mourges: Dawn was very well known. She was on *Hullabaloo*. *Hullabaloo* dancers were amazing. You know, the regular troop. They were fine dancers, very accomplished dancers. Much more so than me and all our friends. They worked in Broadway shows. They danced, danced, danced. Very studied. I studied with some of the same people, but their accomplishments were tremendous. That's why Dawn was the lead dancer.

Bobbie Molina: Two or three months passed, then lo and behold, I got this letter in the mail from *16* magazine. Inside were four tickets . . . yellow with their pictures on them . . . and a letter that said, "Congratulations, Barbara. You won the tickets through *16* to see The Beatles in concert that you requested in your dream."

I was stunned! Oh my God! I'm going to get to see The Beatles! So with that, I told my family, my mother, my father.

"Pa, I'm going to go see The Beatles."

He said, "You're only thirteen. Ask your cousin Margaret if she wants to take you. If she says yes, then you can go. But that's the only way you're going to go. You're too young to go all the way into Flushing."

My cousin was very conservative. She listened to other kinds of music. I was the only one in the family to like this "new music." I pleaded with her to take me. Finally, she agreed . . . and then I had to wait the whole summer for the concert.

A New Jersey rock and roll band called the Rascals was packing them in at the Barge, a floating bar with live entertainment in the Hamptons.

Joy Musiker Cohen grew up in Northeast Philadelphia, a daughter of liberal parents, the oldest of three children. In 1965, she was fourteen years old and a full-fledged Beatlemaniac.

Joy Musiker Cohen: I can't remember how I heard about the concert—either our local radio station or the "bible": *16* magazine. And that's probably more likely. That's where I got all of my information.

Our local radio station, WIBG, had a contest, and since it was ninety-nine on the dial, they had ninety-nine winners. All I had to do was send in a postcard, and back then it was a penny a postcard. I sent twenty-five, so it cost me all of 25 cents to go to Shea Stadium. I was the third winner picked. [After] the first two winners were picked, I was moping around the house thinking, "I'm not going to get picked," and sure enough I did. You might have thought I had won the lottery when that happened. We had ten minutes to call back the station and I had somebody else do it because I was too nervous. Then we called my dad at work to tell him to listen for my name on the radio. The DJ mispronounced our last name, which everybody did back then, and my father's only concern was, "Those bastards mispronounced our name." That became legend in our house.

A few days later, a friend from my homeroom, Joyce Montgomery, called me. She was also a winner. That was very nice because back then I was painfully shy, and thank God I had somebody to go with.

In mid-June, the British press announced that The Beatles were to receive the MBE from the queen. For the first time in history, nine other recipients of the honor returned their awards.

The Beatles' British tour promoter, Arthur Howes, believed the honor for the boys was well-deserved.

Arthur Howes: The biggest thing The Beatles did was to open up the American market to all British artists. They alone did it. I had brought over lots of American stars, but nobody had gone over there. They just weren't interested. By opening up the States, The Beatles made an enormous amount of money for this country.

Ringo: Some old soldiers sent their medals back. They just thought that it was too much.

George: I brought it home and put it in the drawer; later I wore it on the *Sgt. Pepper* album cover. So did Paul.

In 1971, John admitted to Paul in a letter that the thought of accepting the MBE had him "squirming" with discomfort. He gave the medal to his Aunt Mimi, who proudly displayed it over her mantle until John took it back. He returned his in 1969 with this brief note:

November 25th, 1969

Your Majesty,

I am returning this MBE in protest against Britain's involvement in the Nigeria-Biafra thing, against our support of America in Vietnam and against "Cold Turkey" slipping down the charts.

With love,

John Lennon

While the controversy continued, The Beatles got down to recording the *Help!* album.

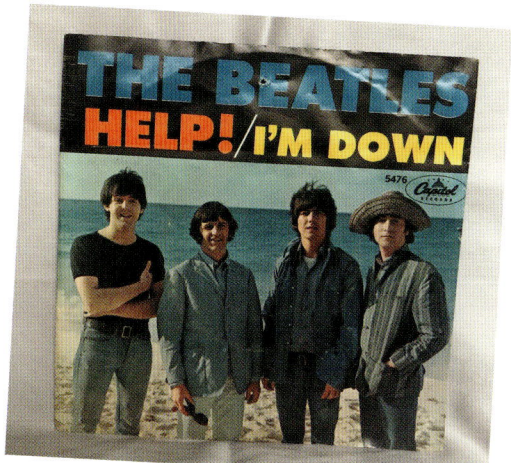

John: Most people think it's just a fast rock 'n' roll song. I didn't realize it at the time—I just wrote the song because I was commissioned to write it for the movie—but later I knew, really, I was crying out for help. *Help!* was about me, although it was a bit poetic. . . . The whole Beatle thing was just beyond comprehension. I was eating and drinking like a pig, and I was fat as a pig, dissatisfied with myself, and subconsciously I was crying for help. It was my "fat Elvis" period.

The seeds of John's discontent had already taken root. He felt constrained by the group and his departure was inevitable. In 1965, he already had one foot out the door. With hindsight, the future for each of The Beatles seemed clearly drawn even then. Indian music would change George's life completely. Ringo had discovered his acting chops and that he liked being out in front of the drums. And Paul? He was about to put forth the most important song of his career.

At the studio that morning in mid-June, Paul played "I've Just Seen a Face" for the guys. George Martin pronounced it not yet ready, and the rest agreed.

Paul then enlisted the other Beatles in a rip-snorting version of "I'm Down" while doing his best impression of one of his idols, Little Richard. It was like the Hamburg days! They tore up the joint. There was no topping that. Everyone broke for dinner.

After dinner, the plan was to record "It's Only Love" and "Act Naturally," but first George Martin cleared the studio. After two years of work on "Scrambled Eggs," Paul was finally ready. Alone in the middle of the studio with an acoustic guitar, he recorded "Yesterday" for the first time. Two days later, Martin added a string quartet, a first for a rock and roll song. The album was completed a few days later.

SHOOTING SHEA

Epstein and Sullivan finalized details for their deal to film the Shea Stadium concert. Time was short. The men needed to quickly move forward with production plans. Sullivan recommended the producer of his own show, son-in-law Bob Precht, to head the production.

> **Vince Calandra**: He [Precht] was a very special guy. Very well-liked by everyone. But also great taste and Sullivan trusted him implicitly.

> **Bob Precht**: In the summer of '65, the Sullivan staff was on hiatus, having taped several shows in advance. One day, my wife Betty and I were at the Century Country Club in Westchester where I was playing tennis. We both remember vividly Betty coming out to the court to tell me I had an overseas call. It was Brian who told me he was planning on a concert at Shea Stadium, and he asked if I could film it. The timetable was short, but of course I jumped at it. Shock time! Though I had directed film programs as specials from Alaska, Ireland, and Portugal in '59, I had never undertaken anything this big. First order was to pull together a film crew, and for that I went to Clay Adams, a veteran film man I'd worked with before. Clay's credentials were impressive, the acclaimed series *Victory at Sea* among them.

> **Vince Calandra**: We were supposed to go on vacation and Precht called me in the office and said, "Look, Sid Bernstein is producing Shea Stadium, but Brian Epstein just called me and said he wants us to film the show." So Bob

Precht literally put that show together in the space of four days, with not television cameras, but 35-millimeter cameras. You know, the big film cameras. So that's how we started putting it together.

The first of many production meetings was held with producer/director Bob Precht, producer Clay Adams, and cinematographer Andrew Laszlo, ASC, to figure out how to film the unprecedented event from every angle. Naturally, multiple cameras would be needed, but how many and where would they be placed? How would the crew be able to communicate with each other?

The men agreed that several cameras had to be placed in front of the bandstand, hidden from the audience by a shade much like a duck blind. They would also place several cameras with long lenses around the infield and in strategic spots in the audience. These vantage points should allow them to capture "the unexpected and unusual." These cameras were all to be connected by state-of-the-art radio communications, but should that fail, the men knew what to do.

There weren't going to be any second chances here, so Precht wanted the best he could get. He turned to veterans including Gordon Willis, who would go on to shoot all three *Godfather* films, *Annie Hall*, and *Manhattan*; Jack Horton, who shot *The Miracle Worker*; Peter Gabarini, who would shoot *Endless Love*; and Emmy-nominee Harvey Genkins and Michael Rayhack, who shot the 1956 classic film *Rock, Rock, Rock*.

More meetings followed, each one larger and longer than the one before. The chief of stadium security and his staff warned of the possibilities of a full-scale stampede, which could result in thousands of injuries and even death. Laszlo was beginning to regret accepting the job.

Andrew Laszlo: Just moving around in the stands called for an armed escort for the camera crews. Staff on every level were told never to run, no matter the urgency, because it could trigger a riot.

Meanwhile, life was coming at The Beatles at a furious pace. They hadn't given Shea Stadium any thought. What with all the location work for the film and recording the album, they'd barely had any time for family. And now family would have to wait again as they prepared to leave for what would be their final European tour: fifteen concerts in thirteen days in France, Italy, and Spain.

SET LIST FOR THE EUROPEAN TOUR

"Twist and Shout"   "Baby's in Black"   "Rock and Roll Music"
"She's a Woman"   "I Wanna Be Your Man"   "I Feel Fine"
"I'm a Loser"   "A Hard Day's Night"   "Ticket to Ride"
"Can't Buy Me Love"   "Everybody's Trying to Be My Baby"   "Long Tall Sally"

They opened in Paris with the first concert they'd given in six months. The reception was low key, with smaller crowds at the Paris-Orly airport and only fifty fans waiting at the elegant George V hotel.

The Beatles played two concerts at the Palais des Sports, at 3:00 p.m. and 9:00 p.m. The English rock band the Yardbirds opened for them sans Eric Clapton, who'd left the group to play in John Mayall's Bluesbreakers. Rising-star Jeff Beck had replaced him. Both shows were recorded by French radio station Europe 1; the second was transmitted live. The evening performance was also filmed in black and white by television channel 2 for an October airing.

The crowds may have been small, a total of six thousand for both shows, but they were enthusiastic, collapsing several rows of seats in their excitement. They screamed and sang along in English with some of the songs, especially "Can't Buy Me Love."

At night, the boys were visited in their hotel suite by popular French singer Françoise Hardy, whom Paul and George had met in London. Her pop hits in France climbed the British charts, and on her regular visits to London, she rubbed shoulders with some of rock's biggest stars. Mick Jagger declared Françoise his "ideal woman," while Bob Dylan dedicated a poem to her. Not to be outdone, Paul and George invited her to dinner. Françoise was really rather shy. She found herself drawn to George, whose quiet style matched her own. They had a great visit; The Beatles had the following day off and took advantage of it. After dinner, they went to the Castel nightclub on Rue Princesse, where they partied until early morning.

The following day, the group gave an interview in their hotel room to Chris Denning for Radio Luxembourg's weekly show *The Beatles*. For their last night in the City of Lights, the lads returned to the Castel nightclub.

The next morning, they left for Lyon. It was a similar arrangement there: one show 8:00 p.m. and another at 10:00 p.m. at the Palais d'Hiver de Lyon for a total of seven thousand people.

Then it was adieu to France. The group flew to Italy for two shows in Milan, 4:30 p.m. and 9:30 p.m. at the Velodromo Vigorelli. The arena held twenty-two thousand people, but neither of the concerts sold out. In fact, only seven thousand tickets were sold for the afternoon performance. Low attendance was blamed on the fact than most Beatle fans were in school or work. The evening concert attracted a respectable twenty thousand.

Next stop was Genoa, barely one hundred miles away. The boys were thrilled by their method of transportation. Each was driven separately in a brand-new Alfa Romeo by a member of the Alfa Romeo racing team.

Despite the unique arrival, the results were the same. One show at 4:40 and one at 9:00 at the city's Palazzo dello Sport, a twenty-five-thousand-seat arena. Only five thousand saw the afternoon show. The evening show drew just ten thousand.

Combined attendance at all eight shows in four cities barely equaled what awaited them in New York for one thirty-minute performance. Brian Epstein wasn't sure Sid Bernstein could really pull it off. Rome had to be better. In fact, Brian was so sure crowds in the Italian capital would be bigger that he'd added a second day at the Teatro Adriano in Piazza Cavour. Again, the concerts took place at 4:30 p.m. and 9:30 p.m. He might have had two sold-out shows if he'd left it to one day. Instead, The Beatles played four shows to half-empty houses though they barely noticed. The screaming sounded like a full house.

The next morning, The Beatles and their entourage—minus Brian—flew to Nice, France, for another one-night stand at the Nouveau Casino's Palais des Expositions. Brian had "disappeared" in Rome on an assignation. This happened with regularity. He'd catch up eventually.

After the concert, the group went to La Fiesta nightclub, which featured a go-kart track where the boys spent the evening racing each other and members of their entourage.

The Beatles arrived in Madrid on July 1 with time to see some of the city. Brian was waiting for them when they arrived at the hotel. His absence was never mentioned. While he attended a bullfight at the Plaza de Toros de Las Ventas, where the lads were to perform the following day, The Beatles visited the Jerez de la Frontera vineyard.

After the 8:30 p.m. concert, The Beatles were troubled by the intensity of violence leveled at the fans by the police.

The boys land in Madrid. Alf follows close behind.
BY IBERIA AIRLINES - LOS BEATLES / WIKIMEDIA COMMONS

Ringo: The thing I remember about Madrid where we played another bullring was that the police were so violent. It was the first time I'd really seen police beating kids up.

The last show was in Barcelona with a concert at the Plaza de Toros Monumental. Scheduled for 10:45, the performance was delayed more than thirty minutes.

Paul: I remember playing a big bullring in Barcelona, the Plaza de Toros, where the Lord Mayor had great seats and all the rich people had seats but the kids, our real audience, were outside. We used to get upset about that: "Why are we playing to all these bloody officials? We should be playing to the people outside. Let them in." But, of course, they wouldn't.

After two weeks on the road, The Beatles were more than ready to head home. The last show was July 3 in Barcelona. The next morning, they boarded a plane bound for their beloved England. A few hours later, they were welcomed by a thousand screaming fans at Heathrow.

HIDE AND SEEK

July 1965
- The US single release of "Help!" will reach number one and remain there for three weeks despite an outcry from some fans who are disappointed with the new direction the group is taking.
- The Rolling Stones' "Satisfaction" reaches number one in the United States and stays there for four weeks.
- Dylan uses an electric guitar at the Newport Folk Festival. Folk-rock is launched.
- World premiere of The Beatles' second film, *Help!*
- Cigarette makers are required to put health warnings on all packages.
- Lyndon Johnson sends fifty thousand more soldiers to Vietnam.
- Rehearsals begin for The Beatles' North America tour.

Exhausted in overdrive, John, Paul, George, and Ringo desperately needed time to unplug. Brian called for a media blackout, canceling TV appearances on *Ready, Steady Go*, *Top of the Pops*, and *Thank Your Lucky Stars*. Fans expressed upset, but the boys had to have a break—and, frankly, so did the public. The times, they were a-changin'. Summer was passing at lightning speed. The postwar hand-holding of 1950s was a memory. Life had become more complicated and so had music. A new generation wanted something different, something deeper, and the boys wanted to deliver. For that, they needed time to themselves and time to experiment in the studio.

Eppy wanted to deliver to the youth of the day, too. He'd added several pop artists to his roster and had been successful with them. In fact, business was never better. But his personal life was chaotic. The more success he achieved, the more he punished himself. His drug and alcohol intake had more than doubled. His drugs of choice had grown from pot and amphetamines to include LSD, Seconal, brandy, and more. He even had his suits tailored with small interior pockets to hold his pills. He was moody, prone to outbursts. His sexual liaisons grew more dangerous and violent. He sometimes showed up at work with bruises or a black eye. One "trick" he brought home robbed him. He laughed it off, but friends grew increasingly concerned.

Despite the backlash following The Beatles' MBEs, the awards kept coming: five Novellos for John and Paul. The Ivor Novello Awards for songwriting and composing had been presented annually in London by the British Academy of Songwriters, Composers and Authors (BASCA) since 1955. This year, the awards were to be presented at a ceremony emceed by David Frost at the Savoy Hotel on the Strand. John chose to lay low and sit this one out. Paul agreed to go then forgot about it and arrived forty minutes late. He accepted the awards on behalf of John and himself saying, "Thanks. I hope nobody sends theirs back now."

On July 29, ten thousand fans descended on Piccadilly Circus to see the group arrive in a black Rolls-Royce for the royal premiere of *Help!* Inside the Pavilion, they met Princess Margaret and Lord Snowdon, who had delayed their summer holiday for the event.

After the film, The Beatles, director Richard Lester, Princess Margaret, Lord Snowdon, and the other cast members attended a black-tie party in the Orchid Room of the Dorchester Hotel.

Despite the kudos, the boys yearned for privacy—even from one another. The nesting instinct overshadowed everything else. As the month ended, Ringo and Mo closed on a new home around the corner from John and Cyn in Weybridge. Sunny Heights was a large, elegant estate with extensive grounds and a bar called the Flying

The Stones appeared in court in July 1965 for the March incident at the gas station. They were not charged with public urination but with trespassing and insulting behavior. A customer in the store supported the attendant's account of their conduct; however, he admitted to egging them on by calling them "disgusting." In the four months since their transgression, the band had reached number one in the United Kingdom with "Satisfaction." But that was no reason for them to think they had "the right to act like this," rebuked the chairman of the magistrates. Even so, the punishment didn't amount to much more than a stern scolding. Bill, Mick, and Brian were all found guilty of using insulting behavior that may have disturbed the peace. Bill was found not guilty of using insulting language. They paid a minor fine and moved on. The incident didn't hurt their record sales. If anything, it only increased their popularity with young people who applauded this harmless flaunting of authority. Their "bad boy" reputation stuck, and they continued to live up to that reputation over and over again.

Cow. And John bought a house for his dear Aunt Mimi, who raised him. In gratitude, he gifted her with a home in Poole with panoramic views of the English Channel. Even Paul felt the need to spread his wings. He moved out of the Ashers' home into a newly renovated Regency House at 7 Cavendish Avenue near Abbey Road. For the next few weeks, The Beatles were quiet.

BEST-LAID PLANS

August 1965

    The Beatles break their media silence with only one live TV appearance to promote *Help!* on ITV's *Blackpool Night Out*. Paul plays "Yesterday" for the first time publicly.

    UK album release of *Help!*

    Lyndon Johnson doubles the monthly draft numbers.

    Bobby Vinton's latest single stalls at number seventeen.

    The Dave Clark Five arrives in the United States for a promotional tour and television guest spots on *The Ed Sullivan Show*, *The Dean Martin Show*, and *Shindig* for their film, *Having a Wild Weekend*.

    Lyndon Johnson signs the Voting Rights Act, prohibiting voting discrimination against minorities.

Racial tensions explode in Los Angeles in the Watts riots. Amid the flames comes the chant: "Burn, baby, burn!" During the seven days of rioting, thirty-four people are killed, eleven hundred people injured, and four thousand arrested, with an estimated $100 million worth of damage.

The Beatles leave for the United States.

For weeks, a friend of Sid Bernstein's had been pestering him to go hear this new local group. Frankly, he'd made a nuisance of himself. Finally, to appease him, Sid relented and joined his insistent friend to hear a new group on a floating club called the Barge in the Hamptons. He was glad he did. Not only did he enjoy a delicious turkey club sandwich, but the Rascals were terrific. He agreed to manage them on the spot.

Felix Cavaliere is a founding member of the Rascals.

> **Felix Cavaliere**: Immediately he [Sid] doubled our pay [at the Barge]. Because we were working and bringing the people in, and we were making nothing. So that happened. And then he started bringing in record companies that were interested in signing us. So immediately we were in the music industry instead of just a workhand. It was an immediate reaction, and you know, it was very exciting.
>
> Our parents, and of course Sid and his wife, Gerry, we would have holidays together. We would make sure we had special events together. My father and Sid, they really hit it off.

After contracts were signed, Sid paused to appreciate the moment. Everything with Shea was moving smoothly. The Rascals were going to explode onto the music scene; he could feel it. He and Gerry were expecting another child. His life was full of blessings. Standing in Washington Square Park, munching on a pizza slice, he felt like the luckiest guy around.

As the concert drew closer, preparations heated up for those planning to attend. Marc Weinstein, a seventeen-year-old junior in a Baltimore high school, was one of them. He suffered with a significant hearing impairment but had learned to live with it, even make it work for him at times. Marc loved photography and wanted to be a photojournalist.

TOP OF THE MOUNTAIN

Marc Weinstein. COURTESY MARC WEINSTEIN

Marc Weinstein: I was in Young Democrats for Johnson in 1964. We took a bus trip up to Atlantic City to the convention, and the very first thing I got pictures of was LBJ's daughters and a full-frame shot of Hubert Humphrey. When I came home and showed the pictures, I was an instant celebrity to my family and kids in high school. I was hooked from that point on.

Then The Beatles came in September that year to the Baltimore Civic Center. Right away, I wanted to take pictures. I had a two- or three-year-old bar mitzvah suit that was already getting too small on me. But it was my lucky suit, so I was wearing that. I had a phony press pass from the radio station WCAO. I took a business card from the station and put my picture on it. I flashed it to this police officer at the front of the stage and he let me into the orchestra pit. I was the only one in there. They had an armed gate around the orchestra pit behind me! The Beatles played about thirty minutes, and I took pictures. Out of a roll of thirty-six, I probably had about eight or nine good shots.

The Beatles in Baltimore. PHOTO BY MARC WEINSTEIN

Marc planned to try the same thing at Shea Stadium. He entered contests, made some phone calls, and somehow managed to get a ticket through the radio. The station was providing buses from Baltimore to the concert, solving his transportation problems. For the press pass, he again created something official-looking by using another business card from the radio station. This time he had it laminated. Finally, thinking of the captive audience of Beatlemaniacs he'd have on the bus, he chose his best shots from the Baltimore concert and had hundreds of three-by-five prints made to sell on the bus.

During the weeks leading up to Shea, Cousin Brucie ramped up the excitement daily on WABC, or as it had become known W-A-Beatle-C radio in New York. Beatlemania soared with the summer temperatures.

Cousin Brucie: I used to get people calling me all the time. A kid from the Bronx would call me, "Hey Brucie, this is Harold from the Bronx. Wanna play a record? My girl Suzy wants to hear the Everly Brothers." Two weeks later, after The Beatles arrive and after all the hype, . . . this is what happened. Another caller, "Is this his majesty, Sir Brucie? This is Sir Harold of Bronxshire. Would you please play a record for me and me bird by The Beatles?" What I just said to you, with a little levity, was that speech patterns changed. People were emulating the British sound. They were speaking as being Anglophiles. They were all suddenly noticing the Union Jack and becoming British. Because sociologically, as I said, we needed something to latch on. And they latched on to this English thing that was happening, this sociological phenomenon. It was not just music. That's important to remember. It goes way past music. Music alone cannot do it. It can do it for a while, but not like what happened with The Beatles. And it's still happening with The Beatles. They still hold a special place on Mount Olympus, the musical Mount Olympus. Because it surpassed just their music. Hair, dress, speech. Lipstick, nail polish, underwear. You name it. It's there.

Beatles for Sale. COURTESY SUE MUSE COLLECTION

COURTESY SUE MUSE COLLECTION

COURTESY SUE MUSE COLLECTION

These boots are made for Beatles!

Andrew Laszlo began attending night games at Shea with a small camera to experiment. He was most concerned with exposure. Going during a game was only "partially useful" because he could not go onto the field to measure the light. The stage was not the big problem. That would be well lit. But what about the audience? He concentrated on filming the baseball fans.

> **Andrew Laszlo**: When there was no game and the lights were off, turning them on even for a short time cost thousands of dollars. But I needed to know; and the lights were turned on for me. I experimented with exposure, faster lenses and handheld lights . . . until we came up with a formula that was going to allow me almost unlimited opportunities to film the audience. Indeed, some of those shots—tears running down both cheeks of a teenaged girl, kids jumping up and down and more—became interesting highlights of the show.

Meryl Streep stood before her parents trembling with excitement. A boy she knew invited her to see The Beatles at Shea Stadium. She begged her parents, but they were reluctant to say yes. Queens was a long way to go on a date, not like going to a local movie. They would have to think about it. Meryl, desperate to go, devised a campaign to earn permission that included washing dishes, walking the dog, keeping her room spotless.

George Orsino, thirty-seven, was a professional portrait photographer in South Philadelphia. He had a lot of work from the neighborhood—and what a neighborhood. Chubby Checker was next door. Bobby Rydell and Fabian were a few blocks over. George did many shoots with all of them. They became his friends. He had a few great shots of visiting celebrities, a doozy of Princess Grace, but beyond that, he didn't pursue show business shots. He was happy in his own backyard. So when a friend in public relations suggested he go to Shea Stadium, he said no. He wasn't even a fan of The Beatles.

> **George Orsino**: I'd shot Bobby Rydell, Fabian, and other local celebrities. I shot Fabian's wedding. But I wasn't much of a Beatle fan. A friend of mine, Mike Alfredo, a promotion man, asked me if I wanted to go to Shea Stadium to view The Beatles. I was completely uninterested. I turned him down.

Bartender Buddy Perst came home one night from his job at Delmonico's with a surprise for his thirteen-year-old daughter, Renee: four tickets to The Beatles at Shea Stadium. She immediately erupted in screams of joy, leaping, jumping, and bouncing off the walls. Without question, it was the most thrilling thing to ever happen in her brief life.

Renee Perst: I was an only child. I came from an Italian, very protective family, and there was no way in hell my mother was going to let me go to Shea Stadium alone.

As a teenage bobby-soxer, Renee's mom, Elsie, used to go to the Paramount Theater to see Frank Sinatra. She remembered yelling "Frankie! Frankie!" and feeling weak in the knees when he cast those baby blues her way, sure that he had looked right at her. The idea of seeing her daughter swoon over her idols just as she once had sounded like so much fun. She called her best friend, Ida, whose daughter, Linda Ghigonne Marotte, was around Renee's age.

Renee Perst: [Ida and Elsie] were best of friends. We never even thought about who would go. It was Linda and her mother, Mom, and me. So that's how we came to it. It made it easy, almost like taking a relative, because if I had had to choose a girlfriend to bring, I would have lost all my other girlfriends.

Linda Ghigonne Marotte: Renee was a very good friend. We go back. We say we're the oldest living friends. Our parents were friends before we were even born. We've stayed friends the whole time. In 1965, she was almost fourteen and I was almost twelve.

Renee Perst: Of course, Paul was my favorite Beatle at the beginning because he was so cute. But then Ringo became my favorite because he wasn't, if you know what I mean. He was cute in how funky looking he was. I was a real fan. I mean I read everything. . . . I did like his story. You know, he was a sickly child, and I loved the way he literally just stumbled into this group and what a great story that was. The whole big picture captivated me about him.

Linda Ghigonne Marotte: I was very much into George.

Renee Perst: My father was a bartender, and he always worked in very good places. He worked at Delmonico's for a time in New York City, and one of his regulars came in one day with a box and plopped it on the bar. It was full of tickets to the Shea Stadium concert, and he handed him four tickets right off the top. He was in the printing business and had just printed them. That's what Dad had always told me.

I repeated this story to my mother just three or four days ago.... My mother gets this grin on her face and starts to laugh. And I said, "What's so funny?" She said, "I really suspect that he got the tickets from Blackie." "Who is Blackie?" She said, "Blackie was one of his best customers and they were really good friends. He'd come in all the time. Blackie was a Mafia guy." I had never heard the name Blackie in my whole life. I guess my father kept that a secret. Mom just laughed and said, "I bet he got the tickets from Blackie, and he told you that story because he didn't want to tell you he got the tickets from some Mafia guy." However it happened, Dad was king of the castle for weeks after.

Linda Baker LaFlamme was a high school senior in Long Island, though her attendance there was spotty. Voluptuous at a young age, Linda had been assaulted at age twelve. Deeply affected, depressed, traumatized, and with nowhere to turn, her self-esteem was nonexistent. Music was what saved her, music and her boyfriend, Willie, whom she met when she was fifteen. Without him, she'd have been alone. At eighteen, when her stepfather began salivating over her, her mother tossed her out.

Linda LaFlamme. COURTESY LINDA LAFLAMME

Linda LaFlamme: I pretty much left home in 1965 and lived elsewhere. I spent most of my time in the Village hanging out, living in communes with other runaways.

Linda would eventually sing for thousands of people around the world and leave her mark on rock history. But in 1965, she was fighting to survive. In early August, Willie handed her an envelope. Inside was the greatest present she'd ever received: two tickets to see The Beatles.

Linda LaFlamme: I couldn't believe it! We were both so excited, we were counting the days. It was so refreshing for our age group to have something this big to look forward to.

GOING FOR BROKE

Sid Bernstein's phone rang. Sid washed down the last of a corned beef sandwich with a few gulps of an egg cream. He breathed deeply and picked up the receiver. It was Mayor Wagner's office. He smiled. For once, they were asking *him* for a favor. They wanted to send an intern to shadow him on the day of the concert. Their thinking was that if the city ever tried something of this magnitude again, they'd have someone who'd been through it.

"Sure," said Sid. "Who are you thinking of?"

"We've got this young man. He's fifteen years old, very sharp. His name is Jeffrey Katzenberg."

"Fine," said Sid. "I look forward to showing him the ropes."

One day, young Mr. Katzenberg would be running his own Hollywood studio. In 1965, he would take his cues from Sid Bernstein.

Eric J. Adams: I had just turned nine years old. My father was a foreign correspondent working for the *City Morning Herald*, an Australian newspaper. He was working in New York in Times Square in the *New York Times* building. One of his colleagues was a woman whose name was Lillian Roxon. She wrote the book that was called *The History of Rock and Roll* or the handbook. It was, at the time, *the* source material for rock and roll. And probably the first one ever done. And I, of course, fell in love with her because at the time she was meeting with The Beatles and, you know, all these bands. And she was so kind. . . . So my father was able to get tickets to the concert. And he promised to take my sister, Denise, and me.

Roxon's Rock Encyclopedia.
COURTESY BARBARA REW

Whoopi Goldberg was also just nine years old.

Whoopi Goldberg: I heard about the concert, and I asked, "Can we go?" And my mom said, "We don't have the money for this." And then . . . I don't know how she did it . . . [welling up] I don't know how she did it, but she got two tickets and she didn't tell me.

Meanwhile, George Orsino had begun to rethink what his friend said. Everyone was talking about this concert. Sounded like it could be a big deal. Maybe he'd made a mistake. So when his friend called again, George made the decision to go to New York.

George Orsino: Turns out Mike was not going to let me turn down the opportunity. He had already arranged for me to travel there on a bus full of radio contest winners.

Joy Musiker Cohen: We had a meeting for all the [radio contest] winners and there were three buses. Three buses would take us up to New York. We were supposed to have time to go to the World's Fair first, which was right across the street from Shea.

Ronnie Schneider had settled in an apartment in New York and taken a job with ABKCO Records, his uncle, Allen Klein's company. There, he was responsible for handling the likes of Neil Sedaka and Bobby Vinton. In August, Klein informed Ronnie that he would be touring with a group called the Rolling Stones, in charge of them and their money. Klein was taking two of its members out on his yacht with Vinton and some clients and friends on Sunday, August 15. He wanted Ronnie there.

Meryl Streep cried tears of joy when her parents finally gave permission for her to see The Beatles. She immediately set about making a sign to carry.

Meryl Streep: In August 1965, after I cried for about three days and promised that I'd do the dishes for the next four years, my parents finally relented, and they let me go into New York on a date for the first time to see this new English band that we were all so emotional about.

That was the first big stadium concert. People had concerts in concert halls. Nobody had a concert in a baseball stadium; it was unheard of . . . and they thought no one would come. . . . Oh, it was thrilling!

Fanning the flames of anticipation during the month before the US tour, there was a flurry of record releases on both sides of the Atlantic. *Beatles VI* was released in the States and went straight to number one, followed shortly by a single of "Help!" backed with "I'm Down."

Before they could travel to the States, the boys and their entourage had to get vaccinated. Alf also needed an International Driver's License. He was sitting with the lads, filling out the forms, and asked, "How do you spell chauffeur?"

John answered, "Put musical director." John was always the one who made Alf laugh the most.

The evening of August 12, Sid and Gerry, pregnant again, had a quiet birthday celebration at home for Sid's forty-seventh. It was the lull before the storm. Their phone, which had been ringing incessantly all week, was uncharacteristically silent. All details for the Shea Stadium concert were taken care of. Everything was in place. All there was left to do now was to wait for The Beatles' arrival—and pray it all went as planned.

The night before The Beatles and their entourage were to leave, Neil, the tour manager, paid a visit to Alf's home. Inside, he handed Alf a carton of cigarettes, a large bag of marijuana, and some rolling papers. He instructed Alf to split open each cigarette, replace the tobacco with pot, and seal it all back up.

Alf was up most of the night and into the wee hours rolling joints. He slipped the cigarettes back in the packs, wrapped the cellophane around them, and sealed it with a warm iron. He did the same with the cellophane around the carton. At the airport, he carried the carton under his arm, naive to the serious consequences he would have faced if he had been caught.

CROSSING THE POND

The morning of August 13, Eppy, The Beatles, and their group checked and rechecked luggage and paperwork. In a scorching heat wave, they headed for Heathrow, where more than a thousand fans had gathered to see them off. The Beatles climbed aboard TWA's Flight 703 and piled into the Royal Ambassador Section, first class. Brian sat a few rows ahead, as did Mal, Neil, and Alf. The flight took off around noon for The Beatles' second tour of the United States.

Nothing had been left to chance. Brian had planned every detail of the flight. More than a month ago, a public relations rep from TWA had flown to London to meet with him. The flight crew had been handpicked and flown in the day before so they would be well-rested.

Behind the partition in coach sat 120 other passengers—"Beatlenuts" TWA's *Skyliner* magazine called them—the majority of them fans who'd somehow found out about The Beatles and scrambled for tickets on the flight. Now they were dying to get a peek at them. One or two occasionally screamed. But when they all received autographed photos and a 45 of "Help!" signed by each of The Beatles, they quieted down. There was no disturbance for the rest of the flight.

The boys behaved themselves, too, playing card games, eating chateaubriand and lobster, and drinking lots of wine and champagne. There was a brief food fight started by Ringo. Even the non-Beatle first-class passengers got in on it. Then they all settled in to watch Sophia Loren in *Operation Crossbow*.

As he approached New York, the captain opened a sealed envelope containing secret instructions for landing. Tight security measures were in place.

The boys, along with Neil and Mal, leaned hard on their armrests as the island of Manhattan loomed large beneath them. On August 13, 1965, at 2:30 p.m., The Beatles arrived in the Big Apple.

The Shea Stadium concert was only two days away.

4

THE BEATLES TAKE NEW YORK

It was Friday the thirteenth, a not-so-lucky day for thousands of screaming girls who descended on John F. Kennedy International Airport to greet The Beatles when they landed.

The captain opened the envelope, which contained eight possible spots to deplane the group. He gave a code word to the tower and was instructed to continue past the international terminal to a remote spot two miles away.

As they taxied past the main terminal, the passengers on the plane couldn't help but notice the lack of a crowd. In fact, only a dozen or so girls gathered to welcome them. "Where is everyone?" Paul wondered. "What's wrong?" The energy among the entourage immediately deflated. *This was New York. Where were the fans?*

There were actually thousands of screaming fans, but the controllers at JFK Airport refused to let the band use the main terminal, a move that infuriated the boys, who had hoped to greet their American fans.

A fleet of limousines awaited them on the tarmac to take them away without entering the main building. The boys posed for photos with the press then they piled into one of the cars along with the rest of the group and headed to the Warwick Hotel with a full police escort.

Once inside, Ringo asked the driver to turn on the radio. Cousin Brucie was broadcasting live from the Warwick with help from WABC's program director, Rick Sklar. Sklar had the genius idea to rechristen the station W-A-Beatle-C. In return, WABC got Beatle songs before the other stations, and Cousin Brucie got coveted access to broadcast live from The Beatles' suite on the thirty-third floor of the Warwick.

Cousin Brucie: Okay, so Sid and Rick and myself make the deal with Brian. And we get access to the Warwick Hotel. We were the only radio station that was going to do a live thing. People got them for a couple minutes with recordings and taped them or whatever in those days. But we were there live and the boys were aware of Cousin Brucie and what we were doing.

Outside, police were . . . it was a camp. It was a military camp. We got into the hotel and there's more police all over the place. It looked like a military zone. Every time The Beatles came around there was always some kind of problem, so the hotel security was wild, nervous as hell. We got into the elevator, and right away we noticed something moving on top of the elevator. It was kids! Kids riding on top of the elevator! We quickly got out because we all said, "This kid is going to get killed." But worse than that, we stopped at a floor before we got up to our suite where we were going to do the broadcast and in comes a maid who looked a little strange, pushing one of those hampers—you know, those little carts with dirty linens and things like that. The security guard that was with us says, "Ma'am do you work here?" And she was obviously a kid, looked like an older sister of somebody who made-believe she was a maid. She got a uniform. She started fumbling and the security guard picked up the dirty linen. Two more kids were in the hamper.

This was just part of it. They were all over the place—any[where] they could. They'd have parents check into the hotel. And, of course, every floor you'd hear screaming and yelling. And we thought we would never get up to our suite.

The Warwick.
COURTESY DAWN MICHAELS

Bill Angelos lived next door to the Warwick.

Bill Angelos: It was at 45 West Fifty-Fourth, the first building going down Fifty-Fourth Street toward Fifth. The Warwick was on the corner of Fifty-Fourth and Sixth. And, of course, the Sullivan Theater was just a block up and across the street. It had to have been four or five days they were at the Warwick. I could see the whole scene from my apartment window, and I absolutely remember the crowds. It was almost as if they were bound together; they kind of moved in a crowd. They would come down the street and you would see them coming. I didn't see any boys. My nieces reminded me that I got them tickets to the show. And to this day they cannot understand why I didn't go. I try to explain to them that I heard that screaming for a number of days . . . even after the crowds were gone!

Once in the safety of his room, Cousin Brucie and Rick set up their equipment, which was simple in those days. Once on the air, he tried to convey the scene outside to his listeners.

Cousin Brucie: In those days they didn't have wireless microphones, so I'm leaning out the window with a microphone while Rick is standing behind me holding me by the seat of my pants, by the belt. And across the street herded behind police barricades and horses were five or six thousand kids. That's over where the Hilton was. The Hilton at Sixth Avenue at that time was still planked with wood because I guess the subways were just going in there. But the kids were herded behind these barricades, all of them knowing The Beatles were going to be coming to the Warwick.

So picture this: all of a sudden, a Bentley pulls up. I'm on the air and, "Here they come, folks! Hey, everybody! It's Cousin Brucie. We're here on the eighth floor of the Warwick Hotel, and we're going to be giving you an eye-witness account of what's happening." Every kid in that crowd had a transistor radio they were listening to. And you hear, "Arrrrrrgh." It was unbelievable. I'm saying, "Here they come." And the Bentley pulls up—If I'm not mistaken, it was a beige Bentley. That seems to be ingrained in my skull, a beige Bentley—and the doors are opening and the police are rushing in, security's rushing and the kids are straining behind the horses. The kids are screaming and I'm screaming, "Here they are!" Four mop tops came running out and they make it into the lobby unscathed.

The hotel management swarms them, trying to get them out of the lobby and into the elevator when someone takes a good look at the group.

Cousin Brucie: It turns out, it's not The Beatles. It's a group called the Teddy Bears. The Teddy Bears were a band. They were wannabe Beatles. They wanted to cash in on the Beatlemania, so they decided to do this. They knew where they were staying and they came in with a Bentley. All I can tell you is the Teddy Bears have never been heard from or seen again. My feeling is, they are probably chained up downstairs in the basement of the Warwick Hotel.

In 1965, the Teddy Bears were the house band at Sybil Burton's hot new club, Arthur, the precursor to Studio 54. She chose the nightclub's name based on an exchange between a reporter and George Harrison. When asked what they called "those haircuts of yours," George answered, "I call mine Arthur."

Linda LaFlamme: I knew the Teddy Bears! They were a Beatle look-alike band—very cute guys. They weren't soundalikes, but they did the same kind of pop music. I dated the lead singer for a little while. He was British. He asked me to go back to London with him. . . . Maybe that's what happened to them after that stunt. I never heard that story, but that is absolutely something they would have done. The Beatles had us all doing crazy stuff!

The Fab Four were listening to all of this in the limo and roaring with laughter. After the long flight, they were just a little slaphappy and this episode had them in hysterics. But what they didn't realize was that the crowd was now in overdrive. When they finally arrived at the hotel a short time later, the scene was absolute bedlam.

Cousin Brucie: Then of course the actual event happened. The cars, the limos came. The kids across the street at this time were so pent-up that they broke through the police barricades. I was watching as all this was going on, describing it on the air. There must have been six thousand kids there—a sea of people—and every one of them was listening to a transistor radio. . . . When I announced that The Beatles were really arriving, they screamed and surged forward through the barricades and into the street. . . . Everybody wanted a piece of them.

I was on the eighth floor looking down. I was frightened Rick would let go of me. I was holding onto one guy and a microphone and I'm about three-quarters of the way out of a window. I was explaining how the police barricades were coming down. It looked like an ocean opening up, like waves coming up, people flooding Sixth Avenue. I saw horses, ready for this, I'm talking horsey-horses, not wooden horses, go down. Nothing stopped them. I don't know if you've ever been in a crowd that's panicked. But this was like positive panic. They wanted to grab them. So they run across and by this time the guys are getting out.

The Beatles barely made it safely into the lobby, where they were quickly shepherded to the elevator. For security purposes, they had an entire floor. Guards were posted at the elevators and at stairway exit doors. All of the opening acts would move in Saturday and Sunday. Alf, Mal, and Neil shared a room a couple doors down from the boys. These three men were the group's most trusted confidants and their first line of defense—their *only* line. Their previous driver had sold his story to the tabloids, a betrayal that cut them deeply. It was a tremendous relief to be able to trust this trio implicitly. There was nothing they wouldn't do for them. The boys knew it and were grateful for it.

Dave Glyde: Neil was a gorgeous man who stuck by through everything. He was always there. He took care of everything. He was management personified. If you had a problem, he took care of it. Such a lovely guy. Mal was the guy who picked it up and put it down. He was a big guy and did all that. He was the original roadie. And their driver . . . Alf was there, but he was mostly in the car.

Susan Silva: Mal was like what I would call an armor bearer—like a major guard, a big guy, always a protector . . . a very happy person. He was a doll, so, so nice.

George: Alf was a friend, protector, bodyguard, and confidant. . . . Alf, along with Neil and Mal, was priceless. Their contribution to the "Fabness" of us four was immeasurable.

Waiting in the suite to greet the group and Brian were Sid and the American promoters and managers, Norman Weiss, Ed Leffler, and Ira Sidelle. Cousin Brucie was there too.

Cousin Brucie with the lads in their suite. COURTESY BRUCE MORROW

After their harrowing entrance at the Warwick, Brian Epstein expressed deep concern about security at the stadium. Sid did his job, assuring him that he had nothing to worry about. But as Sid watched the frenzied mob in the street, he wondered how he could promise that the fifty-six thousand fans heading to Shea would behave.

Despite the long flight from the United Kingdom, a press conference had been arranged by Tony Barrow downstairs in a packed ballroom.

Tony Barrow: It was heaving wall to wall with a mixed assortment of noisy, chattering press photographers, television cameramen, journalists, deejays, a lot of technical lighting and sound equipment—and scores of overexcited teenage competition winners! I brought in the boys to tumultuous prolonged applause.

Barrow fielded the questions. And although the boys had been awake for more than twenty hours, they proved they hadn't lost their sense of humor.

Question: Ringo, what are you gonna name the baby if it's a boy or a girl?

Ringo: Uhh . . .

John: Charlie. [Laughter.]

Ringo: That was John answering, not me. We don't know yet. We're still talking about names.

John: How about Lyndon?

Ringo: How about it? [Laughter.]

Question: Is your popularity fading?

John: Go and ask the record people.

Ringo: Well, you all seem to be back again. [Laughter.]

Question: Do you think you're setting styles in pop and op art?

George: Maybe unconsciously.

Ringo: Yeah, we're always unconscious.

Question: Is matrimony in the immediate future for the two unmarried members of your group?

Paul: Matrimony is not in the immediate future.

George: [Jokingly] Paul won't have me.

Question: Did you fellas do your own skiing in the [*Help!*] motion picture?

John and Paul: Some of it.

Paul: The clever bits we didn't do.

George: We did the bits falling over. The falling-over bit.

Question: Who do you consider the best actor among you?

John: Ringo.

Question: Is this movie as good as *Hard Day's Night*?

John and Paul: It's better.

Question: You Beatles have conquered five continents. What do you want to do next?

Paul and John: Conquer six. [Laughter.]

Sid Bernstein, ever the promoter, had a plant in the crowd.

Question: The American press has compared you Beatles with the Rascals. Have you heard of them or seen 'em?

John: No.

Paul: We've never seen them.

Finally, the conference came to an end, and the boys headed back to their suite. Bob Dylan stopped in to visit. They got stoned, caught up on news of friends, and, of course, talked music. Dylan suggested to John in particular that he write deeper, more personal songs.

Dave Glyde: It was a crazy time thinking back on that. We never considered touring with The Beatles as being big-time. They were our friends. We just thought we can do a lot of drugs. We can have a lot of sex. We just go down, get on planes. We fly. Everyone takes care of us. There's cars to pick you up. There's people to take care of you. If you sneeze, there was someone to take care of that. It was a magic time.

Sounds Incorporated. COURTSEY DAVE GLYDE

TAPING *THE ED SULLIVAN SHOW*

Neil and Mal woke the group the following morning. They had a big day in front of them, taping an appearance on *The Ed Sullivan Show*. Work always came first, and they tumbled out of bed and shook off their drowsiness.

After a hearty breakfast, they were ready to head over. The New York Police Department had decided in advance of The Beatles' arrival that it could be dangerous for them to be stuck in traffic. So, although it was barely a block and a half to the studio, The Beatles required a police escort to get through the massive crowds gathered around the hotel and lining the streets all the way to the studio. Ringo loved it.

Rehearsal at CBS-TV Studio 50 began at 11:00 a.m. in front of a live audience. They were to perform six songs: "I Feel Fine," "I'm Down," Ringo's solo "Act Naturally," "Ticket to Ride," Paul's solo "Yesterday," and "Help!"

At 7:00 p.m., another audience would be brought in for the show taping, which was to air on September 12. Close to a thousand more kids who were unable to procure tickets filled the streets outside Studio 50, moaning, shouting, and weeping. It was a hot day, and police worked hard to hold their tempers. Many were overheard to mutter, "If I had a daughter like that, I'd . . ." What they didn't realize was, more than likely, they *did* have a daughter exactly like that. In fact, more than a dozen of New York's finest asked for autographs for their kids.

Vince Calandra: I was the main contact with the stage manager, Mal Evans, and Neil Aspinall. I was the go-to guy. I was the guy that gave John Lennon nickels for the Coke machine when he was at the Sullivan Theater. That was the stuff that I did.

The Stones were jerks. The Doors were jerks. The Byrds were jerks. There were a lot of jerks. The Stones were jerks because I had to go up and tell them to change the lyrics of their song that day, and Mick Jagger wasn't very nice to me. He used an Anglo-Saxon word that I'm not going to repeat. But that's why I felt he was a jerk.

Oh my God, The Beatles were perfect. Great guys. They were gentlemen. They were a class act. Everyone loved them. Listen, I worked that show seven years before they got there, and we had a crew of backstage guys and stagehands and everything. Ninety-eight percent were Italian and were in the union. The kids were in the union. And that's the first time in my life they actually went and got urns to make hot tea for the guys. They sent out to some restaurant to get them cucumber sandwiches. They didn't know what a cucumber sandwich was.

TOP OF THE MOUNTAIN

The Beatles' popularity with the crew dimmed a bit that day when the boys expressed dissatisfaction with the sound and insisted on recording their songs again and again.

Tony Barrow: Saturday's rehearsal took almost ten hours because of horrendous sound problems that the boys insisted upon sorting to their satisfaction. A year earlier when The Beatles did their first appearance on Sullivan's show, I doubt his people would have let us go into so much expensive studio overtime in the pursuit of better quality sound. Sullivan himself was far more friendly to us than last year, which helped to ease the atmosphere.

During the rehearsal, John practiced on his Vox electric organ, running up and down the keyboard with his elbow.

John: Most people can do that sort of thing with a thumb. But I'm not a good pianist. It hurts my thumb. So I use my elbow.

Eventually, to everyone's great relief, the problems were solved, and a fresh audience was brought in for the taping. The Beatles, now experienced professionals, gave a spirited and, by all appearances, spontaneous performance while the girls screamed, cried, and called out the names of their favorite Beatle.

Paul's a doll!

SATURDAY NIGHT

The Beatles returned to the hotel again via police escort to freshen up. Capitol Records, their label, had arranged a dinner that evening in the Rainbow Room, the iconic dining and entertainment venue on the sixty-fifth floor of Rockefeller Center. Brian and the boys dined, signed autographs, and entertained record executives and their guests. They enjoyed the spectacular views of New York—just about all they got to see of the city, which was a good sight more than they got to see of most American cities they toured. Exuberant fans made that impossible. The dinner was a subdued affair. The Four Fabs, as Paul liked to say, excused themselves close to 10:00 p.m.

Back at the Warwick, they decided to have a quiet little gathering, just a few friends. Neil Aspinall, The Beatles' longest-term employee, quickly realized that his job to insulate The Beatles was suddenly far more challenging in New York. He was in charge of access, and he adopted a policy, essentially, of no access unless The Beatles wanted to see you.

Mick Jagger and Keith Richards arrived close to 1:00 a.m. with their manager, Andrew Loog Oldham. By then, the party was in full swing, people everywhere, including Bob Dylan. Alf tended bar, ready to offer help to anyone who may need it and to smoke cigars near the doors to mask the smell of marijuana.

🥾🥾🥾🥾

After the party early the same morning, the phone rang in The Beatles' suite despite a request to hold all calls. Only Paul was still awake, and he was just trotting off to bed himself. The operator told him that Mr. and Mrs. Sammy Davis Jr. were in the lobby with champagne and wished to come up. Paul told her that everyone was asleep and asked if they could come back later. Paul's message must have gotten lost in translation because the Davises left in a huff and the New York press reported that The Beatles had snubbed one of America's biggest stars.

While The Beatles slept, thousands of others were wide awake, tingling with anticipation, spending the day preparing placards, creating gifts, and choosing the outfits to wear to Shea in hopes of catching the eye of their favorite mop top.

Meryl Streep: I had a little sign that said, "I love you forever, Paul!" I don't think he saw it.

Linda Ghigonne Marotte: Renee's father was our god and by a miracle, we were going to see The Beatles. All I kept thinking was, "This is going to be the best day of my life, and nothing is ever going to top this day."

Ronnie Schneider: On the morning of August 15, my uncle, Allen Klein, told me, "You're going to be business manager for a group I just signed—the Rolling Stones. You'll meet them tonight on my yacht and we'll all go catch The Beatles at Shea Stadium."

Linda LaFlamme. COURTESY LINDA LAFLAMME

Linda LaFlamme: It was the biggest thing that ever happened to me as far as I was concerned because The Beatles—they were it. They were what's happening. Everything else was moving at such a fast pace. To have them come on the scene and get us through the Kennedys and all the political stuff that was going on at the time. . . . My boyfriend felt the same way. I could barely sleep the night before.

Brian Epstein couldn't sleep either. He paced the floor in his hotel suite, worrying about the myriad of things that could go wrong. He reached for his pills but thought better of it. Only one person could help relax him. He looked at his watch. Midnight in New York. His mother, Queenie, would just be getting breakfast. He reached for the phone and had the hotel place an overseas call to her.

Vince Calandra: My job was sitting outside the Warwick hotel shooting B-roll for the documentary of the crowds and all the people coming into the hotel. I wasn't allowed to go up to the floor where they were hanging out. I remember a lot of airline stewardesses coming there. I remember Sammy Davis Jr. came in there with a big magnum of champagne.

Marc Weinstein went over his checklist: his camera was ready, he had plenty of film, the laminated business card from the radio station that he believed would look like a real press pass was finished, his lucky suit pressed, his concert ticket, bus ticket, and two hundred three-by-five prints of his Baltimore concert photos. Would it all be enough to fool security? He hoped it would.

It all seemed like a dream, but in just twenty-four hours, all of them would be sharing the same air, the same space, with John, Paul, George, and Ringo.

5

THE CONCERT

HERE COMES THE SUN

Bobbie Molina: Finally, the month came, the date came, and I was just so anxious.

Linda Eastman: I loved The Beatles right from the start. I saw them when they made their American debut on *The Ed Sullivan Show* in February 1964, I bought their first album when I was living in Arizona, and I saw them along with fifty-six thousand others, when they played what was then the largest outdoor concert in history, at Shea Stadium, New York, in August 1965.

Shea before the onslaught. COURTESY DAWN MICHAELS

The duck blind constructed near the front of the stage. Bob Precht is far left. Andy Laszlo third from left.
PHOTO BY GEORGE E. JOSEPH

A heat wave roasts New York. By noon, it is a sweltering 87 degrees with 72 percent humidity—and the air is electric. All the energy, all the emotion directed toward this one day, this one event, all the hopes and dreams, time and sweat invested by thousands of people will be crowded into this sold-out arena—a volatile situation to be sure. No one can predict what will happen when it all comes together. Sid says a little prayer, finishes his bagels and cream cheese, and heads to Queens.

Bob Precht and his team had been setting up since early morning headed up by Andrew Laszlo and his team of twelve cameramen. Despite having a camera crew that included future Oscar-winning cinematographer Gordon Willis and the talented Warren Rothenberger (*Live and Let Die*, *The Turning Point*, *Trading Places*), the director of cinematography, Andrew Laszlo struggled to get the job done. He could never have predicted the hardships of the shoot.

The crew set up a type of duck blind in front of the stage to cover several big cameras then strategically placed the rest throughout the stadium. Within a short time, they are already shooting all the activity as Shea prepares for the arrival of The Beatles. So as not to miss a single note, the crew tapes their own microphones to those that The Beatles will be using onstage.

Bob Precht (l) and Andy Laszlo.
PHOTO BY GEORGE E. JOSEPH

Bob Precht: The time was short, the event enormous. We had to move fast. It was seat-of-pants! I don't know how I got Andy Laszlo as my director of photography; Clay may have made that call or I asked for him because I knew him. It was a good choice. He did a great job. How we determined the number of cameras—all 35 millimeter except for a couple of 16-millimeter Arriflex—worked out the power, lighting, and audio is a blur. I do remember a big concern or fear was the audio, hence double mics. But everything had to be done quickly. This was a time before sophisticated computerized lighting, gigantic sound systems, special effects, and pyrotechnics. We were breaking new ground. I think the approach was shoot or record it all, anything and everything possible, including the stage setup in an empty stadium and the boys' comments as they flew over Manhattan. Because most of the Sullivan staff were on vacation, the only production guys I had to help were Vince Calandra and my production manager Tony Jordan. Vince was fantastic in everything that he did. He had special insight. He was with the boys a lot, interacting with them. We anticipated audience reaction, screaming, etcetera, but nothing like what happened. Security was a major concern. Sid's people along with people from GAC [General Artists Corp] dealt with that issue as did we. We were very worried about the cameramen's safety and equipment.

As Sid Bernstein checks his final preparations, he is shadowed by city intern, fifteen-year-old Jeffrey Katzenberg, who years later will found the powerful Dream-Works Studios with Steven Spielberg and David Geffen.

Seth Zimmerman: Sid treated him with real respect. He took time to explain situations and the possible solutions. He asked his opinion, what he would do. That's who Sid was—even with the incredible pressure he had to be feeling that day. Jeff never forgot that kindness.

Years later, I was traveling with Sid, sharing a hotel room with him. I answered the phone one morning and a voice said, "Is the nicest man in the world there, please?" It was Katzenberg calling for Sid.

Sid had double-checked everything, so he was a bit worried when he saw Shea Stadium staff approaching him. "Mr. Bernstein, what about the message board? What would you like it to say?" The message board that flashes continuously to the crowd! He hadn't even considered it. Of course, what an overlooked opportunity! In an instant, it comes to him. "Tell them to flash: *The Rascals are coming! The Rascals are coming!*"

A large number of cars are already in the enormous parking lot and a never-ending chain of others are arriving. Kids are getting out of sleeping bags near the ticket windows. Some are already inside the stadium.

Andrew Laszlo and his crew film the groundskeepers, security people, and New York police as they set up wooden barricades around the stadium, in front of the audience, and in other key positions. Laszlo's crew

Police get ready for the arrival of fans. COURTESY DAWN MICHAELS

TOP OF THE MOUNTAIN

Fans line up to to get in. COURTESY DAWN MICHAELS

Calm before the storm. PHOTO BY PETER SIMON/PETERSIMON.COM

is aware that if the crowd decides to run for the stage en masse, these barricades will be tossed aside like toothpicks, and they will all be trampled. As if he had read their minds, a security officer shows Laszlo and his crew four possible escape routes in case of a large-scale riot.

Sid circles the stadium interior, checking and rechecking every detail.

Bill Angelos: It was an event that was very carefully put together. Very carefully. And Sid Bernstein is to be commended for that.

Here comes the sun . . .
COURTESY DAWN MICHAELS

Fans in the upper tiers let the boys know how they feel. PHOTO BY PETER SIMON/PETERSIMON.COM

THE CONCERT

Dancer Denise Mourges arrives hours early with her sister. They emerge from the dugout and step onto the field to view the stadium. Fans have already started to arrive. Some hang bedsheet banners declaring their love for one Beatle in particular or for all of them. A few girls wore sandwich signs—one of which urged: "Paul, Don't Marry Jane."

Denise's sister, with her long red hair and mod outfit, was mistaken by some female fans as Asher.

Denise Mourges: I was allowed to bring someone, so I brought my sister. She and I both had bangs and red hair. We used to dye our hair red, like these twins. My sister went out there and she was wearing this dress. Very Carnaby Street, you know, Mary Quant type, Paraphernalia [a mod shopping district, fashion designer, and boutique popular at the time]. We looked like, little, oh my God, we were fashion plates, and they thought she was Jane Asher. Some fans started yelling at us and booing. One group threw things at us. We were so stunned, like deer in the headlights. They all started screaming, "Jane, Jane," you know. And the cops were afraid the girls were going to leap over the fence. Finally, a security guard grabbed us and pulled us back in the dugout.

Dawn Michaels: We went there in the morning. My cousins Ronnie and Debbie were like my sisters, my family. I had tickets for them, front row. My father went with me. He really got off on all this stuff. I always had to tell him to put the camera away and stop taking pictures. Thank God now he did.

Dave Glyde: We got in. We were flown to the stadium during the day. Suddenly we could hear this saxophone playing, this huge sound. And we were walking around the halls trying to find it and there was King, playing underneath the bunkers there, and it was incredible. We loved it. King Curtis was a legend for us . . . on so many of the early rock and roll records. We just loved him so much, a great man.

Dawn and Ronnie Schwartz arrive at the check-in gate.
COURTESY DAWN MICHAELS

Dawn's cousins eagerly anticipate the show.
COURTESY DAWN MICHAELS

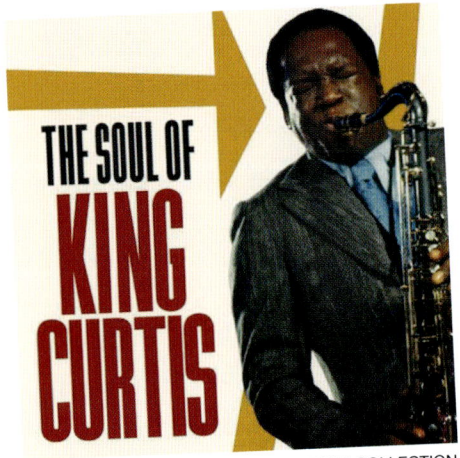
COURTESY DONDI BASTONE COLLECTION

COURTESY DONDI BASTONE COLLECTION

Bobbie Molina: I got all dressed up nice and pretty. I was wearing one of those '60s-style dresses, empire with a big bow. It was maroon on the bottom and white on the top with a big beige bow across my chest. . . . It was a square neck, and I had white shoes with little, tiny pumps. I had my hair in a flip. I used to tease my hair and make it into a flip. I had a little bow in the front.

Marc is on the bus from Baltimore with his 35-millimeter camera and phony press pass. The fans sing Beatle songs the entire way.

Marc Weinstein: The concert was sponsored by a radio station. If you bought a ticket for the bus, the price of the ticket for The Beatles concert was included. [The bus ride] must have been about two and a half hours, I believe. The bus was filled with mostly girls, but there was a mix of people in there.

Some recognized Marc as the guy who photographed The Beatles in Baltimore the previous year. His pockets are stuffed with three-by-five copies of his prints from that concert; on the trip, he sold more than $200 worth of them at 50 cents apiece.

Marc Weinstein: Oh, yeah, I was getting a name for myself selling pictures of other rock groups that I was taking pictures of at the Civic Center. As they came through the Civic Center, I would take pictures at the front of the stage. But they weren't as good as the ones I did of The Beatles and the Rolling Stones. There were five buses of fans as I recall. I later regretted not having people on the other buses selling pictures to the girls.

THE CONCERT

George Orsino: I had a four-by-five press camera with a big strobe and a big battery pack. It was a very intimidating camera. No one had a camera like I had. You only see them on the late show. I packed up and left to catch the bus. We left from . . . I think it was the Suburban Hotel in South Philly. Three buses, ninety-nine kids, and they didn't know what my job was. They had all the winners there and chaperones. Some of them were pretty fanatic about The Beatles. I had a pass Mike had given me and I went in. I knew some of the people, the chaperones. I got on the bus, no problem.

One of those "fanatics" on board was Joy Musiker Cohen. Just fourteen, her parents dropped her at the hotel and hugged her.

Joy Musiker Cohen: They were behind the whole Beatles thing. My mother was a big fan. My mother went with me in 1966 to see The Beatles in Philadelphia. My Dad bought me my first Beatle magazines and the little buttons and stuff. I didn't have parents I had to fight with. They were good. I got my outfit from Gimbel's mod boutique—a turquoise sleeveless, A-line dress with a lime green scalloped collar. And lime green shoes to match. It was cool back then.

Joy Musiker Cohen, Beatlemaniac. COURTESY JOY MUSIKER COHEN

Bobbie Molina: My cousin Margaret and I took the number 7 train that connected into Queens. I was thirteen and she was about eighteen. This was my first time to go to Shea Stadium. As we approached Flushing, we saw this beautiful light from the World's Fair. It was gorgeous. That was to our right coming into Flushing. Then to our left was Shea Stadium. And to our left we heard all the noise below, like "We want to see The Beatles." And my cousin Margaret said, "Oh my goodness, look at all those girls!"

Linda Ghigonne Marotte and Renee Perst traveled from Staten Island with their mothers, disembarking the Staten Island Ferry, all dressed up to go into Manhattan.

Fans continue to arrive. PHOTO BY PETER SIMON/PETERSIMON.COM

107

Renee Perst: We lived near a train. The Staten Island Rapid Transit, which is a train to the ferry. We take the ferry over to Lower Manhattan and then we get onto the appropriate subway.

I wore a shift dress. A dress, of course, because you always dressed when you went to the city. You know, it was back in those days. We were going to be in public, so it was still at that time when you dressed.

They excitedly descend into the subway and wait for the train. When it arrives, the doors slide open and the girls do a double take.

Renee Perst: It was nothing but girls—on the escalator going up and down, and the platform, and the subway cars—nothing but teenage girls. That's all that were there. Thousands of them! And they were all thirteen years old . . . and their mothers and a few disgruntled fathers. But for the most part, it was a sea of teenagers as far as the eye could see. And the din. Everyone was so excited. So excited. The "Ayeeeeee," you know. That's what it was.

Linda Ghigonne Marotte: The day was the most exciting day in my life. Having to take a subway train, which I hardly ever took, was a big deal. So that was exciting in its own way. And then we get on the train and there's nothing but thirteen-year-olds . . . and so many people on the subway train that you have to stand. Getting to Shea Stadium, you felt like the cows had been let loose at the farm.

Linda LaFlamme: My boyfriend's father was a Supreme Court judge and his mother was an important attorney. I'm sure that had something to do with the box seats we got. He managed to borrow his parents' Lincoln Continental with suicide doors to drive us to the stadium.

As soon as Meryl Streep arrives at her seat, she unfurls her "I love Paul" banner. She and her date chatter excitedly about the crowd.

Sid had invited his latest discovery, the Rascals. When they arrive, Sid ushers them through the dressing rooms to the third-base dugout to be as close to the action as possible.

THE CONCERT

Felix Cavaliere: For us, it was exciting just to be there, ya know. Because we were kids looking at the potential to be a part of this world and business world and music world. So, yeah, it was exciting.

Kids in the stadium see the Rascals' long hair—just as Sid had hoped—and make a beeline for the dugout. Even when they discover it isn't The Beatles, they still want their autographs. Fans rush the dugout, but Sid is ready for them, handing out thousands of buttons saying, "I'm a Rascals Fan" and lining them up to get the Rascals' autographs. Between announcements, the scoreboard flashes "The Rascals are coming! The Rascals are coming!"

Sid assembles the security people for final instructions, stressing that no matter how much they may be provoked, the fans must be handled with kid gloves. Under no circumstances are they to use force. The infirmary is through the first-base dugout.

Gates open at 6:00 p.m. Thousands of people are lined up to get in. Three buses from Philadelphia arrive at their destination.

Sid Bernstein talks with Felix Cavaliere of the Rascals. COURTESY DAWN MICHAELS

Joy Musiker Cohen: We never made the fair because of the traffic on the New Jersey Turnpike. But nevertheless, we got to the important part. We got to the concert. We had so much fun on the buses. We were singing songs and it was like going to camp.

George Orsino climbs off the bus, happy to leave the exuberant girls behind. He is clueless as to what awaits him.

Renee Perst: A sea of girls and of course the stadium is really big. Now, my father was an avid Yankee fan, and he had taken me maybe once or twice when I was younger to a ball game. Of course, it was Yankee Stadium. I mean, the Mets, no, no, no. So the stadium itself was new, and almost deco looking outside. I remember being fascinated by just the stadium itself. And by the way, I'd never seen that many people in my whole life. Just coming up to it, you could see in and a lot of people were already seated. Again, I had never been in any kind of a venue that was so big. But, yeah, rivers, rivers of girls.

TOP OF THE MOUNTAIN

PHOTO BY PETER SIMON/PETERSIMON.COM

And the excitement. You know, when Linda and I were talking, it was not details that I was really recalling. It was feelings. It was just being so excited that you felt like you could just jump out of your skin.

Linda Ghigonne Marotte: Renee and I couldn't understand why our moms had to go with us. But when we got there, we realized it was a good thing they were with us because we were completely overwhelmed with the amount of people and the noise, even before The Beatles got on. It was just a mob. It just felt so surreal. You were going to see The Beatles. You didn't expect what it was going to be like until you walked into that stadium and saw how big the stadium was. But it was just the crowds, the electricity in the air was just ridiculous. Everything was at its peak. It was really amazing—like nothing could top that day. This was going to be the best day of my life and nothing was ever going to top that day.

Beatle fans come in all shapes and sizes.
PHOTO BY PETER SIMON/PETERSIMON.COM

Mod boy fans. PHOTO BY PETER SIMON/PETERSIMON.COM

THE CONCERT

Marc Weinstein: I went to the ticket taker and gave him my ticket, but I wasn't going to my seat. I had to get to the locker room. I looked around and saw a stairway going down. That was the right direction, so I took it.

Dawn Michaels: My father was bursting with pride. Dad shot pictures of me on the stage because I had to set everything up. You can see the clock behind us. The clock is visible throughout the day getting later. Dad was into everything. We got closer, closer, closer to the time and we rehearsed. We put on our little tights and our sparkle tops and our white boots and that was it.

Top: Denise, Dawn, and Ronnie near the dugout.
COURTESY DAWN MICHAELS

Bottom: The Discotheque Dancers check out the stage.
COURTESY DAWN MICHAELS

Whoopi Goldberg: So this is what happened. Mom said, "We need to go." I said, "Where we going?" She said, "I'll let you know when we get there." So, we're on the train and I'm not paying any attention. And we get out and I say, "Where are we?" And she says, "We're at Shea Stadium." And I said, "Why?" And she held up two tickets and all I remember is my head going *poof*!

LEAVING THE WARWICK, 7:00 P.M.

The Beatles and their entourage are taken by limos and police escort to a Manhattan heliport.

> **Vince Calandra**: And then that night when we were leaving to go to Shea, Bob and I, we had a car take us. My job literally was to coordinate The Beatles leaving the Warwick in limos to the heliport to take them over to Shea Stadium. I was the guy that was on the phone with the pilot and the helicopter and La Guardia airport. The coordination had to be down fairly good because I had to tell the director of photography like, "Hey, they are twenty minutes away or thirty minutes away," and then we would set our cameras up. Because we wanted the helicopter to fly over the stadium so you could get these crazy fifty-five, sixty thousand people going nuts. That's basically one of the jobs I had to do on the show. It was madness! All I could do is make sure the limos were there and they had police protection. I mean, I wasn't there physically; I was on the field coordinating all this at Shea Stadium.

COME FLY WITH ME

George, a notoriously bad flier, is very anxious about the helicopter and has to be coaxed inside. One of the cameramen from the Sullivan crew is along to film it. In the air, the other three lads express regret at not having seen much of the city. The pilot detours from the route, swooping in for a bird's-eye view of Manhattan that terrifies poor George.

> **Tony Barrow**: We flew in by helicopter, which was sheer magic, over Manhattan and the East River. For George and John, it was a white-knuckle flight. I said, "We've asked the pilot to fly around the city," and George said, "Tell him to forget about that and go straight there. I don't want to be impaled on the top of the Empire State Building."

> **Vince Calandra**: George doesn't like flying. He especially hated helicopters. What happened was, the guy, the captain or whoever was flying it decided he was not going to just go to Flushing and land. He just started doing a tour of

Manhattan, flying in between the skyscrapers. George was having a shit fit. George almost threw up. He was so scared. And he was screaming, "Land this, land this damn plane. I don't want to do that!" That was the background stuff.

Moments later, they fly over Shea Stadium. "Can you go around again?" John asks. This time, they all look wordlessly at the enormous crowd below.

Tony Barrow: Thousands of flashbulbs popped off simultaneously to create a momentary display of dazzling light that lit up the evening sky. For the first time as we looked down at this unforgettable sight, it dawned upon four awestruck Beatles that this might just turn into the greatest gig the group had ever done.

Bobbie Molina: Then, all of a sudden, we saw a helicopter circling Shea Stadium. And I wasn't too sure The Beatles were in there or not. But it was circling, circling, and the crowd started going, "Whaaaa, Beatles! Beatles!" Then a couple of minutes went by after that happened; there were still entertainers, and we were so psyched. The music was not really too clear, but everybody was screaming. . . . I noticed everybody sharing the same feeling that I'm sharing right now. We loved them. We loved The Beatles, and we were there because we loved them. They had put us in a trance, and we are in love with them. We're just out of it. We just have to see them. We want to touch them. I mean, I wanted to touch them and everything, but I had a little bit more control. I noticed that everybody was like my age group, the younger girls, like thirteen, fourteen, fifteen who definitely had it. But I noticed there were adults who probably took their kids there. There were older teenagers who were sort of—I don't know—they were there because they were interested, but they were not so enthused as . . . the younger ones. . . . It was unbelievable. It was like this thrill inside. It's so hard to explain. It's something that, I could just sit down and meditate on it right now and I can go through the whole feeling. And it's a beautiful feeling.

The plan was to land at the heliport at the World's Fair, but hundreds of kids were waiting there. The pilot makes a last-minute adjustment and instead brings them down on the roof of Terrace on the Park. The Beatles and their entourage, which included Brian Epstein, Mal, Neil, and Alf, take the elevator to the ground floor, where thirty-four-year-old John Lociano, a security specialist, is waiting for them.

John Lociano: The Pinkerton Detective Agency wanted to contract to police the World's Fair with twenty-six hundred armed men. I was with the special events squad, which was sixteen men specially trained to handle security for executives, dignitaries, to work with the Secret Service and with the pope when he showed up over there, and quite a few people. The other Pinkertons are only security guards. When we trained on the grounds of the World's Fair, they had classes there for police. We were New York City police officers.

One day, they called us in and told us that The Beatles were going to show up at Shea Stadium, but they were going to land at the heliport at the World's Fair. And they said, "You guys have to escort them into Shea Stadium this week with about three hundred thousand people on the grounds." So when we saw all the crowds, we got there early.

The copter landed and they had about twelve people with them; Epstein was in the back with them.

KEEP ON TRUCKIN'

Sid Bernstein arrives by limo with another in tow to oversee the transfer to the stadium. It is only then that the entourage realizes the limo will be mobbed by fans. They'll never get through. An unhappy Brian tenses up. Everyone stands frozen.

John Lociano: I saw an armored truck. I figured one of our men worked for the armored guard service at the World's Fair, picking up all the bank deposits at night from all the restaurants. And I went over there and asked him if we could borrow the truck because nobody would suspect they would be in an armored truck. So he says, "Sure, but I have to drive it because of the insurance." I drove it up to the top of the fair restaurant there where the heliport was, and we backed it up into the service elevator and they walked right in.

George: I didn't think Wells Fargo were still going; I thought the Indians had got them all years ago.

THE CONCERT

John Lociano: George was the only one who gave us any trouble about it. Brian Epstein and Sid Bernstein complimented me on getting the truck. They thought it was the best security they'd ever seen. But George argued with Brian. He said, "I don't want to ride in that thing. I'm claustrophobic. I'd feel like I was in a cage." Brian and Sid had to convince him that there was no other way to get into the stadium and that it would only be for ten minutes. It took twenty in traffic. Ringo thought it was fun.

Brian rides in a van loaded with their instruments and some equipment.

John Lociano: So we got them in the truck and I had one of the patrol cars escort us to Shea Stadium through the fairgrounds and nobody stopped us. They all got out of the way, including the photographers. That's why there's no photos of that. If you watch one of the clips of the Shea Stadium concert, you'll see an armored truck next to the bandstand with me standing in front of it.

I just did it on my own because it was a quick thing. There was no chance of running into the Wells Fargo executives. I closed them in and I rode as a passenger. I rode with the driver. I found four badges up front and—don't say it too loud—but I gave them each one.

They complimented me. "That's the most beautiful uniform." Because the uniforms were tailor-made and we were noted to be the best dressed uniformed police in the United States.

They were just four skinny little boys to me. With a British accent. And they were hungry. That's all they kept complaining about. "When are we eating?"

Vince Calandra: So the truck took them to the center field opening and then they proceeded to walk, as the other bands were getting ready and playing. They proceeded to walk from center field through the infield and into the dugout, getting ready to make their appearance. Of course, the crowd went absolutely berserk.

The Beatles arrive!
PHOTO BY PETER SIMON/PETERSIMON.COM

A police officer talks to Ed Sullivan.
COURTESY DAWN MICHAELS

Cousin Brucie: "I was standing in the dugout with Sid Bernstein and Ed Sullivan waiting for the boys to get there. Finally, they were brought in by an armored car. And John Lennon came over to me and said, "Coo-sin, is it dangerous?" And I knew what he meant by that because there was such a cacophony. And Paul chimed in, "Is this going to be alright?" And I said to them, "These people are here for one thing, it's love, and they are here to share this space with you."

They didn't get that; they didn't understand that then—the power that they had. They were not ready for what greeted them at Shea Stadium.

Once inside the stadium, Sid guides The Beatles and Brian to a quiet observation point. The boys look around, pointing out banners and the martial artists. As he scans the crowd, Brian catches sight of the flashing message: "The Rascals are coming! The Rascals are coming!" His hand strokes his chin.

Felix Cavaliere: The billboard—we knew nothing about that. Meanwhile, there was this one person helping out with publicity, handing out Rascals buttons, cups, and pens. We were trying to take advantage of the math—you know, fifty-five thousand there. Well, we were back there with Epstein when he saw the sign. And Epstein was very controlled, and he put his hand to his mouth, and he stroked his chin, and he said, "Yes, clever . . . I see . . . um, Sid, if that message about the Rascals is not off in ten seconds, there will not be a show. No one rides on the backs of The Beatles." [Laughs.] He was ticked! Sid, he would do things that were a little off-the-wall like that. Sid apologized and had it shut off.

BEHIND THE SCENES

Sid escorts Brian and The Beatles to their dressing room underneath the stadium. The crowd is in a frenzy already, screaming so loud they can be heard underground. The "claustrophobic Beatle" is grateful to be on solid ground in the dressing room, where all the creature comforts he and his mates requested have been delivered: twelve bottles of Coke, four army cots, and a small black-and-white TV for Ringo. He loves American television.

THE CONCERT

Vince Calandra: The other job I had was going into the dressing room where The Beatles were on the third-base side of the stadium and getting a list of the songs that they were going to perform that night.

The four young men squabble. Eppy has never seen them this nervous. They even forgot to make a set list and hurriedly put together the songs they will perform that night, writing their list on a scorecard they find in the dressing room.

"Twist and Shout"
"She's a Woman"
"I Feel Fine"
"Dizzy Miss Lizzie"
"Ticket to Ride"
"Everybody's Trying to Be My Baby"
"Can't Buy Me Love"
"Baby's in Black"
"Act Naturally"
"A Hard Day's Night"
"Help!"
"I'm Down"

George, happy to be on solid ground under the stadium.
© 2003 BY GEORGE ORSINO

Vince Calandra: Now, no one knows whatever happened to that piece of paper. That scorecard. No one ever found out what happened to that piece.

I remember the four guys sitting there and talking, and they got these Nehru jackets on. I remember John saying, "I don't want to wear this thing. I don't like it. It's a military jacket. I'm not going to wear it." And they said, "You gotta wear it because you've got to match." So he deliberately opened the jacket up, and you never saw him onstage with the jacket buttoned because he just really didn't want to wear it. Paul remembers the Wells Fargo badges and they each pin one on.

Paul points to his new badge and warns that he is the new sheriff in town. © 2003 BY GEORGE ORSINO

George Orsino attended a Beatlefest decades after Shea to sell copies of his photos. The man in the booth next to his took an interest. "He saw the shot I got of Paul McCartney looking right down my throat. The guy in the next booth sells uniforms. He's from Maryland, Russ Lease. He saw that picture and he says, "You know, I'd give anything for that picture." I say "What do you mean? Why?" He says, "Because I own the uniform." "You're kidding me?" He says, "I paid $22,000 for it. It's up in my room right now. You want to see it?" So I said, "Yeah. Why not?"

So he closed the stand down and we went up to his room. He took it out of a plastic bag, with rubber gloves. He said, "Do you want to take a picture with it?" And he held it in front of me. And I said, "Oh, why not?" I held it in front of me, and he took a Polaroid picture of it. I laid it out on the bed and I said, "Where's the pinhole?" He asked me what I meant. "They all had the Wells Fargo badges on." I laid it on the bed and I searched around and sure enough, the pinhole was there. I say, "Wow, there's the pinhole." He said, "George, you're something else. You just authenticated my jacket." Which I did. It was the jacket.

Despite all the security at the stadium, George Orsino somehow makes his way unhindered into the bowels of the stadium. A man who has never done anything like this before suddenly decides he's going to get close to the biggest act in the world and ends up in their dressing room armed only with a camera. Brian Epstein would have exploded.

George Orsino: I was walking through the hall. I kept walking and a security guard put his hand up to stop me. I raised my camera like I was going to take a picture of something behind him, and he kind of slid over to the side, thinking to himself, "Am I supposed to stop this guy or what?" I just kept bumping my way through it.

Further on, I tried a door and I'm in the dressing room! It wasn't a dressing room. It was a bullpen, the ballplayers' hangout room. And they're all in there. Ringo's sitting down drinking a soda. Paul McCartney and George Harrison were talking to a couple PR men by a table. And one of the girls who followed them was sitting there. There was a drink on the table. There was no beer. There was soda bottles and Coke bottles on the table. And one of the security guys said, "Can you give me an autograph for my daughter?"

I don't want to be a fan because then I put myself in a different category. So I just hung around there doing pictures. I didn't want to be obnoxious taking pictures because I wasn't supposed to be in that room to begin with.

If I was actually supposed to be there as a photographer, then I would have been taking all sorts of pictures. But I was just kind of in there not making any fuss. Ringo is sitting on a little bench there, and I said to him, "Can you give me an autograph for the security guard's daughter?" I gave him my pen. He signed it, gave back my pen, and I gave the autograph to the security guard. He flipped. He was pretty happy, and that was it. I took a few more shots and tried to stay out of the way.

THE ROLLING STONES

A yacht, the *Princess*, cruises around the isle of Manhattan by way of the East River. Aboard are manager Allen Klein and his clients: hitmaker Bobby Vinton and newly signed Mick Jagger and Keith Richards of the Rolling Stones. Also aboard are Klein's nephew and the Stones' new road manager, Ronnie Schneider, record promoter Pete Bennett, and writer Chris Hutchins.

> **Chris Hutchins**: As we lazed on the deck in the sunshine, Mick told me: "I don't envy The Beatles. Look how much freedom we have and they're locked up in their hotel rooms." . . . Then he played Bob Dylan's latest single—pressed secretly for eager maniacs—and danced on the deck in the androgynous style that identifies him on stage. It seems likely the song Mick gyrated to was "Positively 4th Street," which was recorded in New York on July 29, 1965, and wouldn't be released officially until September 7.

When Klein suggests to his guests that they stop to see The Beatles perform, Mick fairly leaps at the chance. Klein has a bit of a questionable reputation. You either love him or hate him. Secretly, he hopes to lure The Beatles away from Epstein. This will be his first pass at them.

> **Bobby Vinton**: In those years, Allen Klein was my manager. Pete Bennett was my promotions man, as well as one of my best friends. I figure he fits into the story somehow. Allen was with me from the beginning. So when The Beatles came along, the big history about it was Allen Klein was my connection because I was his first major artist. When a lot of the English groups would come, like Herman's Hermits and the

Animals and all that, Allen had a reputation of, you know, be careful with him. I always stuck up for him and told them he was a good man who did me good service, and anybody who's a number-one singer, he can really take care of. So that was kind of our click.

And as a result, the word spread to a lot of English groups coming along, and eventually Allen got the Rolling Stones as well as The Beatles. I was kind of tied in with them. When they would come to Allen's office, I would be there, we'd say "Hello," and of course when they came to Shea Stadium, we were all to go. In fact, I went to Shea Stadium with Mick Jagger on a yacht.

Ronnie Schneider: We were able to dock right outside the stadium and walk to it. We went right in.

Bobby Vinton: Allen, Mick Jagger, Keith Richards, and The Beatles were all going to have a big party that night. And when we got to Shea Stadium, it was such a hectic thing that when we got backstage to see The Beatles, it was just hello and goodbye because there was so much action going on and everyone was very uptight about how the show was going to go.

In fact, what I really remember is, I'm walking with Mick Jagger past all these kids buying refreshments, and they say "Look, it's Bobby and Mick Jagger!" And they didn't like Mick Jagger, so they started punching him. Yeah! These tough guys from the Bronx. . . . And at the time, Mick was one of these bad boys that you weren't supposed to like, so they were punching him as we were walking along. He started to run, and then I started to run, and then I figure, "Why am I running? They don't want to punch me. They want to punch Mick."

Ronnie Schneider: I've been with Mick when he got punched two times. Oh yeah. He got punched in Dallas when we were going up an escalator, and he got punched at Altamont when we were walking in. Actually, there were probably other times. . . . You get guys that think they're going to be cool, and you know. Just drugs. One guy shot Lennon, so you know. Another came to stab Harrison. It's a rough business.

When we were getting ready to go into the dressing room, it was just a mob. It was like going through a Macy's parade. I think there was one cop

THE CONCERT

on either side of the door—it was a big doorway, but they were surrounded by people pushing in. But there was nobody to usher. It was a zoo. I couldn't see anything happening at the time. I was lucky because Mick and Keith were right by me, and I walked in, in between them and right by the cop. All of a sudden, I heard from about two or three people behind me, "Ronnie, Ronnie!" And of all people, the cop had stopped my uncle—the man who brought us there! I looked at the cop and instinctively said, "He's with me," and the cop let him go. We laughed about that for ages because who the hell was I?

Vince Calandra: I was in the dugout with Sullivan, Bob Precht. But Brian had a thing about celebrities. He did not want celebrities hanging out with his guys. Yeah. Because he always felt celebrities taking pictures with them and they always took advantage. Celebrities would take advantage of The Beatles. He didn't like people taking advantage of The Beatles.

John, Paul, and George will carry guitars onstage, but the time has come for Mal to bring additional guitars onstage. He needs help. Alf grabs two and goes with him.

Bob Precht talks with his father-in-law, Ed Sullivan. PHOTO BY GEORGE E. JOSEPH

Alf Bicknell: We went down this long winding corridor into a tunnel. . . . Seconds later we were in the open air. That's when it hit us—this wall of noise—so loud, it was physical.

The men just keep their heads down and hurtle toward the stage. Alf leaves the two guitars and runs back toward the dugout. He arrives visibly shaken. George asks what's wrong. "Well, the place went mad at the sight of your guitars. Lord knows what will happen when the four of you go out there."

Crowd behind net.
PHOTO BY GEORGE E. JOSEPH

Young boy being pulled away from Ringo's drum kit. COURTESY DAWN MICHAELS

121

Fans urge officer to get them autographs from whoever is in the dugout.
COURTESY DAWN MICHAELS

In the dressing room, Mick asks Sid Bernstein if the Rolling Stones are big enough to play a stadium. "Not yet, Mick," Sid responds. "Give it another year or two."

Felix Cavaliere: We came in through the players' entrance and through the dressing rooms to the dugout. And nobody really knew what was going on until we got to the field and we heard this nonstop, high-pitched screaming. What was going through my mind was the Chinese Xian hordes coming over the mountain in the war. That's what they did; they had this insistent battle screech to scare their opponents. That's what it sounded like.

It's amazing that we were around that time. . . . I said to George one time, "Do you realize how powerful you guys are in the world? I mean, if you go to the right, everybody goes to the right. If you go to the left . . ." And he just kind of sat there and looked at me and said, "Yes." They had to carry that with them wherever they went.

THE VIEW FROM HERE

Bob Precht: Ed and Sylvia were in the audience along with Betty and two of our children. We got them out early, concerned about the madness that was transpiring. Of course, Ed loved The Beatles—their appearances had given his show a huge shot in the arm—he was delighted to have been asked to introduce them that night.

THE CONCERT

Joy Musiker Cohen: They were not the best seats—nosebleed seats, upper box section 40, box 848A, seat 5. But we were there. And we were sitting literally in the clouds. Literally on cloud nine. I still have my ticket stub.

Linda Ghignone Marotte: Our seats were amazing. We were right behind the first-base dugout. We literally had the best seats in the house. Ed Sullivan's family was *behind* us. . . . We were so impressed with that. It was amazing.

Renee Perst: That's how good these seats were. Our sodas were sitting on the dugout. We had the first row. Ed Sullivan spent the entire concert—that was his spot—the first-base dugout. That I vividly remember. "Oh, my God, it's Ed Sullivan! He's five feet away from me!" The whole time. He kept talking to this whole box of people behind us. Come to find out that was his family.

Above left: Ed Sullivan, Bob Precht and Betty Precht, with her back to camera, peruse the crowd. COURTESY DAWN MICHAELS

Above right: Joy Musiker Cohen's ticket stub. COURTESY JOY MUSIKER COHEN

The crowd grows more restless.
COURTESY DAWN MICHAELS

Unknown couple in dugout.
COURTESY DAWN MICHAELS

Linda Ghignone Marotte: And then we looked into the third-base dugout—Renee had binoculars—and we're looking into the third-base dugout and that's where they were all congregating. You saw Ronnie and the Ronettes and you saw Murray the K standing out there. And, of course, we were all like, "Oh my God look at that. There's Murray the K and there's this one and that one." So it was just overwhelming.

Bobbie Molina: We went in the doors. And when we went in, I was so surprised that *16* magazine had given me such good seats. I was so happy that we were down in the box seats at the front. It was left field and all the way to the front, not at the top bleachers or anything. Then I saw the field. I saw the grass, and I saw far away, the stage. It looked far away.

Meryl Streep: I remember I sat about the 116th row, and I had a better view of New Jersey than I did of the little stage that was set up on center field.

Meanwhile, Marc Weinstein has great luck finding his way into the inner depths of the stadium. That part was easy, but inside is a maze of long, silent hallways with many doors.

The Rascals are on the far right of these unkown women. COURTESY DAWN MICHAELS

Marc Weinstein: The lower concourse was like a big, empty cavern. Nobody was there. I started walking and tried to open every door I passed. Everything was locked. I went to the left and, again, everything was locked, but I kept trying.

I continued my search in another hallway of doors. To my amazement, the knob on the third door I tried turned in my hand. I pulled it back a little bit and peeked in. Oy vey! It was a locker room full of policemen. I shut the door and thought, "What am I going to do?"

I got myself together. With my phony press pass I'd made hanging around my neck, I screwed up my courage, opened the door, and walked up to the first police officer I saw. In the best British accent I could muster, I said, "Excuse me, sir, I'm with The Beatles' entourage and I got separated from the group. Can you help me to the stage, please?" He looked at me in my too-tight, too-short bar mitzvah suit and said, "Sure, follow me."

THE CONCERT

The officer led me out into the hall and through another series of halls past several more officers, saying, "Hey, guys, move out of the way. This guy is with the group. I'm taking him out there." It was like the Red Sea parting before me. I couldn't believe it. There were police officers from all over the place. It was full of police officers. And I just followed him. Finally, I saw the little three steps up to left field. And I saw the sky. I just could not believe it.

He took me to the steps and told the left gatekeeper to let me out in the field. And as soon as my feet hit the grass, I was just electrified. I was wearing a suit similar to [those worn during] the '64 concerts and I had a big nose. Girls started screaming. They thought I was Ringo. I looked in their direction and the screams died down when it was obvious that I wasn't. Then I walked out to the stage.

OPENING ACTS

The anticipation is at a peak and emotions are beginning to spill over. At 8:00 p.m., the gates close, leaving two thousand ticketless fans in desperate straits. In a sudden swoop, they descend on the barricades meant to hold them back, carrying them to the stadium wall. Before the stunned police can move, they begin scaling them like ladders, leaping over the wall and into the stadium. At least fifty make it over and into the crowd before security could pull them down.

Perhaps inspired by the girls who'd climbed the wall, ten or twelve boys scramble over the fence at center field and make a run through the outfield for the stage. Fans cheer them on, but they are quickly rounded up and tossed out.

Inside the stadium, the opening acts are minutes away.

Cousin Brucie: It was like a variety show, which was pretty standard in those days.

Brenda Holloway: Jackie DeShannon did The Beatles' European tour and I had done background for Jackie. I said, "Hey, Jackie, when you talk to them, tell them I want to be on their show" . . . and she did! So they contacted Motown and got me. I was so grateful that she did that. It was just a treasure.

Dawn Michaels: We were all lined up, ready to go on—all of us: King Curtis, Brenda Holloway, Cannibal and the Headhunters, Sounds Inc. Murray the K went out to get the kids riled up but realized they didn't need that! Instead, he actually tried to calm them, "Let's not have anyone get hurt tonight."

Susan Silva: We had to get an official Beatles pass to get in. . . . I still have mine.

The golden ticket, the authorized pass for the tour. COURTESY OF SUSAN SILVA

Dawn Michaels: I had this heavy white makeup on so my face could be seen since they wouldn't be able to see any expression on my face. I told all the girls to do it, but they didn't care. I just wanted to be professional. The Beatles had us come in and we were introduced—you know, "This is who you're touring with." Then they went back to their dressing rooms to get ready. Paul was cute and we sort of had the eye for each other.

Onstage, King Curtis is introduced. He plays the national anthem and brings 55,600 excited fans to their feet to sing along. W-A-Beatle-C's Cousin Brucie welcomes the crowd and introduces beloved DJ Murray the K, who brings on the Discotheque Dancers. Dawn, Susan, Denise, and rest of the troupe run onto the field and up on the stage. The enormity of the audience, the noise, the event absolutely takes their breath away.

Dawn Michaels: Time to go on. Steve and I led the way out of the dugout with the rest of the girls following all the way to the stage. My father told me, "I was so proud of you. All those people and you just marched out there."

The Discotheque Dancers open the show. COURTESY DAWN MICHAELS

Denise Mourges: It was shocking. It was something like out of a dream.

The group dances to a medley of hits: "It's Not Unusual," "Downtown," "Can't Buy Me Love," "I'm Telling You Now," and closes with "A Hard Day's Night."

Susan Silva: The band played too fast! We were out there shaking our behinds . . . [It] probably didn't matter.

THE CONCERT

Denise Mourges: I messed up on some steps because I was so shocked. . . . I just was startled into not doing the steps I was supposed to. I turned a different way when everybody else was going one way and there I am. "Whoops, okay" and I got back to what people were doing and got back into the routine. But I was shocked out of it. And when you are on that stage, it was a postage stamp. It was tiny. There was room for the band and for us to dance. That was it.

Dawn Michaels: Denise is in the back laughing so hard because we had rehearsed but not with the orchestra at all [King Curtis], and it was so fast we could hardly move. We were laughing because it was so ridiculous. It was so fast. We straightened that out for the next night. No one wanted to see us anyway.

Denise Mourges: They [the crowd] kept screaming their [The Beatles'] names. They didn't care. They didn't want to see us. . . . All they wanted to see was The Beatles. I totally understood. If it was me, I wouldn't want to see me, either.

Dawn Michaels: It was just very fabulous to me. I loved it—thrilling! The stage was so tiny, and they had all their instruments there, plus King Curtis and his band. It was ridiculous. And the noise was crazy. You couldn't hear anything but the screaming. It was surreal. I had only been in one other situation where police had to set up barricades and hold crowds back, and that was for Soupy Sales at the Paramount Theater.

The Dancers return to the dugout. COURTESY DAWN MICHAELS

Susan Silva: After we finished our stuff onstage, I recall standing in this tunnel, an alcove, and watching The Beatles running to this platform, and that's when it struck me . . . the craziness of it, the screaming. I was never into rock groups, so this was a whole new thing for me. . . . I was in shock, amazed at the whole thing, just frozen. I never thought, "I just did that on this platform." What came to me was what was going on with these girls . . . total amazement. I was eighteen, had never seen anything like that in my life.

Cousin Brucie then introduces Scott Ross of WBIZ and husband of Nedra Talley, one of the Ronettes who first met The Fab Four when they toured England in 1964 with the Stones as their opening act. Nedra, Estelle, and Ronnie are all there. Scott introduces the King Curtis Band, who takes the crowd through a rip-roaring version of "What'd I Say," "The Branch," and "Twist and Shout." The legendary Curtis wails away on the sax, trying to engage the audience.

Marc Weinstein is at the edge of the stage. He avoids the film crew and tries not to draw attention to himself, fearful he will be discovered and thrown out. He does get the courage to get autographs from Brian Epstein, Murray the K, and Ed Sullivan. Not one of them questions this teenager whose pants are three inches too short. He has unfettered access to the stage.

Marc Weinstein: I primarily avoided any contact with anybody in authority or anybody who was competition to me. I kept milling around the stage and checking my camera. Just trying to look like I was doing my own thing, because I didn't want to risk getting kicked out of the area.

Cousin Brucie introduces WMCA's Frank Stickle who, in turn, brings on the WMCA "Good Guys" to harmonize on a Beatles/WMCA jingle. For the crowd, it is mercifully short. They introduce Cannibal and the Headhunters to a warm welcome. One of the first groups out of East LA to make it big, they rock their way through "Out of Sight," "Now Lady Now," "The Way You Do the Things You Do," and finish up with their current hit, "Land of 1,000 Dances." The crowd responds enthusiastically, singing the "na-na-na" chorus. They are so well-received that The Beatles move them to last in the lineup—right before them—for the rest of the tour.

Richard "Scar" Lopez was a member of Cannibal and the Headhunters.

THE CONCERT

Richard "Scar" Lopez: The audience didn't go for us like they went for The Beatles, but I didn't hear any boos. And after we played, Mick and Keith came backstage to tell us how good we were.

Dave Glyde: Cannibal and the Headhunters really impressed us. Because we learned from Americans right in the beginning, you better have stage presence and show. You can't just go up there. You had to have an act. Those guys were the kind of guys who made us go "Wow!" They had this thing when they finished their act, they'd turn into this kind of caterpillar, and they would go off in a whole line. They were great. I thought they would do more.

Bill Angelos: God, what was it like for those poor kids who were on the same stage as The Beatles? And they were just five kids who did what The Beatles did, but somehow they didn't do it the way The Beatles did it.

Audience calls for The Beatles while invited guests gather at the dugout where the boys will be. COURTESY DAWN MICHAELS

Dave Glyde: When you do a show like that and people are only really there to see The Beatles, you're pushing shit uphill—you know that old adage. Go and do your thing, but people aren't really watching.

Brucie returns with DJ Hal Jackson, who then introduces the Motown artist Marvin Gaye. Gaye waves to the crowd but does not perform. Brucie returns to introduce an up-and-comer at Motown, Brenda Holloway backed by King Curtis.

Brenda Holloway: Oh my God, I'll never forget Shea. . . . Girls were fainting. . . . I wanted to faint too when I met them. . . . I was too young to know anything [about being nervous to perform].

The great Marvin Gaye shot his own movie footage. COURTESY DAWN MICHAELS

And perform, she does—five numbers for the impatient crowd: "Shake," the Stones' "Satisfaction," "I Can't Help Myself," "You Can Cry on My Shoulder," and her hit song "(What Are You Gonna Do) When I'm Gone." All through her act, girls scream the names of their favorite Beatle. "I know, I know," she responds. "We all want to see them. They are coming soon."

Renee Perst: And how interminable the opening acts were. They kept coming! And who cared? It was so rude. I mean, I really hope you interview some of those people if they're still with us, because how rude was it that no one paid any attention to them at all? I mean, they were performing, but they were just invisible. They were. Now I remember King Curtis and I think the Young Rascals were there, too. Right? I was there for one reason only.

Joy Musiker Cohen: Oh, those poor acts. People weren't paying much attention. You know, a lot of people screaming, "We want The Beatles! We want The Beatles!" I felt bad for some of the warm-up acts. Teenagers aren't exactly the most, you know, nicest of people.

Cousin Brucie and fellow W-A-Beatle-C disc jockey Charlie Greer introduce Sounds Incorporated. The instrumental group tears it up with Major Griff West (David Glyde) virtually airborne through four rollicking numbers, all hits for them in the United Kingdom: "America" (from *West Side Story*), Little Stevie Wonder's "Fingertips," "The William Tell Overture," and "In the Hall of the Mountain Kings."

Dave Glyde is airborne as Sounds Incorporated rocks.
PHOTO BY PETER SIMON/PETER SIMON.COM

Tony Newman was the drummer for Sounds Incorporated.

Tony Newman: It was bedlam from the time we started playing, but we couldn't tell if they were cheering for us or if they were just excited because The Beatles were coming soon. But also, we were from England. So that made them more excited about us than they would have been otherwise.

THE CONCERT

As Sounds roar through their numbers, Sid is in the dressing room with John, Paul, George, and Ringo, explaining how it is going to go down. When he finishes, they grab their guitars and follow him out—and into a mob scene! The outer room is packed with people. Mick Jagger and Keith Richards grab John and Paul to introduce their manager, Allen Klein. Miniskirted girls vie for attention. Denise and her sister are there, too. Like an ocean current, the crowd begins moving toward the dugout. Bobby Vinton is swept up in it along with everyone else. George Orsino runs ahead. He is walking backward, snapping photos.

John makes his way through the crowd toward the dugout. © 2003 BY GEORGE ORSINO

George Orsino: I had to wind the film after each photo and I'm walking backward, trying to stay in front of them. People are coming from every direction, and I call out to John Lennon, "Slow down! You're going to run over me!" He laughed and said, "That's not my problem."

Ronnie Schneider: I'm telling you, there wasn't an inch. It was cramped. Plus people were smoking cigarettes. It was like backstage now at any of the big events for the Stones or anything. That was just like a giant greeting area. Everybody was there well-wishing. You know, here come the Stones and the press, etcetera. It was just crazy. I mean, they may have had private moments at some point, but we were in there, and then we all got out, and they were going to go onstage, so they didn't have that much of a peaceful moment.

The crowd moves as one toward the dugout like a tsunami picking up everything in its path. The boys are barely able to move. Paul and John push their way toward the front with George not far behind, but Ringo—where is Ringo?

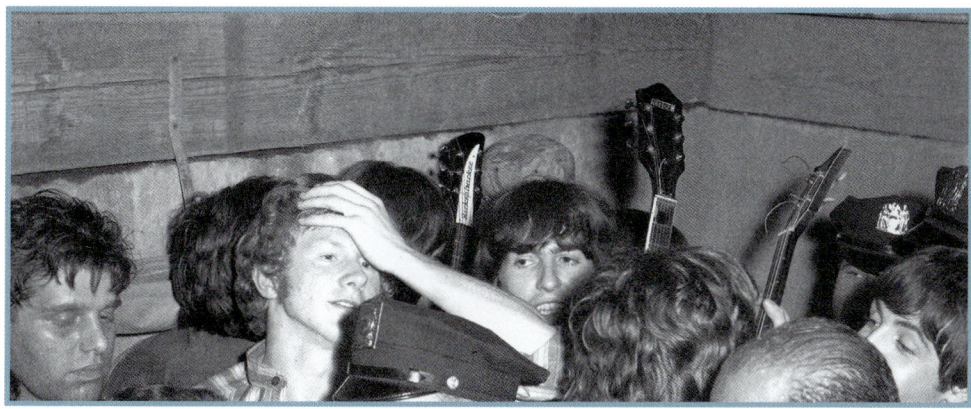

Where is Ringo?
© 2003 BY GEORGE ORSINO

George Orsino: They're walking through this hallway and it's kind of getting jammed up and . . . people they knew got in. Mick Jagger, Bobby Vinton, and a couple recording company owners are in that crowd. And I'm walking through the hallway. Now we got jammed up because the guard was at the door and was taking them out to the field and holding it shut so he could round up all of The Beatles and get them all out front. Ringo was way in the back somewhere.

Bobby Vinton: Everybody was there and I'm sure a lot of the press people I knew were just as surprised to see all this happening as I was. It's sophisticated today. It's hard for us to relive anything about those days. But you know that was fifty years ago. There was never that many people.

The diminutive Ringo has been swallowed up in the crowd. He has to fight his way to the front, where the others were waiting for him so they can all take the field together.

George Orsino: I couldn't move with my camera and my big strobe, so I saw these swinging doors on my right-hand side. I pushed them open and there were the commodes for the ballplayers. I said, "Wow. Okay, I'm private now." I stood on one of the commodes and I'm hanging over the cinder block wall. I'm getting these nice shots. Well, they weren't great but there's shots of Mick Jagger, Bobby Vinton, and some of the crowd there. I unloaded my film there, and I went down to the guard, and I said, "Listen, I have to get over by the stage and load my camera up." He opened up the door and let me out.

George has heard the din while underground, but when the door to the field flew open and the screams of fifty-six thousand girls hit him, he is momentarily stunned.

George Orsino: That was a blow to my head. Wow, you know. Lot of people. I couldn't hear a thing. I just ran to the stage and loaded up my camera. I think I had eight or nine more shots left.

Peter Bennett and Allen Klein are behind Bobby Vinton and Mick Jagger is in front of him with Keith Richards (back of head). George is ahead and John is barely seen on the upper right . . . but Ringo?? © 2003 BY GEORGE ORSINO

TAKING THE STAGE

The crowd is chanting, "We want The Beatles." Bedsheets turned into banners hang throughout the stadium proclaiming love for one or all of them. The air is heavy and sticky. Police mop their foreheads and survey the crowd nervously. They already have endured more than an hour of DJs and opening acts. They want The Beatles—now!

>**Eric J. Adams**: The Beatles played at second base and there was a seemingly impregnable line of policeman facing the crowd. They stood arms-length apart, forming two phalanxes, one each from the edges of the stage to the foul poles in left and right fields. These somber men in blue remained unearthly still, as if any small movement or loss of symmetry might encourage one, two, one hundred, ten thousand teenaged girls to jump the fence and begin a stampede toward the boys. How could you stop it?

Mal is onstage arranging amplifiers and setting up John's portable Vox Continental organ. He stands up and looks around. Sweat drips down his forehead, and he wipes it from his eyes as he stares out at the immense crowd. He looks toward the barricades and the lines of defense and says a silent prayer.

Cousin Brucie tries to entertain the impatient crowd. The police keep a wary eye on the stands, and the judo masters stand at attention. Some fans spot Mick and Keith in the dugout and start chanting for the Stones. Bottles and other debris are thrown onto the field. Suddenly John isn't sure about going out there. Brian fears it isn't safe. He looks around for Sid, but it is too late; he is already making his way to the stage.

>**Cousin Brucie**: People ask me, "What are the highlights of your career?" Probably one of the most important and earth-shattering one was The Beatles at Shea Stadium. That feeling is still in my body. I still feel that reverberating. That was the day I believe that Con Edison could have shut down its turbines and plants and there would have been enough electricity generated from Shea Stadium to light the entire city. I'll never forget what it felt like in my diaphragm and my belly. You felt the power of this audience, and I never realized that before. In fact, today I can sit down while I'm talking with you and conjure up that feeling that I had in my body. I've never felt anything like that, and I've never felt anything like that since. There were fifty-six thousand

some-odd amazing fans, most of them female, by the way. And those fans were all waiting for one thing: to share space with their new heroes, those mop tops from England. There was such a cacophony, such an electricity in the air that you felt it. When there's electricity in the air like that you can feel it, the pressure in your body, the vibrations.

I asked the boys prior to this concert what it was like, and they described things. But they never felt the energy that they felt that day at Shea Stadium. Because with all the riots and all the things they'd been through in Europe, they never, never experienced what happened there at Shea Stadium. That I know. They were very nervous, very nervous, shaking—especially John. He never understood the power he had—the power of a poet to get people to share a space with him. He never took it for granted, very honestly. I've always thought that.

The moment is here. At 9:10, Sid and Ed Sullivan walk across the infield and climb the steps to the stage. The two men responsible for introducing the lads from Liverpool to American audiences are the last two standing between the audience and their idols, and everyone knows it. The crowd is delirious. Cousin Brucie does not keep them waiting. He motions to Sid.

"Let me introduce Sid Bernstein, the man who brought The Beatles to America." A roar goes up. Flashbulbs pop. Only Sid's family and closest friends know what he's been through. Without Sid, the concert at Shea Stadium would never have happened. But Bernstein is not one to blow his own horn or seek credit—even credit well deserved. In his modest fashion, he turns the reins over to Ed Sullivan.

John, Paul, and George make it to the top step, and finally Ringo is able to break through the swarm of people to join his mates at the field entrance of the dugout.

Sid Bernstein: One of our finest newspapermen, the number-one showman of the world, and most important of all, a truly great American, Mr. Ed Sullivan.

Ed Sullivan takes the stage as the fans go wild.

Ed Sullivan: Honored by their country, decorated by their queen, and loved here in America . . .

THE CONCERT

The Rascals pat the boys on their backs as they spill out of the dugout and onto the edge of the field.

Ed Sullivan: Ladies and gentlemen—The Beatles!

From the moment The Beatles take the field, it is sheer pandemonium. The screams are deafening. Andrew Laszlo, wincing in pain, pushes his earplugs in further, but they are useless. Thousands of flashbulbs light up the stands as The Beatles look around in complete wonder. If there is one moment in their touring career that is indelibly etched forever in their memory, it is the instant they hit the field at Shea. They'd never played for a crowd even half this size. It is stunning. The documentary captures the moment their trepidation changed to awe.

The fans go wild! PHOTO BY GEORGE E. JOSEPH

Paul hits the field. COURTESY DAWN MICHAELS

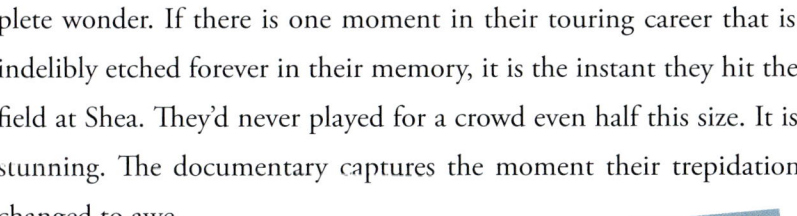
The Beatles are awestruck.
PHOTO BY PETER SIMON/PETERSIMON.COM

Paul steps back to let John take the lead.
PHOTO BY PETER SIMON/PETERSIMON.COM

TOP OF THE MOUNTAIN

Chris Hutchins: Keith and Mick were present when the band was introduced. If the stadium had had a roof, it would have been blown sky-high. Never have I heard such a blast. The screaming, shouting, whistling, and stomping swelled into a crescendo that sent me and the Stones reeling backward in the aisle. The Beatles had literally rolled the Stones.

Joy Musiker Cohen: I also remember Sullivan introducing them. The really big show. And that was very exciting because Ed Sullivan was the epitome of cool back then.

Linda's view from first base.
COURTESY OF LINDA GHIGNONE MAROTTE

Linda Ghignone Marotte: Electricity filled the air. And when Ed Sullivan introduced them, the roar, . . . it was like standing next to a freight train. . . . People started throwing things from up above. I got hit with a sandbag Beatle doll—I wish I'd kept it. It was beautifully done. Books, lipstick cases, flowers rained down on us. It felt like the whole stadium shook.

Bobbie Molina: Then all of a sudden, they came out of the dugout. I was looking and in my heart I was seeing them walking. I had viewed them before through the magic of television. And when you actually see that person, in person, walking: "Yeah! That person does exist." They're walking. I saw their brown hair and it was so nice and shiny. And they were waving and then they ran up to the stage and they got on there. Ed Sullivan shook their hands and then they started singing.

John looks around in wonder at the size of the crowd.
PHOTO BY PETER SIMON/PETERSIMON.COM

Brian Epstein stands alone in the middle of those around the stage, nervously staring at the crowd. PHOTO BY PETER SIMON/PETERSIMON.COM

THE CONCERT

I'm not too sure which one was the first one they sang, because I do know that they sang, like, "Twist and Shout" and a couple other songs that were on the new album they had. It was like, "*Wow! This is super fab!*" And everybody was just cheering and yelling and screaming. I saw on the field, people climbing the fence. They got into Shea Stadium and on to the grounds and they were running to the stage. Then the police got them and took them away. Then Ringo turned around and he waved to that person. You know, he probably felt bad. He turned around and he waved. Then there was another person; the second one who climbed over and tried to get to the stage. But that person didn't make it up either. They just kept on playing and playing.

Precht, hands on hips, watches the stage and the clock.
PHOTO BY PETER SIMON/PETERSIMON.COM

At the time they were playing, you heard the music, but the sound system wasn't sophisticated like it is now. It was raspy and choppy and everything. It was just all screaming and crying and everything. But still in my mind and my silence and my heart, I just saw them. I was just so satisfied just viewing them and acknowledging, "There they are. There they are. All four of them. I'm seeing them here and I'm just so happy." I was very calm. I mean, why would I want to scream? I was just tranquil, like, "wow." Yeah. It was probably just a daze. But it was fun.

Linda LaFlamme: Seeing them run out was so cool. I never screamed for anyone. I was more a fly-on-the-wall type. I preferred to take it all in, absorb it.

Meryl Streep: As indelibly as the words of those songs are written across my heart, I can remember the sight of those four boys running across the grass to the stage. And I can remember the downbeat and the first few chords of "I Saw Her Standing There" and I can remember the roar that just rose up and surrounded those four boys . . . for the next twenty-five years of our lives.

TOP OF THE MOUNTAIN

Bobby "Rabbit" Jaramillo was "Cannibal" of Cannibal and the Headhunters.

Bobby "Rabbit" Jaramillo: We were standing right next to the stage when The Beatles played, and man, it was awesome. There was this roar, and then the flashes started going off from the cameras. And it never stopped.

Pain, sadness, and ecstacy—it's all there. PHOTO BY GEORGE E. JOSEPH

Ronnie Schneider: When we were standing there outside listening to the music, we couldn't hear anything and we left. We didn't stay for the show. We stayed for maybe three songs. We tried to, but the crowd. You just couldn't hear the music at all. It was ridiculous. "Let's get out of here." My feeling, what it made me feel, was like, it was just silly. Basically, I just thought, "Look at these girls screaming." I mean, the line we always had was, "When the girls stood up the seats were wet." That's how we looked at it. No offense, but that was it. This was just crazy.

Linda and Renee's view. COURTESY OF LINDA GHIGNONE MAROTTE

Renee Perst: My mother was a nonentity, I have to say. Really, because Linda and I were so excited. Elsie was there and she was the chaperone. And my mother and I had a wonderful relationship then, still do now. I asked her,

Linda in green and Renee with binoculars. COURTESY OF RENEE PERST

"Do you have any real memories of it?" And she was like, "Not really. Other than the noise." That was a major part of it. That sound of fifty-five thousand screaming high-pitched voices was something that is truly indescribable. This I vividly remember is that my ears rang for over twenty-four hours. I had that sound in my ears like, you know, the ocean. I think it's called tinnitus. It's like when your eardrums have been assaulted.

For over twenty-four hours I could hear that roar, but it wasn't a roar because a roar is low. This was high pitched. I can't even describe it. And it never stopped. You couldn't even hear the music. And we had those stupid little skinny speakers right in front of us. And more than anything I just used my binoculars because I wanted to be closer. I just wanted to see them. I wanted to see them sweating and, you know, everything about it. But that din was indescribable. Really. And that is one of my most vivid memories.

Eric J. Adams: The screams allowed only intermittent waves of music to reach my father, sister, and me. Even with our great seats [behind the plate, lower level], I don't recall hearing any particular song. But who cared? The sound of female enthusiasm was far more exhilarating.

Paul: Linda [Eastman] was also there—but as she was a real music fan. She was quite pissed off with everyone screaming. I think she enjoyed the experience, but she genuinely wanted to hear the show. That wasn't the deal though. Not then.

Linda Eastman is not the only future wife of a Beatle who attends the concert. Barbara Bach at seventeen is not much of a Beatle fan. She prefers Dylan and Aretha, Ray Charles and the Stones; and she goes to Shea only to chaperone her little sister, Marjorie, who attends complete with a Beatle wig.

Barbara Bach: She was crazy about The Beatles!

In yet another remarkable coincidence, Marjorie's future husband is also at the concert. Imminent guitar legend Joe Walsh, also seventeen, of Eagles fame, wouldn't have missed it for the world.

TOP OF THE MOUNTAIN

Joe Walsh: I took one look on *The Ed Sullivan Show* and it was, "Fuck school. This makes it!" I memorized every Beatle song and went to Shea Stadium and screamed right along with all those chicks.

I ended up playing bass for a band called the Nomads most of my senior year. My parents still have a picture of me all slicked up, with a collarless Beatle jacket and Beatle boots, playing at the prom.

COURTESY DAWN MICHAELS

COURTESY DAWN MICHAELS

COURTESY DAWN MICHAELS

COURTESY DAWN MICHAELS

COURTESY DAWN MICHAELS

COURTESY DAWN MICHAELS

THE CONCERT

Linda LaFlamme: The Beatles completely changed my life, a whole new lifestyle. I was more into R & B, Otis, Wilson Pickett. Then all of a sudden there were these white boys with beautiful music and lyrics. They were like me, and I wanted to be like them. I started smoking pot, changed the way I dressed, skipped school. I just loved the music and only wanted to be around that. Willie, my boyfriend, was going off to college and law school. He wanted to get married and have kids. Nope, not me, no thank you. Within a year, I was living upstate in a communal house with Jimi Hendrix and a bunch of other musicians.

Steve Van Zandt: I was in New Jersey and the night I saw The Beatles changed everything. I had seen Elvis before and he had done nothing for me, but these guys were in a band. When I was thirteen, my favorite Beatle was George Harrison. From the age of fourteen, thirteen, I guess, I wanted to be a rock and roll star. And that was it. I wanted to make a living playing rock and roll, and it was a ridiculously impossible dream at that time.

Mikhal Gilmore: That August in 1965, we didn't fathom where the power in this sort of communion might lead. We didn't know where we were going with The Beatles, and they didn't know where they were headed.

PHOTO BY GEORGE E. JOSEPH

Ringo: I never felt people came to hear our show—I felt they came to see us.

George: When you're competing with fifty-six thousand people. It's ludicrous. . . . We weren't sure if anybody could even see us, let alone hear us.

Paul: It was like being in a washing machine.

John: It was like being in the eye of a hurricane.

Felix Cavaliere: I don't think anyone really screamed the way they screamed for The Beatles. You know, it's a different scream. You have to take it up a few decibels. This was hysteria. . . . And when you hear fifty-five thousand of them. It just didn't stop. It just, it was sound. And it was eerie because it was not controlled by any stretch of the imagination. It was like a hysterical scream that didn't stop. So they played. I can't honestly tell you I heard the music. But it was really strange, you know.

Elliott Gordon has known Rascal Gene Cornish for many years.

Elliott Gordon: Gene did tell me, and I'm quoting him, I asked him, "What did the sound sound like?" And Gene said, "It sounded like I was sitting by an engine of a 747, the most explosive sound I've ever heard at a concert in my life."

Felix Cavaliere: Yeah, I mean, there was no way to describe it, because at least in our years, there was no precedent for that.

Whoopi Goldberg: It's what they elicited. I mean, it didn't matter where they went. And so at Shea with a gazillion girls, you're part of this giant machine and screaming.

Marc Weinstein: What I did was what I instinctively do in a noisy situation. I turn my hearing aid off. I was born with a hearing loss. Nerve deafness. I've been wearing hearing aids all my life. I was wearing a hearing aid then. So usually in noisy situations I just turned it off. I still heard it, but it was vastly

PHOTO BY GEORGE E. JOSEPH

reduced. It wasn't piercing my ears. Many rock and roll band members have severe tinnitus and hearing loss. I have tinnitus as well.

Joy Musiker Cohen: My favorite Beatle was Paul. That goes without saying. Thankfully I was sitting on his side. And again, that was just how the luck fell. They were just little teeny tiny ants, because of course back then we didn't have the big screens. And, of course, you couldn't hear them because those amps today are what you would have at a house party. It kind of makes it all the more charming.

Bobby Vinton: You just couldn't get over all these people coming, and like I said, when the music started, you could hardly hear. Because, first of all, they didn't have great amps—one mic by the drums and one mic by the guitar amp. As a musician, I wanted to hear more. But it didn't matter; there was excitement. It was probably one of the greatest events that I went to because it was a first of its kind.

Bill Angelos: It was a watershed moment in global cultural history.

Overhead, the Goodyear Blimp floats in circles above the stadium while flashing Fab Four–related messages like "Welcome Beatles" and "Help!"

PHOTO BY PETER SIMON/PETERSIMON.COM

Joy Musiker: A sea of humanity and extremely excited young ladies. Who knew that this was history? We didn't think back then that fifty years later this would be such an amazing thing. There were a lot of teenage boys as well. But it was, I'd say, mostly girls. Screaming young ladies having a wonderful time . . . the time of our lives.

The cops are not prepared for the noise. Some cover their ears with their hands in an attempt to stem the pain.

The Sullivan crew tries to cover all the action. Andrew Laszlo and Bob Precht give direction to their crew, most of it by sign language and a notepad. The noise surpasses imagination, rendering the state-of-the-art communication system worthless. Laszlo stuffs more and more lens-cleaning tissue into his ears, but nothing helps abate the noise.

Meryl's date squeezes her hand. Both teens smile ear to ear.

Marc shoots photos of The Beatles all around the stage. The screaming is overwhelming but not for him.

Linda screams her lungs out while her friend Renee watches in tears. Their reactions are filmed for the documentary.

Renee Perst: In awe. That would be it. Linda was a screamer. I never screamed. I was a silent adorer. You know, my mouth was probably hanging open for half the concert. I am just staring adoringly. That's exactly what it was for me. . . .

I just remember thinking to myself, "It's really them! They're here. We're breathing the same air." It was so amazing to me that they were in front of me. It was real. And it didn't matter what they sang. It didn't matter if they sang.

COURTESY OF RENEE PERST

COURTESY OF RENEE PERST

It was just this excitement that . . . I don't know. It certainly is in the top-most exciting things that has ever really happened in my life. And what's funny is if it comes up in conversation and you tell people you were at that concert, they look at you with reverence, if you know what I mean. It's like, "Really? You really saw The Beatles at Shea?" And then I'll tell them I was in the front seat; not only that, I have proof because I can put a video on and see myself there. That's the best part. It really, really is. Because although I remember, it's like, "*Wow*, there I am!" And the crowd, you know. It's just so very cool. I can't even tell you.

Linda Ghignone Marotte: I hadn't planned to scream, but when they came out, I couldn't help it. My mother, Ida, was mortified at my behavior. She told Renee's mom she was just flabbergasted at my reaction, and she could not believe how I screamed so much. For three days I couldn't even speak, and Renee couldn't hear. So Elsie was like, "I don't think these girls are ever going to these concerts again." But, of course, we went.

Andrew Laszlo: Long before The Beatles finished, the extra-large first-aid area created especially for this event was overflowing with injured, bandaged, and still-weeping kids and their terrified mothers.

Unidentified policewoman: They're psychos! Their mothers ought to see them now.

Renee Perst: The dugout where we were sitting was where they brought most of the girls who had fainted. And I remember just seeing these passed-out girls being brought in. They were bringing them in for resuscitation, into the first-base dugout. They were probably bringing them many places because there were probably many. I just thought, "Poor them! They're missing the concert!"

Linda Ghignone Marotte: There were a few girls to the right of us, and I remember one girl being pulled across the dugout by one of the policemen because she had fainted. That was the only way he could get her: . . . standing on the dugout and try[ing] to pull her up over the fence. And I'm like, "Boy, they are going above and beyond." The poor guy.

Bobby "Rabbit" Jaramillo: We went backstage, and there was a first-aid area where a bunch of the kids were just laid out. There wasn't room for them all, so they were sitting in the hall, sitting on the floor. . . . [I]t looked like a hospital scene from World War II or something. And they were moaning. It wasn't just the girls, but the boys were also moaning about their favorite Beatle . . . "Oh Paul . . . Oh, Ringo . . ."

PHOTOS BY PETER SIMON/PETERSIMON.COM

Linda Ghignone Marotte: Some tried to run to the stage, but the police were right on them. The amount of police force that was there was amazing. They did some job holding them back. It was great, I don't think anybody ever reached anywhere near it.

Felix Cavaliere: Sid was a fairly big man, and he was even bigger in those days. I remember some kids charged the stage, and I saw him chasing after them, running on the field so they wouldn't get hurt. Seriously. Oh yeah, I mean, he was a very caring guy. He was a very gentle soul. But he was way too big to be running across the field following these kids. And of course, they're like in their teens, so they could outrun him pretty easily. I'll never forget that, seeing him just chasing after them, huffing and puffing. I'm sure he just didn't want them to get hurt. You know, some security guard might hit them or something like that. But it was quite a day. [Laughs.]

John and Paul stop a couple of times to watch the runners and cheer them on only to see them overtaken and carried away by police.

George Orsino snaps several shots from the side of the stage.

Ringo scans the stadium from his perch: all the banners, the flashing bulbs from cameras, girls carried by police to the

© 2003 BY GEORGE ORSINO

The boys launch into "Twist and Shout."

Look at the runners!

All photos this page: © 2012 Adam Kushner photographed by Marc Weinstein

Eppy watches the crowd.

All photos this page: © 2012 Adam Kushner photographed by Marc Weinstein

The boys wipe away the sweat from the hot August night.

All photos this page: © 2012 Adam Kushner photographed by Marc Weinstein

Ringo's view from the stage.

"I'm Down."

Ringo shoots Marc a look.

Mal is bottom right, there to help if needed.

HELP!

All photos this page: © 2012 Adam Kushner photographed by Marc Weinstein

Paul's intro cannot be heard.

Ringo tries to hear George.

Thank you and good night all!

Ringo sings "Act Naturally."

John and George lose it!

All photos this page: © 2012 Adam Kushner photographed by Marc Weinstein

infirmary. This is real. This is Beatlemania. He later said the only way he could tell what song they were playing was by the way the other three wiggled their butts.

Sid and Brian stand on the field below the stage.

Paul plays his way through the music, a look of pure amazement on his face. He glances down at Sid and winks.

Sid takes it all in—this surreal, record-breaking night. Despite all the problems and fears and naysayers, Sid has done it—it is the night he dreamed of. He is the man who made this happen. His chest swells with pride as he allows himself this moment of satisfaction. Just then, Brian leans over and asks, "How are we going to get out of here?" Sid laughed.

> **Marc Weinstein**: Yeah, yeah. It really went by fast. Although it seemed like a long time, it did go by pretty quickly.

> **Tony Barrow**: Brian Epstein's face glowed with pride. Tears of joy ran down his cheeks long before the boys finished their set.

Larry Kane was a radio personality who had traveled with The Beatles in 1964 and was invited to return in '65.

> **Larry Kane**: Brian was very relieved, and he was elated that they'd filled it up and pulled it off safely. And when I talked to the band afterward, they called it collectively the greatest moment of their career together. . . . The Beatles never got over the spectacle, the grandeur, the chills they felt at Shea Stadium.

The Beatles, drenched in sweat, have poured their all into eleven songs. The electricity from the audience travels across that field and rains down upon them. John especially is delirious with excitement. He speaks jibberish during several introductions, acutely aware that it doesn't matter what he says, what they play, or even if they are in tune. He raises his arms over his head, laughing with a wild look in his eyes. Then they launch into their last number, "I'm Down," which they are playing live for the first time with John on the organ.

> **Ringo**: John just went mad. . . . If you've seen him, he was playing the piano with his elbows!

John: I felt naked without my guitar, and George couldn't play for laughing [laughs]. I was doing it for a laugh . . . biggest crowd we ever played to . . . biggest live show . . . ever done up until then . . . and it was fantastic.

Marc Weinstein: When they did "I'm Down," John ran over to the organ. Moments earlier, he had thrown his arms up in complete amazement. He couldn't hear a thing and he knew the audience couldn't hear either. He knew he could play anything, and he just went goofy, running his elbow up and down the keyboard, laughing. I ran to that side of the stage. A folding wooden chair was right next to the stage there. I quickly scrambled on the chair. One more step and I'd have been on the stage. I got a full-frame shot of John from the elbow up.

George tried hard to remain serious through all of this, but when he saw John, he lost it. I ran around to the front of the stage and grabbed the very last shot of the night. Little did I know it would be the best shot of the concert: George and John laughing hysterically, having the time of their lives. Looking back, that photo epitomizes the height of their career, the peak of Beatlemania. They were still themselves—no arguments, no controversy—just enjoying their fans and the totally exhilarating moment. In that photo, I see their total uninhibited joy of doing rock and roll.

GOING HOME

Vince Calandra: They came off the stage and the cars were waiting with their doors open. It looked like the getaway from a Steve McQueen movie.

Marc Weinstein: And I went on to try to meet the boys at the car that was to take them away. And I couldn't even get a shot off. Everything happened so fast I couldn't even get the camera ready to snap a shot of them getting in the car. There was so much commotion going on.

Bobbie Molina: When they finished singing, they got off the stage and a white station wagon came to the stage, and they got in there. Then they started coming out and I noticed they were coming out toward where we were in left field. Because it's near the picnic area. There's an exit near there.

They started coming and I'm like, "Oh my goodness, the car is coming by!" And the crowd started getting so excited behind me. They started climbing over me, and my cousin said, "Oh my God. They're climbing over us!" I felt a shoe on my shoulder go over me. And they stepped on my cousin and my sister. And I said, "Whoa!" All of a sudden, the cops were in front of us saying, "You better get back or we're going to hit you!" Some guys, they didn't care.

Actually, it was guys that jumped over the wall to get to them. I was surprised. I remember there was one fella who almost got near the station wagon, and the cop grabbed him and twisted his arm and ripped his T-shirt and then had to club him to get him down. Then a whole bunch of cops came and started locking their arms, one in one, to prevent the crowd from going further to the station wagon. The station wagon slowly passed by, and Paul took out the handkerchief to wave goodbye. I was so thrilled to see that. Then all of a sudden, the station wagon quickly jetted off to the exit. Then the cops came to take care of the crowd in the field.

They are very lucky, The Beatles. Because security was not how it is now. And how the crowd was over there at that time. If they hadn't done it that way—in the white station wagon instead of them walking back to the dugout—they would have been in danger. I was just waving and I was just happy. My cousin Margaret at the time couldn't understand, "Why are they crying and screaming?" and "Yes, they are nice fellows, but why is this happening?" She didn't have Beatlemania. Everybody else had Beatlemania. And then they left. And after they left, I felt a sense of satisfaction. I had seen them. I got to see The Beatles. My dream came true. It was just wonderful.

Nedra Talley left the stadium in her own car. Estelle and Ronnie Bennett (soon to be Ronnie Spector) left with Nedra's husband, Scott Ross, and his manager, Jerry Shatzberg, in his Bentley. The friendship between the Ronettes and The Beatles was well known. The girls were spotted by fans climbing into the British luxury car. Someone cried out, "Over here!" and suddenly hordes of fans descended on the car.

THE CONCERT

Ronnie Spector: We had just enough time to slam the doors shut before the kids were climbing all over our car, screaming and yelling and bouncing it back and forth . . . on the fenders, the hood, even on the roof. . . . They were pounding on the windows with their fists . . . and kicking at the glass with their heels.

Eventually, the Bentley pushed its way through the crowd to freedom.

Ronnie Spector: After that day, I'd had a little taste of what it must have been like to be a Beatle, and it was scary as hell.

George Orsino: I made it back to the buses and got on one. When they found out I was with The Beatles, I had to get off that bus. I remember fighting my way off the bus when they found out I was with The Beatles. They attacked me. I got onto the next one. No problem getting a place to sit on the bus. But then they found out I was with The Beatles and they were jumping on me. Touching me, grabbing me. Just touching someone who'd been near a Beatle. In fact, I remember Ann Wix—I remember her name, Wix—was one of the chaperones that I believe worked with the station, WIBG or WFIL, one of the stations. And her daughter was there. Fourteen or fifteen years old and she was crying, "I didn't get to see The Beatles or get an autograph. I had a note I wanted to give him." They all had something they wanted to give to The Beatles—letters or notes or something. And she was crying, and I'm with her and Ann Wix, and I said, "By the way, this is a pen that Ringo Starr signed an autograph with. You can have it." And she grabbed it and she thanked me. And even her mother thanked me. This girl, she's gotta be in her sixties now. She probably still has the pen. I wish I had it. It [The return trip] was a lot different from the ride down. A lot different. They were singing Beatles stuff and talking about what they should have did and could have did.

Felix Cavaliere: It was unique, I'll tell you that. And it was over. It was over rather quickly as a matter of fact. You could feel this sweep of emotion after. I believe they took off in a plane or a helicopter. And then it was like this—[long sigh]—ya know? And then the aftermath was like, you know, after an argument or after a thunderstorm. It was very strange, very strange.

Vince Calandra: That night at Shea was just unbelievable. I remember kids climbing up the backstop. Kids trying to jump on the field. Meryl Streep told me years later she was in section 18 screaming her lungs out. I remember after we shot all this stuff and this hysteria walking by the first-plate area. There were all these kids who had passed out and [were] hyperventilating. Bob [Precht] turned to one of the guys and said, "Jesus, how did we miss that?" And I said, "Bob, are you out of your mind? You just created history, man. And you're worried about some kid that is passing out and wetting their pants? Look at what you've got on film." He doesn't realize to this day. I told him yesterday when I did that Beatlefest in New York, how much people consider *The Beatles at Shea Stadium* as one of the all-time classic television specials in rock and roll history. He still doesn't get it. He said, "You're kidding?"

As far as explosive excitement, it's number one. I did something like sixty-five specials after that. I did a lot of stuff for the American Film Institute. I did CBS's "One Hundred Years, One Hundred Great Movies." The Monte Carlo–produced film for Rainier and Grace Kelly and all that kind of stuff. But *The Beatles at Shea Stadium* is the top of my fifty-seven years in the business.

I put the top down on my convertible, and the drive home to Long Island that night was the most exhilarating feeling I'd ever had. I thought, "My God, I was just part of history."

Bob Precht: It really was an incredible experience and, looking back on the things I've been involved with over a lot of years, that probably was the most exciting time I can remember.

Andrew Laszlo was grateful to be able to contribute to this once-in-a-lifetime event, but he paid a price. He suffered damage that night that would result in permanent hearing loss.

Andrew Laszlo: To say that my ears were buzzing would be the understatement of the century. The pain was excruciating . . . and continued for days afterward.

I look back on that experience with pride, knowing that I was part of "being there." . . . I have worked with several other rock groups since, including John Lennon after The Beatles broke up at his concert in Madison Square

Garden. . . . None of these concerts, as good as some were, even came close to the excitement and the extraordinary experience of filming the granddaddy of all rock concerts, *The Beatles Live at Shea Stadium*. And nothing ever will.

Bobby Vinton: Was it the most exciting event I've ever attended? It was. I mean, I've seen a lot of big shows. I've seen Michael Jackson at Madison Square Garden when he came with the big show. . . . He was on balloons and dirigibles and all that. . . . This was forty years later with all the effects and all the sounds. But it still couldn't match up to The Beatles, because like I say, it was the birth. It was the happening of stadiums and this new music with people going crazy. I've never seen anything like that in my life. To tell you the truth, I was happy for them. They were my competitors taking my airplay away, but I had to shake my head and say, "God, they really have something." I'm delighted for them.

Joy Musiker Cohen: It was a magical night. When people talk about Shea, you know instantly what it is. People who have *met* Beatles have said to me, "Oh! You were *there*?!"

BACK AT THE HOTEL

When the boys left the stadium, they were literally on fire, babbling to themselves about the amazing night, the crowd, the police, the runners, the sound, the insanity—a night that had exceeded all their dreams.

George: I've never felt so exhilarated in my life. . . . [I]t was unbelievable that so many people wanted to see us.

Paul: Once you know you've filled a place that size, it's magic; just walls of people. Half the fun was being involved in this gigantic event ourselves.

One night years later, John reminisced with Sid, telling him, "That concert in 1965 at Shea Stadium, I saw the top of the mountain on that unforgettable night."

Tony Barrow: The four boys expressed complete satisfaction with the show, something that rarely happened on tour. As we travelled along . . . I was already reliving highlight moments of an evening that would stand forever as the most vivid memory of my six years with them. Shea Stadium '65 was in a class of its own. This was the ultimate pinnacle of Beatlemania.

Mick and Keith had asked them to join them on the *Princess*, but the boys opted to return to the hotel. The yacht would certainly have been a more peaceful choice. The scene outside was a madhouse. Thousands of adoring Beatlemaniacs surrounded the Warwick to show their love for The Beatles through shattering, hysterical cries for hour upon hour.

The limos carrying the lads and their full road crew—Eppy, Tony Barrow, Mal, Neil, and Alf—arrived at the hotel. Everyone scrambled into the elevator and headed for the thirty-third floor, all of them euphoric. Just two years ago, the boys were playing lunches at the Cavern, and the year before that, the smoky, dark clubs of Hamburg. How did they get here? When Ringo and Mo married just six months earlier, they talked about opening a chain of hair salons when this rock and roll thing fizzled out, when the bubble burst. But this crowd! And this paycheck! God bless America, this was going somewhere! Okay, so the fans couldn't hear the music tonight. They'd heard it before. That's why they came. This evening had been a joyful embrace of The Beatles' spirit, their message, and, yes, their music, a confirmation that their fans can't wait to see and hear what the band does next. The Beatles, four young men in their early twenties, couldn't process it all that night, but they could celebrate it, and celebrate they did as various friends dropped by throughout the night and into the early morning: Del Shannon, the Exciters, who had opened for them in '64, and the Supremes, whom the boys had never met.

Mary Wilson: Okay, so the whole situation started with us when I think we were rehearsing for *The Ed Sullivan Show*. We were there for a week. You were usually there for a week and you rehearse and you have a few times off. Our PR people . . . suggested or got the idea that these two super groups should meet. Since The Beatles obviously could not come out of the hotel room because of all the screaming people and this and that and the other, they say maybe the Supremes should go to their hotel. So that was all arranged.

THE CONCERT

We drove up to their hotel in a limo and there were these screaming girls all over the place. There were just girls . . . *Ayyyyy!* So, we pull up and of course it was in a big limousine, and they now all of a sudden run to the limousine thinking perhaps it was one of The Beatles. When they saw these three black girls, they had no clue who we were and didn't care. They all . . . went back to screaming for The Beatles. So anyway, we were whisked upstairs.

The whole city was just wired for this concert they were having. Girls don't scream over other girls. They scream over guys. We never had that kind of attention from the fans. And we never had girls lined up or guys lined up at our stage door. It was a whole different—and it still is—a different dynamic for female groups or females as opposed to guys.

So, we're whisked upstairs. I don't know what floor it was. And I don't know what room. We open the door and . . . we're accustomed to a sort of higher plateau of—how do you say—meet-and-greet type thing: lots of lights, lots of champagne, lots of photographers, lots of bright "ta da." It's a wonderful thing. That's what we were accustomed to around the world. So, we come there . . . and it was not that. It was a little dark, maybe smoky. It was just not really a festive thing that we thought it was going to be. It reeked of marijuana. We were at the time very classy young ladies, and we didn't do any of that kind of stuff. We were introduced, but there was generally no excitement about us being there. There was a little something . . . I guess we were not who they thought we were going to be, being black girls, that we would be hip. But we were not hip at all.

So pretty soon, we asked our people, we said, "We're ready to go," or something like that. I don't know the words we used but we were ready to get out of there. It wasn't really what we expected. And I guess we weren't what they expected. And that was it. That's all I remember.

Years later when I spoke to George Harrison—he and I became very dear friends after that—he said, "You guys were just, you know, we thought you were going to be hip girls from the projects. We were surprised. We met all the other girls and they were really down and you girls were just different."

Dawn Michaels: We got to the Warwick. We were all on the same floor. I roomed with Ronnie Schwartz, one of the dancers, a sweetie. And that was probably one of the wildest nights I've ever spent in my life. . . . The chanting in the streets was unbelievable. And Paul came to our room that night with Ringo. They were still wearing their jackets open, bare feet, and they came in looking for a hair dryer. Yeah, right! Next, they started jumping on our beds. . . . I was like, "Stay!" but Ronnie said, "No we don't. Get out!" A wild night, wildness like you never knew.

Denise Mourges: I know that Steve Levitt, our dancer, hung out with them more. Because he was a guy, he could get in and out where we couldn't. He smoked pot with them. I think he might have turned them on to his pot, so he was like a big whoop.

Dave Glyde: I left around 4:00 a.m. I had a girlfriend in New York and took a cab to her place so I could get some sleep.

At 8:30 a.m., the boys were still up, record player blaring, TV on with the sound turned down, the boys still fooling around. While most New Yorkers were downing coffee, ready to face a new week at work, The Beatles were heading for bed, having just put in the hardest day's night of their career.

6

AFTER SHEA AND BEYOND

MONDAY MORNING

Sid had slept like a baby, the first carefree night he'd had in months. Monday found him in his office surrounded by deli food, pastries, and all the New York papers. Reviews were great. Accolades poured in. So did record company offers for the Rascals resulting from all the hoopla Sid created about them. They signed with Atlantic Records a short time later.

> **Sid Bernstein:** We turned down the great Phil Spector. He became angry, stormed out and kicked either a stone or a fire hydrant and broke his foot. I recommended that they go with Atlantic. Ahmet Ertegun [cofounder of Atlantic] didn't have any white acts at that time. He said to me, "Sid, other record companies want the Rascals. We *need* them. That's an advantage you should not forgo." I agreed.

Sid, without question, had an eye and an ear for talent and for knowing what would be popular. And he had some damn great ideas for venues. As the man who brought The Beatles to America and ushered in the British invasion, Sid Bernstein changed the face of rock and roll—and in doing so, changed the entire culture.

Dr. John Kane is a professor of design and media at the New England College Institute of Art and Design, an expert in concert sound, and the author of *Pilgrims of Woodstock: Never-before-Seen Photos* and *The Last Seat in the House: The Story of Hanley Sound.*

John Kane: Sid gave us concert arena rock and roll. He saw the potential to fill a stadium with music of that genre. He was a smart guy.

Felix Cavaliere: He was a visionary. Now the other side of that coin is the everyday business you have to attend to and what you have to do to get them where you want them, and that's where he was not so great. Listen, there are not many managers in the entire music world who are great. The ones who are great you can tell because their groups are legendary. Peter Graham with Led Zeppelin, legendary, Brian Epstein, Colonel Parker, but there are not many people who have it all—I mean, who does? So the knock on him is that he didn't know what to do once we were there. But in the meantime, he made us visible. He connected us with our record deal, and he fought for us all the way. I have nothing bad to say about him except that he was an imperfect human being like the rest of us.

Shea is a perfect example. Bernstein should have been a producer on the documentary. After all, there would have been no documentary without him. Rather than make waves with Sullivan or Epstein, Sid remained satisfied as the event's promoter. The Beatles made $160,000 of the $304,000 box office take. Sid cleared just $3,000. He should have been wealthy, but in the end he always found himself chasing the next dream. He missed many opportunities. But Sid was honest and true, a man of his word. And, in 1964, he was the only man in the world who believed The Beatles could fill a baseball stadium.

Seth Zimmerman: For whatever he did screw up, he should at least be remembered for what he didn't screw up. Because, honestly, when he brought The Beatles and the Stones and all those bands, he changed the world. Politics, everything was different from that point on. The world was different from that point on. And he had a key role in that.

A key role in changing the world—now, that's a legacy.

AFTER SHEA AND BEYOND

THE REST OF THE TOUR

Susan Silva: At Shea, I didn't know them yet, but on the plane, we got to know them. . . . Dawn was with Paul most of the time, always on the plane . . . very controversial. I spoke more to John. He was down-to-earth, no phoniness, really something. Ringo was the friendliest. Back area of the plane was where just the boys could go. I actually dated the photographer who was from London—Bob Whitaker—then Epstein fired him halfway through the tour, which really upset me. I don't remember why. I didn't interact with Epstein at all.

Dawn Michaels: We were all on the plane together as one big family. Everyone got along . . . but everyone was in their own little thing, even on the plane. Everyone had their own little niche.

John was very quiet, very shy and subdued. Ronnie sat with him most of the time in the back of the airplane quietly talking. I was the wild one with Paul. I was always with Paul. He was doing push-ups in the aisle, cursing . . . he was very pumped up with himself. Looking back, I guess he was a little conceited, hard not to be. George was quiet, very sensitive. Ringo was a no-brainer . . . he was always there.

Dawn and Ronnie leave New York two days after Shea to go on tour with The Beatles.
COURTESY DAWN MICHAELS

SUMMER 1965 US TOUR

August 15: New York—Shea Stadium

August 17: Toronto (two shows)—Maple Leaf Gardens

August 18: Atlanta—Atlanta Stadium

August 19: Houston (two shows)—Sam Houston Coliseum

August 20: Chicago (two shows)—Comiskey Park

August 21: Minneapolis—Metropolitan Stadium

August 22: Portland (two shows)—Memorial Coliseum

August 28: San Diego—Balboa Stadium

August 29–30: Los Angeles (two shows)—Hollywood Bowl

August 31: San Francisco (two shows)—Cow Palace

Cannibal and the Headhunters pose on the plane with Ringo. COURTESY DAWN MICHAELS

Dave Glyde: You know the reason the dancers were there, don't you? That was one of those things they did in those days, especially on The Beatle tour, and you could, well . . . the normal thing happened. I ended up with the blonde, Judy. One night I ended up getting drunk and threw her into the fountain in the front of the hotel. We were wild in those days.

I believe one of the girls was a dancer in *West Side Story*. But yeah, they were there to keep people happy, so you didn't have to look outside the camp to find "inspiration."

Brenda Holloway: We were on the plane . . . with four beautiful guys. . . . Ringo started pillow fights with me, feathers all over the place. Ringo was the playful one. . . . John was the one who gave us all our meals. He was about details. He was more interested in us eating and being ready to perform.

Dawn Michaels: Everywhere we went, there were screaming girls, and to tell you the truth, it was a little scary. Once when we were on the plane waiting to take off, the fans broke through. Paul lifted up the window shade and there was a face. Some girls had climbed the wing of the plane! They [security] immediately got the boys off [the plane] in the food truck. The rest of us sat there like dummies for two hours.

Susan Silva: The guys were afraid a lot of the time on the tour. . . . There was a fire on the plane. . . . I thought George was going to pass out right there. And when we landed in Houston, nobody was supposed to know we landed. They didn't have enough security because we arrived at 2:30 a.m. The girls [fans] rushed the plane and climbed onto the wings and were banging on the windows. It was very scary. At the Cow Palace, a girl was pressed against the stage and terribly injured.

Denise Mourges: When we were on the tour going into Portland, the engine caught on fire. It was a four-engine plane. I was sitting right by the wing there. I had been sleeping and I opened my eyes and I noticed there were flames coming out of the engine! And everybody was screaming, "Oh my God!" The foam came out and foamed it [the fire] and then we had to land in Portland, where they had more foam. There were a lot of mountains around us. We had to get another plane after that. It was really scary. George was literally green as he walked by me. They got off the plane first. I goof and say that's where he got religion, but, you know, this stuff happens. You could have read about it in the papers. We could have been Buddy Holly.

Brenda Holloway: One time the crowd broke loose . . . when a crowd breaks loose like that, it was like cattle charging if you've ever seen that many people coming at you. And baby, wigs were flying, instruments were flying; and we finally got to a safe place.

COURTESY DONDI BASTONE COLLECTION

Then one night, I was in my hotel room; and somebody knocked on the door. I'm like, "Who is it?" because this was a Beatles tour. Nobody was interested in me. . . . He says, "It's Ringo." I said, "Who?!" and he said, "Ringo." I was shocked. I opened the door and he said, "Can I borrow your hair dryer?"

I was shocked! I said, "You can have it!" And I gave it to him.

Dawn Michaels: That is hysterical! The old hair dryer ploy! [Laughing.] That must have been his thing!

Back then, hair dryers consisted of elastic bonnets big enough to fit over curlers with a long hose attached leading to a base. It's very doubtful Ringo wanted to borrow one of those. Besides, he'd have sent Mal to a drugstore for one. In today's world, the star would send a roadie to bring the girl to his room, leaving no doubt as to his intentions. The hair dryer "ploy" was so innocent that it is clear even fifty-plus years later that Ms. Holloway—then just seventeen—still believes the hair dryer was what Ringo was after. Imagine the jabbing he took back in his suite when he returned not with Brenda, but with her hair dryer.

Denise Mourges: In Portland I fainted. I was very tired. I was going through some physical things, which I didn't know at the time. But I fainted coming off the stage and they took me to the back of the bowels of this giant stadium and put me on a cot bed to just rest and see what was wrong. They had a nurse there for emergencies. So the nurse came and maybe took my blood pressure or whatever. I was just lying there resting, and I opened my eyes and Paul McCartney is sitting in a chair next to me. No shit!

And he says, "How are you?" He had heard about what happened and he came to see how I was. Now you tell me what kind of a human that is? A young man with heart and compassion. That's the way he was. And it showed. Nobody else was back there. There was no camera, there was no nothing. It was him and me. He was a sincere and caring person.

It was just shocking. I remember thinking how good he was, what a good person. It was just such a nice thing. And men weren't so freely expressive and caring. He wasn't holding back who he was. I will always remember that. To be such a young man and to be in such a position of fame and power and to have that compassion for a little dancer. . . . Now if I had any wits about me, this would have been a good time to . . . [laughing]. I was only seventeen. If I had been a braver girl . . . but I was too young and insecure to actually make a move.

Larry Kane: Women came and went from The Beatles' floor in most hotels, but with rare exception, the boys were discreet. . . . Mal . . . was a suave and smooth procurer, able to spot a target with incredible intuition. It was as though he could pick up on the scent of women who were willing. . . . [H]is flair for recruiting included an understanding of the difficulties The Beatles could face if any female companion was underage or wronged in any way. If one could get an Oscar for safely procuring women, Mal Evans would have received the lifetime achievement award.

Dave Glyde: I suppose when you look back, Shea Stadium was a kind of a pinnacle for a lot of the things for The Beatles and the way it was gonna go. That set the future that it [the band's career trajectory] was going to be recording. We were talking about it, and they said, "I'm not going to do this anymore. I'm over this, finished." They weren't traveling; it wasn't going anywhere. They weren't getting the things they wanted back from the music. That's why they made it just recording. And Shea [the tour] was the end of it.

The tour ended on the West Coast, which included several days off in Los Angeles. They met their idol, Elvis Presley, one evening. On another, John and George invited Ringo and Paul to take LSD with them. Ringo said yes, but Paul wasn't ready. They went ahead without him.

Finally, the tour ended and The Four Fabs were on their way back home. It had been a monumental tour in every way. Any doubts that may have lingered about their longevity lay in shreds. Eppy was enormously proud of his boys.

> **Larry Kane:** After fifteen performances watching The Beatles in action and watching the crowd, it's a chilling feeling inside because you know you are experiencing a phenomenon that is the only one of its kind in this century thus far. And they will probably go down in history as the greatest show business example of music and admiration in many, many hundreds of years.

SEPTEMBER 1965

The US single "Yesterday" is released.
Ringo and Maureen welcome their first child, Zak.
The Beatles' cartoon series begins in the United States.

The Beatles cartoon characters ended up on everything.

OCTOBER 1965

John Lennon turns twenty-five.
"Yesterday" hits number one in the United States. It remains there for four weeks, toppled by the Stones' "Get off My Cloud," which was knocked out two weeks later by the Supremes' "I Hear a Symphony."
The Beatles begin recording a new album, *Rubber Soul*.

THE DOCUMENTARY

Executive producer Bob Precht put together a brilliant team from among the best in the business to create the documentary. The guys on the ground, Andy Laszlo and Vince Calandra, had done their jobs beautifully. The film crew shot close to two hundred thousand feet of film that night. Less than 5 percent was used.

> **Vince Calandra:** We were a hundred feet away from the stage. We were on the field. . . . We were in the dugout. We were coordinating all this stuff. And Bob is talking to cameramen, talking to Clay Adams, to the guy who was in charge, Andy Laszlo, the photographer. "Make sure we get this. Make

sure we get that." "Make sure we get the helicopter flying over the airport." We shot with tall cameras. When you shoot with tall cameras, you try to get every angle. And then you take it back to the editing room, and you put it all together. That's how we did it.

Then the production team, led by the Emmy-winning producer M. Clay Cole, took over. Precht wanted Cole because he used 35-millimeter film, which promised a beautiful image. He brought the legendary film editor Sidney Katz on board. The prolific Emmy winner worked in both feature films and television series and would later be recognized by his peers with the career achievement award. Precht had all the pieces. What he didn't have was a concept.

Bob Precht: We realized we needed some continuity for all that we'd shot, hours and hours, and that's when I brought Buz [Kohan] and Bill [Angelos] in. I'd worked with them before on a summer show, admired their work, and knew we would need to make sense of everything to make it into a presentable program. Fifty-plus years later? I loved working with Buz and Bill.

Buz Kohan: We met with Sullivan's son-in-law, Bob Precht. We used to call him the U-boat commander. He looked so airy, like he was dipped in bronze. But a good guy. I mean, he was very square, but a good guy. He took us under his wing. We did a show called *The Al Hirt Show*—a summer show. It was thirteen weeks. We wrote it and produced it. He actually let us produce. At that time Sullivan had brought The Beatles over to America, and of course they became a sensation. And Sullivan had gotten the rights to *The Beatles at Shea Stadium*. And Precht said, "Would you guys like to work on that?" And we said, "Yeah, sure, sure, that will be fun."

Bill Angelos: Bob's the one who called us in. We didn't go through agents or anything like that. He called us directly and he said, "We're going to need some help." But he really didn't know what. We just knew they had contracted to do a one-hour television show. They knew even before the concert [that] The Beatles would only be on for a half hour. The other acts that had been booked couldn't really hold a half hour put together. And we also had footage of them prior to them coming out on stage, in the room downstairs, but they were silent.

So we had to somehow come up with a concept. And the concept came to us. That's how we came up with the idea of literally putting words in their mouth.

Buz Kohan: Somebody knew of this kid, this disc jockey down in Florida [Larry Kane] who knew The Beatles. Because he was one of the first people here, I think, who played their records. So Precht got ahold of him. We called him up and we said, "Listen. Are you available to tour with The Beatles?" He said, "I'm not a performer." We said, "We don't want you to be a performer. We want you to tour with them and take a Nagra tape recorder."

Nagra tape recorder.

It's a Swedish tape recorder, state of the art at the time. It was a little reel-to-reel, seven inch[es]. The quality was amazing, and it was practically indestructible. Back then they cost around $3,000. They weighed about twenty pounds. They were small and aluminum, but still there was a lot of technology went into those things. They were the best. The newsmen used to use them in the field and stuff. And they would survive the wars. We said, "Here's what we want you to do. The Beatles are going to go on tour now. They're going to go around America. We want you to go wherever they go, with your little Nagra and a microphone. And whenever you get a free moment with them—in the bedroom, in the bathroom, anywhere, dinner before the concert, after the concert, walking down the aisle—ask them questions. Ask them anything you can think of. Don't worry about what it means or who you're asking. Just make sure it's a Beatle and you're asking questions. Don't worry about the quality but try to keep it as good a quality as you can. Get that mic in their face because we don't care what you sound like." Well, I don't remember the number of tapes, but I'm guessing—and I don't know how you can check this out—but I think he sent back twenty hours of audiotape.

Bill Angelos: The audiotapes came at the tail end of their trip across country. And, fortunately, they spoke quite a bit about that concert, which gave us the idea to begin the show right after you saw them for a minute or so with the empty stadium and their voices.

And it's really an interesting idea. Before you see anything else, you see an empty stadium and then it starts to build. More people, cops, etcetera. And, fortunately, once that happens, the rest kind of fell into place. Because what we found was that enough footage existed of their actual journey. There is a shot of them in the helicopter. So, you can use that sequence. It's all there. That's how we put it together. The whole thing was put together in Sidney's [Katz] editing facility.

Please mention Mr. Katz. Because he had to take film, fourteen cameras, and get it down to what we could watch. We spent a lot of time with Mr. Katz and he was at least a dozen years older than us. So he was our senior and very, very knowledgeable in a time when film editing was still an art form. Sidney Katz was one of the kings of film editors. He was a giant in the field.

Buz Kohan: We sat down and went over all the audiotapes. And what we did was, we cataloged them and cut out his questions. You know, listed the answers according to who said what, what Beatle said what. And we put them in a file. Maybe we had ten hours of Beatles responses. Then we looked at what available footage we had: The Beatles on the airplane, on the helicopter coming in over New York, and with the mayor, with Sullivan in the plane, arriving at Shea Stadium and backstage, and in the ambulance when they drove them off. And the footage of the kids running onto the field from the bleachers and the police chasing them. We had footage of the girls fainting and the cops lifting them out. And hanging onto fences and mothers wiping tears from their kids' eyes. So, we had all the other stuff. We had stuff of the other acts who performed that night before The Beatles.

Young girl with a big button. PHOTO BY PETER SIMON/PETERSIMON.COM

A fan is "escorted" off the field. PHOTO BY PETER SIMON/PETERSIMON.COM

AFTER SHEA AND BEYOND

So, we took all that footage and we took all our audio stuff, and we just found remarks that had nothing to do with the original questions, but there was the voice of a Beatle saying something that was apropos for the moment. That's how we put together *The Beatles at Shea Stadium* audiotrack.

Bill Angelos: Our contribution was a very good one; I mean it was very strong. We would go every day to Sid's offices, and, remember, this was the predigital era. This was film. So we actually had to watch. There were fourteen cameras there. Now, I don't recall that much footage that we had to look through. But we saw enough of it to realize this was really a revelation. And, in fact, I would go so far as to say it gave the kids who put the *Woodstock* film together the idea for doing it the way we did it—which was to have voiceovers. *Woodstock* did split screens, which came after us, but the idea of building prior to the actual event is very prominent in that film as well.

Part of the film crew shooting the concert.
PHOTO BY GEORGE E. JOSEPH

First it opens with just singing, which is a great idea. But they sing for maybe a minute or two and then Paul says, "We gotta say goodbye." And that's how it begins. And then you've got the titles, and then when it begins again you see an empty Shea Stadium. And as it begins to fill, you hear the voices of the various Beatles doing specific comments about that particular concert.

I do recall we had twelve hours of audio given to us. The disjointed content served its purpose once we had the hook and knew how to put the thing together. Then Mr. Katz had all of this available footage.

And the other lovely thing we did, looking back on it now, was we gave the audience a taste of each of the acts. We did it in a way where in some instances Cousin Brucie introduces the act. But . . . then we cut away from them five minutes in, and then you see footage of The Beatles getting on a helicopter or whatever. And then when we come back, we see the next act. I guess King Curtis was the first act, then it was Miss Motown, whose name I don't recall; we had maybe a minute and a half of her. Then we had the dancers, who were perfect for the era. They were so '60s they reminded me of the dance that Travolta and Uma Thurman do in *Pulp Fiction*. It was so '60s. Amazingly so. So you've captured that era. It's watershed time, folks.

Buz Kohan: And nobody that I know of ever made comment about the fact that The Beatles themselves only did about twenty-two minutes of performance, you know.

But the thing is, if you were there, if you were a teenager in that house that night in Shea Stadium, I don't think you heard anything. Really. All you heard were the kids around you screaming just mixed in with your own screaming and yelling. It was just like a mass response, mass hysteria. It didn't matter if they were on pitch or fun or good. It was just the fact that they were there. This was the end moment of giant height. You know they eventually proved themselves to be remarkable men and musicians and things. It all worked out brilliantly. But at the time they could have been the Three Stooges singing, and nobody would have cared as long as they looked like the four Beatles. That was the amazing thing. Brian Epstein sold them a remarkable package there.

THE SECRET SESSIONS

Precht, Sullivan, and Epstein had agreed that the special should be ready for the 1965 Christmas television season. Two of the twelve songs had been cut from the film. Multiple cameras were forced to change reels of film during "She's a Woman," and it was not covered well enough to include. However, the special still ran long and another song had to go. "Everybody's Trying to Be My Baby," George's only solo, was cut, presumably because it was the only song not penned by a Beatle. From a royalty standpoint, it made the most sense. George understood that it was a business decision, but he felt the slight.

Eppy was sent a viewing copy and, in early December, sent word he was delighted with it. But The Beatles and George Martin felt differently. Though the equipment used that night was state of the art, nothing on that scale had ever been tried. There were technical problems. The film had captured the excitement of the concert, but the sound quality on their songs was not acceptable to the band. The tracks were raw, dropping drums, bass, or both and sometimes dropping out completely.

JANUARY 1966

George and Pattie are married.

Precht did his best to persuade them to leave it as it was. He felt it perfectly captured the pandemonium of the day. Besides, if word got out, he could not sell it as "live." But he was not successful. The documentary would not air in December. Secret recording sessions were arranged in London in January 1966, in which tracks were sweetened, remixed, and in some cases overdubbed or rerecorded. The boys needed to sync their singing and playing to the movie as it was being shown in the studio. They quickly caught on and completed their tasks with relative ease, finishing in two days.

The Beatles at Shea Stadium had its world premiere in the United Kingdom two months later in March 1966 in black and white. But in the States, the sale of the show was met with further delays. Most everyone expected that Ed Sullivan's network, CBS, would pick it up, but in a shortsighted corporate decision, they turned it down. Precht was forced to shop it elsewhere.

THE END OF TOURING

John's offhand statement in a March 1966 interview—"We're more popular than Jesus"—sparked a backlash for the band's '66 tour. Despite garnering little response in England, his remarks created major fallout in the United States when they were reprinted in July. Religious groups held bonfires to burn all things Beatle. Radio stations banned their music, and the boys themselves received death threats.

John: If I'd said television instead of Beatles, I might have gotten away with it.

John's misinterpreted statement, combined with an adverse reaction in the United States to their "butcher block" album cover for *Yesterday and Today* depicting the four lads posing in bloodstained aprons with raw meat, beheaded dolls, and meat cleavers, generated a maelstrom of controversy. Concert promoters for their 1966 tour said ticket sales dropped off almost overnight. When The Beatles returned to Shea just a year later on August 23, 1966, they played to eleven thousand empty seats.

All in all, it was an unsettling time. Against this backdrop, they made the decision to quit touring and concentrate on their music in the studio.

Handed out at the St. Louis concert, 1966.

THE LOVIN' SPOONFUL MEETS THE BEATLES

John Sebastian: We had met in England when the Spoonful played the Marquee Club [April 18, 1966], and John and George, and I think Paul for a while but not for long, were there. We do the show, and you couldn't believe what the audience was. As our publicity agent pointed out, "John, you've got three Beatles, two Stones, and three Yardbirds." I mean, it was a list like that. And in fact Eric Clapton in later years has told stories of meeting George at that particular Lovin' Spoonful concert. . . .

[On that trip] we played *Ready, Steady, Go!*, and we played Tara Brown's birthday party in Ireland. And we also did this show at the Marquee. Only blocks from the Marquee was the hotel where we were staying, a fairly upscale place. There had been this evening in London where John and George ended up in the hotel welcome suite situation with us. It was a little uncomfortable because it was mostly press people watching The Beatles meet the Lovin' Spoonful. . . .

Zal [Zal Yanovsky, guitarist for the Lovin' Spoonful] was beginning to throw small hors d'oeuvres. Keith Moon [drummer for the Who] was egging him on, and then Zal started throwing them at John Lennon. You couldn't believe it was happening. But these were both very transgressive guys as far as their sense of humor. I think John actually retreated from that party when he realized he wasn't going to be the center of attention. It was kind of an uncomfortable moment [laughing].

At a certain point George nudged me and said, "Do you want to get out of here and go over to Brian Jones'?" And I said, "Yeah, I'd love to." So we went, and Brian had a pile of sitars, which at that point George was only slightly familiar with. He was showing me the sympathetic strings and how they rang when you played the corresponding notes and stuff like that. . . . It was like an all-night sitar-playing and hash-consuming night. It was pretty awesome. I have to posthumously congratulate Mr. Jones on the quality of his temple balls or whatever they were called. This is the stuff they levitate mosques with—not just like casual smoking dope. So it turned into quite an evening.

I was there [Shea '66] with my wife, Laurie. We were kind of hustled into the sort of performer's area because I guess we had a pass somewhere along the line . . . through one of the lads or something. We walked into the room and George immediately starts riding John Lennon. "Oh, here's your idol, John. You know you love him. You love him like Elvis." John had started wearing funny round glasses and let his sideburns grow out. I had done the same. So John starts rubbing my sideburns, and as kind of a tit for tat, I begin rubbing his sideburns. So we're standing in the middle of this—they're waiting to go on in the biggest damn place—it was a big deal—and we're standing in the center of the room rubbing each other's sideburns.

The screaming and chaos of the event has kind of blotted out any kind of performance judgment I might have. I was just kind of, "Oh my God, it really is Beatlemania."

My exposure to all of them [The Beatles] has been very limited, but I have always felt great warmth and camaraderie during those days when we would cross paths.

Six days later, the band would play its final concert in San Francisco's Candlestick Park and never tour again.

When he was later asked about the "second Shea Stadium concert," George Harrison replied, "Did we play Shea twice?"

GOING, GOING, GONE!

And, still, the concert film had not aired in the United States after a year and would not air for another four-and-a-half months. The project was being strangled slowly. By the time it finally aired on ABC in color in January 1967, it was old news, nostalgic at best. Their music had grown, becoming more complicated. *Rubber Soul* and *Revolver* had been released, and none of those songs was in the special.

The boys didn't even look the same. In '67, they had moustaches and sideburns. Their matching outfits had given way to the bold, colorful fashions popular on the Swinging London scene. The Summer of Love and *Sgt. Pepper* were around the corner. The Beatles, their fans, and, indeed, the culture had all moved on.

> **Bill Angelos**: By then [there were] all kinds of record-burning sessions all over the country. It was a big news story. You know, all the Christian organizations, blah, blah, blah. They just would not have anything to do with The Beatles. As a result, the show got one of the lowest ratings of any show that year.

Laszlo's film crew had shot the whole weekend of the Shea concert, from The Beatles' arrival at JFK, the Warwick, Ed Sullivan's studio, the helicopter ride, various angles at the concert and of the crowd, coverage of "She's a Woman" and "Everybody's Trying to Be My Baby," and so much more. Six months after the show aired, all unused footage was ordered destroyed. And it seems that it was. None has ever surfaced.

CULTURE

Shea heralded the dawning of a new era for rock and roll, a defining moment in pop culture history and the absolute apex of Beatlemania. The biggest entertainment event anyone had ever seen, it brought about change on a massive scale and launched the modern stadium concert, forcing technology out of the Dark Ages and into the Age of Aquarius with such lightning speed as to be ready for the three-day Monterey Pop Festival just two years later and Woodstock two years after that. This was no passing fad; it was the future, and everyone had better climb on board or be left behind. Madison Avenue followed suit, suddenly awakening to the fact that kids bought a lot more than pimple cream. Fashion went "mod." Barbershops were out and men's hairstyling was in. The movie industry abolished its antiquated censorship rules, allowing nudity and sex onscreen for the first time. And a shaken recording industry did an about-face. Each label now considered it mandatory to have its own long-haired band, preferably with an English accent. A new generation had found its voice and it was being heard. Young Meryl was right, it *was* thrilling!

And the crowd! That hot summer night in Shea, the largest group of Beatle fans—of rock and roll fans—came together in one place *for the first time*. A sheer frenzy of raw emotion, sexual energy, and pure, unadulterated joy ensued. Young Americans were more than fans. They were believers, and Shea Stadium became their temple.

The Beatles felt it too. You can see it on their faces the second they stepped onto that field and took in the crowd. They suddenly grasped the immense power behind the mania. August 15, 1965, was the day they became cognizant of the power they had to sway an entire generation. The afterglow came in waves, with each crest bringing sweeping change—the beginning of an entire culture of change—an international teen culture—starting with the music.

> **Bill Angelos**: Music is a reflection of what's going on in culture and in society. That's what it does; otherwise they can't sell the songs. So to go from Perry Como to those guys . . . this was the beginning of a total cultural change.
>
> When people talk about the sixties, they always think it started in 1960. Well, it didn't. It started in the mid-sixties, probably around 1965, and kind of fell over into the seventies. But that's when things really changed musically and technologically as well. There was no technology in those days.
>
> My son was born in '69. And I can remember playing Beatle songs and rocking him to sleep in our home in Beverly Hills. It's unlike what we've heard

before. . . . There's a certain aspect to The Beatles' music. It's highly melodic and yet rhythmic change. It's different. Very different.

It's extraordinary. I wrote music with Buz for a number of years. We had a Diana Ross number, and we did specials, and we wrote for the Jackson Five, and blah, blah, blah. So, I mean, we were musicians and songwriters. And to watch that happen, it was literally . . . it was otherworldly really. No one has even come close to doing the same thing since. I mean you have the tail end of a tiger doing this particular show. Fifty years later you can look back and say, "Folks, name me something else that happened that matches this." The longevity of their music is extraordinary.

Dave Glyde: They were expected, maybe, if they had a hit record, it might last a couple of months, and it'd be good fun . . . a great time and that would be life. . . . You'd go back to doing whatever you did in life. But look at it now, it's fifty years since we came to Australia . . . and I know I'm amazed I still play music. I mean, [laughs] I'm aghast at that. And Paul and Ritchie still play music. The Stones still tour. All that era is incredibly alive and vital.

World changing, time changing . . . post-Beatles—[it's a] totally different world.

CONCERTS

Shea changed the face of the entire concert industry—the way acts were presented, the way tickets were sold, staging, lighting, security, and, of course, sound.

David Pelletier began his career as an audio engineer on international tours for the Rolling Stones, the Who, John Lennon, Procol Harum, Leo Kottke, Rod Stewart, the Talking Heads, and many others. Since 2002, he has been the exclusive sponsorship agent for Sir Paul McCartney.

David Pelletier: Concerts back then were pretty primitive. Prior to that, concerts were at racetracks, ice rinks, warehouses. . . . Nobody knew how to do them. Sound systems were nonexistent. Lighting was nonexistent. . . . As Chip [Monck, Tony-nominated lighting designer] will tell you . . . all done usually in an incredibly roundabout fashion. I love listening to Chip describe stuff. . . . Chip is the godfather. He was the first guy who got it: basically using movie techniques to make people look good onstage. I try to explain him to people all the time, "None of your jobs would exist without him." There was no "make people look like they do in movies technique" back in The Beatles' days. That didn't come along until probably the Monterey Pop Festival. We had to invent the junk that allowed them to do what they wanted to do and be heard above everybody else. There was a lot of "amateur hour" out there. My company, Tycobrahe Sound, was probably the best of the best at the time, which is why we got to do who we got to do. Then came Clair Brothers and Choco and that end of the industry. And then lighting companies and staging companies and trucking companies. Before, we used to just drive it all ourselves on one truck. Put it up and tear it down and drive all five hundred miles to the next gig.

Bob Spitz is an American journalist and author best known for biographies of major cultural figures, including The Beatles.

Bob Spitz: It forever changed the relationship between the music business and sports stadiums. From that day on, promoters had saucers in their eyes. Seriously. I mean they knew that they could make some money. By the time we hit Woodstock in 1969, the major groups only did big arenas and big stadiums. And it just grew and grew and grew, and it really stemmed from that date that The Beatles did at Shea Stadium.

TECHNOLOGY

John Kane: What The Beatles proved to us was that we needed more power, more wattage to support popular music.

Giles Martin is a music producer, head of audio and sound for Universal Music Group, and the son of George Martin.

Giles Martin: It's hard to think, now, about the technology they had then and how unprepared the world was for the onslaught of rock and roll. The Beatles were the first stadium band when they went to Shea Stadium and . . . Vox built . . . 100-watt amplifiers because they thought that'd be able to cut it. . . . [They] performed club gigs and then took those club gigs and . . . played stadiums. And no one thought about the sound. No one thought about the band being able to hear themselves. . . . The Beatles only had two or three roadies for the whole of that career. . . . [T]hink about road crews that follow Coldplay . . . it's vast. You have lighting guys, sound guys, video projection guys. And it was deeply frustrating for them then actually because they couldn't even hear themselves.

The Beatles were such a huge live band. Someone asked me the other day if I thought they were a good live band and I said, "Well, listen to their records." Because their first three or four albums were of them playing live anyway. I remember remixing "Come Together," which is much later on Abbey Road, and I remember playing it for Paul and he said to me, "God, I remember how good we were on this day." And they were playing live. "Come Together" is a live recording. They could really cut it live. It was just muscle memory. . . . They were just very good at playing their instruments and they just had muscle memory so they could sing and play without being able to hear themselves.

THE BEATLES

Shea was the beginning of the end for touring for The Beatles. Nearly twenty years later, Tony Barrow told Larry Kane that The Beatles enjoyed the 1965 tour more than the others.

> **Tony Barrow:** They were suddenly playing at being superstars. The boys were all smiles. . . . [T]hey were happiest in 1965. 1964 was tough. 1966 was forgettable because they were ready to stop touring, but 1965 was the best for them.
>
> This was the group's brightly shining summer solstice, after which all The Beatles' days would insidiously grow a little darker.

> **Denise Mourges:** I don't think they had even become who they were yet. You know. They were always becoming. That's what was so cool about them. It was a part of their evolution. They were evolving like we were, like the culture was. So Shea was the beginning of this, kind of really a kickoff.

Dave Glyde: It was quite a crazy time, but they were wonderful people, and people forget that, I think, because of the mystique.

They marked a specific time in the history of the music industry and the world. They made an incredible impact. There were so many things they wanted to do, and you've got to make room for that change. The successful acts over long periods—they made changes.

I never considered them anything other than these guys that we knew. They were my friends. I sat with Paul when he was on his bed with his guitar writing "Michelle." They introduced me to a few drugs. I got to travel around the world with them, which I always wanted to do, and they were just really good guys.

Larry Kane: They were very, very sensitive to other people's feelings. All four of them were intelligent people who cared about other people and who had a sense of themselves.

AND IN THE END . . .

Seth Zimmerman: They gave us hope. They showed us the way—peace and all you need is love.

Eric J. Adams: In one cool evening rush, the concert introduced me to the power of a movement, this one musical. I might not have been able to express it then, but I began to realize the power of a zillion people all on the same page, rooting for the same thing, holding hope in their individual hearts, however big the collective heart might be.

Denise Mourges: It was the ingredients. It wasn't just one ingredient. It was all the ingredients. And the ingredients came together at Shea in a way that had not been felt before. And I felt that inside me. We all knew that change was there. Change had knocked on the door. And it wasn't going away.

We realized the power of who we were. That's what the change was that came. It was the power of us. Shea was not just them. Shea was us . . . youth . . . the boomers. It was us.

AFTER SHEA AND BEYOND

Bob Lefsetz: Just four guys, no support, yet it's enough. Greatness is always enough. And the girls are screaming . . . and you're listening, believing you missed something, something incredible.

And then you remember you were there, when Beatlemania took the country by storm, when optimism ruled, when the youth stole the country from the establishment and ran with it.

And it was all powered by music.

And The Beatles were there first.

The Beatles' concert at Shea Stadium—indeed, The Beatles themselves—was a once-in-a-lifetime event. Neither one of them will ever happen again. One man had a whopper of an idea—bigger than even he realized. And before faxes or cell phones or the internet—before *everything*—the power of youth propelled the word around the world. And the lads delivered, boy, did they. And they kept on delivering. And they still do whether they're here on Earth with us or here with us only in spirit. That's because they are more to us than their music. They are part of our lives. They affected everything we did. And our memories of them are filled with emotion and our hearts full of love.

The Beatles changed it all, and the flashpoint was Shea, where for twenty-seven minutes, four young men from Liverpool, England, led 55,600 spirited fans in innocent, unrestrained rejoicing that truly changed the world.

Oh yeah, yeah, yeah.

CAST OF CHARACTERS

Eric J. Adams: The concert changed my life. For one, I vowed to become a journalist if it meant experiencing cool shit like this. I did become a journalist, and, indeed, I was lucky enough to experience so much, from foreign travel to murder trials to leaps out of small airplanes. And I vowed to become a musician, because, man oh man, if it worked *this well* for The Beatles, certainly it might help me elicit a fraction of the attention showered on The Fab Four. I did learn to play guitar, and, by golly, it did help me attract a girl or two.

Joy Musiker Cohen: My husband was also at Shea, but we didn't know each other at the time. We have a son, Matthew, and two beautiful granddaughters, Juniper, four, and Monti, fifteen months. The Beatles have had an impact on every facet of my life. Especially making friends from all over the world. We connect via social media and meet at Paul's concerts. You can't beat that personal contact. Most fun of all is going for a bite to eat after the shows. October 15, 2015, I was one of the lucky ones chosen to go onstage with Paul McCartney. He signed my arm and I now have my only tattoo.

Joy Musiker Cohen with her granddaughter—passing along Beatle love to another generation. COURTESY JOY MUSIKER COHEN

Whoopi Goldberg grew up to become an internationally known comedian, actor, talk show host, and outspoken activist and humanitarian.

The Beatles gave me this idea that everybody was welcome. If you weren't the hippest kid in the neighborhood, it didn't matter because you could be a Beatle fan, and I liked that. And that sort of carried me into these older days where it's like I'm my own person. I can look the way I want. I can be the way I want and it's okay. And I got that specifically from them.

Joy after Paul signed her arm during a concert. COURTESY JOY MUSIKER COHEN

CAST OF CHARACTERS

Linda LaFlamme still living the rock and roll life.
COURTESY LINDA LAFLAMME

Linda LaFlamme was inspired by The Beatles to live her rock and roll dreams. Her boyfriend Willie wanted marriage, kids, and a house in the suburbs. Linda said no, and two years after Shea, she was sharing a communal home in Woodstock with Jimi Hendrix. A few years after that, she joined the rock group It's a Beautiful Day as its lead singer, married the group's founder, David LaFlamme, and continues to perform for their many fans worldwide.

Linda Ghignone Marotte: Linda and Renee Perst have remained friends and in touch for more decades than either will admit. Each has seen Paul and Ringo concerts through the years. Living during that special period in time as a teen and being at Shea that night was obviously a young girl's dream and created memories never to be forgotten. Being able to see themselves on film keeps it as real as their memories of John, Paul, George, and Ringo.

Bobbie Molina: Forty years after Shea, Bobbie won another pass to see a Beatle, this time to a private opening for Ringo's artwork at a New York gallery.

Bobbie Molina today.
COURTESY BOBBIE MOLINA

> I was able to see him up close, to say hello, and to touch his shoulder. I took my daughter, and it was a beautiful night. I was never so close to Ringo in all my life. It took so many years, but I finally got to see him face-to-face. One thing I don't like . . . I don't like him wearing those dark glasses. He should show his pretty blue eyes.

Denise Mourges says her experience with The Beatles filled her with confidence.

Denise Mourges 2014.

> It made me believe that anything is possible . . . because who would have thought in a million years that anything like that could happen to me. It gave my life such a bump as to what can be. And I've had that attitude my whole life. I've led a really interesting life and I could never have imagined some of the things I'd end up doing. That's what I took away from my experience. It gave me the courage to go forth and be an envelope pusher for my generation.
>
> I moved out to LA when I was eighteen after I had seen it with The Beatles. I was one of the first of my group to go out to California. It was our world. I worked at the Whisky a Go Go. I ended up writing for various performance magazines, *Cash Box*, the *New York Times*. We all pursued interests that had to do with culture and expression, just different ways. It was quite a youth movement in general.

CAST OF CHARACTERS

Susan Silva Nikirk suffered devastating injuries in a skiing accident, which ended her jazz dancing career. She became a competitive ballroom dancer who was ranked third in the world and taught across the globe. Her life turned 180 degrees when she gave her life to God in her late thirties. She and her husband formed an international ministry, and doors opened to speak about God all over the world. Susan wrote her life story, *Dancing out of Darkness*, which has been translated into five languages.

Susan Silva Nikirk.
COURTESY OF SUSAN SILVA

> Shea changed my life, but I didn't know how until many years later. Now, at my age, I am more in awe of that—that a nobody from no place toured with The Beatles, performed at Shea Stadium, and ended up speaking all over the world—and it's all because of The Beatles. That opened doors for me I never dreamed of. "I did that." I am in astounding wonderment.

George Orsino: Despite the coup of getting shots in both The Beatles' dressing room and at the edge of the stage, George returned to Philly, developed his film, and put the prints in a drawer for forty years, except for one—not of The Beatles, but the photo he got of Bobby Vinton in the dugout. That one he put in his studio window.

> One day a bunch of teenagers were outside screaming and jumping up and down. I said, "What's wrong?" And they said, "That's Mick Jagger! He's in one of your pictures!" I didn't know. I didn't know who Mick Jagger was until they told me.

George's photos of The Beatles made the cover of *TV Guide* in celebration of the fortieth anniversary of Shea—actually, they made *four* covers. One of each of The Fabs was used, making them all very collectible and still sought after by fans more than a decade later. George loved telling his story of that night to young people and appearing at Beatlefests for many years. He passed away at the age of eighty-six in October 2014.

George Orsino, 2010.
PHOTO BY JOHN ORSINO

Renee Perst: For me, I feel that our mutual experience of seeing The Beatles at Shea bonded Linda [Ghignone Marotte] and me forever in a unique way. It was life changing, especially to a thirteen-year-old, and to have someone who was there with you, that you can remember it with, is truly very special. It has also become a "claim to fame." All you need to do is to mention that you were in the front row at the Shea concert, and you have everyone's attention. Having the photographic proof is the best! The Beatles are, and always have been, my comfort food. Whenever I need a boost, they always uplift me. "Alexa, play The Beatles" is one of my favorite phrases! In so many ways, how very, very lucky we were to have been there!

Mary Louise Streep from New Jersey became the great award-winning actress **Meryl Streep**. In 1990, she was asked to present the Grammy Lifetime Achievement Award to Paul McCartney. She shared her experience at Shea with the audience, every bit as giddy as that sixteen-year-old girl who attended the concert.

Dawn Michaels Switzer: After touring with The Beatles, Dawn moved to Los Angeles and became one of the famed Gazzarri Dancers, appearing on every episode of TV's *Hollywood a Go Go* and on many television shows and specials with stars like the Doors, the Tijuana Brass, and Nancy Sinatra. She remained in contact with Paul McCartney, who continued to call her whenever he was in LA for several years after Shea. She retired from dancing in the early 1970s and became a Braniff Airways flight attendant. Later, she married a pilot and raised a family in Southern California.

Dawn Michaels Switzer today.
COURTESY DAWN MICHAELS

Steven Van Zandt: After Shea, Steven Lento was convinced that rock and roll was the life he wanted, and he pursued it with a passion. Today, he is legendary E Street Band member Little Steven Van Zandt, has his own band, the Disciples of Soul, has played with Ringo in his All-Starr Band, and has been inducted into the Rock and Roll Hall of Fame.

Marc Weinstein loved the excitement. He moved to Los Angeles to be near the music scene there and was one of the first paparazzi photographers, shooting major entertainers of the '60s and '70s.

> The Beatles were the start of my photojournalism career. For many others, it was the top of theirs, but it was the beginning of mine. It was the most momentous night of my life, forever frozen in my mind and psyche.

Marc passed away December 30, 2016.

Joe Walsh: The guitarist, singer, and songwriter for the Eagles, Walsh would come full circle in the early '80s when he produced Ringo Starr's solo album, *Old Wave*. He also joined his first All-Starr Band. And in 2008, the men became brothers-in-law when Joe married Barbara Bach's sister, Marjorie. Walsh told 105.7 WROR how surreal it all is. "He's my brother-in-law, and he wants to involve me in making music, and what am I gonna say? No? I'm really, really, really blessed to . . . be in this family that I'm in that came along with my wife . . . and I still get in the studio, and I'll be playing guitar, and I'll look over and go, 'That's fucking Ringo Starr! I don't believe it!' It still happens sometimes."

"He's not just the greatest drummer in rock history—from the greatest band in rock history—he's also the greatest guy I know and the most kind and helpful friend you could ever want," Walsh said, per *Rolling Stone*.

INDEX

Aames, Nancy, 67
ABKCO Records, 86
Academy of Music, the Rolling Stones at, 38–39
"Act Naturally," 72; at concert, 117; on *The Ed Sullivan Show,* 97
Adams, Clay, 73, 167
Adams, Eric J., 54, *54,* 85, 183; as The Beatles take stage, 133, 139; on changes to The Beatles, 180
Adiarte, Patrick, 40
Ad Lib Club, 38, 44
advertising, for concert, 30–31
Ali, Muhammad, 58
"America," 130
Angelos, Bill, 3–4, 5, 91; on Bernstein, 26; on concert day, 104, 129; on concert experience, 143; on concert filming, 168–70, 171; on cultural change, 176–77; on the Rolling Stones, 64
the Animals, 26, 27, 120
Another Beatles Christmas Show, 34–35
Armstrong, Neil, 14
Arthur (nightclub), 92
Asher, Jane, 43
Asher, Peter, 3, *3*
Aspinall, Neil, 52, 93–94, 97, 99; on helicopter flight, 114; at Warwick Hotel after concert, 158
Atlantic Records, 161

baby boomers, 37
"Baby's in Black," 34, 74; at concert, 117
Bach, Barbara, 139, 187
Bach, Marjorie, 187
"Back in My Arms Again," 57, *57*
Baker, Stanley, 61
Baldry, Long Tall, 44
Barrow, Tony, 45, 94–96, 98; on changes to The Beatles, 179; on concert experience, 152, 158; on helicopter flight, 112, 113
BASCA. *See* British Academy of Songwriters, Composers and Authors
The Battle of the Baritones, 3–4
Beatlemania, 5–15; at concert, 152; Lennon marriage and, 43
Beatles '65, 38
The Beatles at Shea Stadium (documentary): audiotrack for, 171; filming of, 53, 72–76, 156, 167–72, *171,* 175; secret sessions for, 172–73
The Beatles' Christmas Show, 33–34
The Beatles: Eight Days a Week—The Touring Years, 36
Beatles for Sale, 64
Beatles VI, 65, 86
Beck, Jeff, 74
Bennett, Estelle, 154
Bennett, Michael, 40

Bennett, Peter, 119; on concert day, *132*
Bennett, Ronnie, 154
Bennett, Tony, 17
Bernstein, Sid, 17–23; as The Beatles take stage, 134; Carnegie Hall and, 24–26, 30; after concert, 161; concert and, 29–31, 37; on concert day, 103–4, 114, 116, 131; concert experience and, 152; concert plans by, 51–53; Epstein and, 23, 29, 38; financial problems of, 27–28; General Artists Corp (GAC) and, 21, 22, 26; *Hullabaloo* and, 39; Katzenberg and, 85; mail box of, 31–32; office staff of, 32–33; the Rascals and, 79, 108–9, *109,* 116; the Rolling Stones and, 63–64, 122; on truck to concert, 115; as visionary, 162; wife of, 21, 22, 28, 31, 79
Berry, Chuck, 5, 6
Best, Pete, 13; Epstein and, 24
Bicknell, Alfred "Alf," 43, 57, 59–60, 63; on concert day, 121; Harrison, G., on, 94; on helicopter flight, 114; International Driver's License for, 86; marijuana and, 87; at Warwick Hotel after concert, 158
Blackpool Night Out, 78
Block, Martin, 3–4

189

INDEX

bobby-soxers, 4
Boone, Steve, *2*, 2–3
Boston Globe, 10
"The Branch," 128
British Academy of Songwriters, Composers and Authors (BASCA), 77
Bron, Eleanor, 48, 49, 59
Brown, Tara, 174
Buckley, William F., Jr., 10
Bunetta, Al, on Bernstein, 20, 21
Burton, Richard, 37
Burton, Sybil, 92
Bury, Cyndy, 56
the Byrds, 3; Calandra on, 97

Calandra, Vince, 72–73, 97; on Bernstein, 19–20; on concert day, 103, 117, 121; on concert filming, 167–68; on departure from concert, 153, 156; on helicopter flight, 112–13; on truck to concert, 115
Cameron, Barrie, 12
Cannibal and the Headhunters, 45, *45*; as concert opening act, 126, 128–29; on US tour, *164*
"Can't Buy Me Love," 11, 34, 74; at concert, 117
Carnegie Hall, 24–26, 30; the Rolling Stones at, 64
The Carol Burnett Show, 3
Cavaliere, Felix, 79; on Bernstein, 18, 22, 162; on concert day, 109, 122; on concert experience, 142, 146; on departure from concert, 155. *See also* the Rascals
Cavern Club, 3; Cox at, 45; Epstein at, 24
A Cellarful of Noise (Epstein), 24, *24*
Charles, Ray, 17

Charney, Suzanne, *41*
Checker, Chubby, 82
Choco, 178
Christie, Julie, 44
Clair Brothers, 178
Clapton, Eric, 74; at Ad Lib Club, 44
Clark, Petula, 45, *45*
Cogan, Alma, 60, *61,* 61–62, *62*
Cohen, Joy Musiker, 69–70, 86, 183; as The Beatles take stage, 136; on concert day, 107, *107,* 109, 123, *123*; on concert experience, 143, 144, 157; on concert opening acts, 130
Cole, M. Clay, 168
"Come See about Me," 38
Como, Perry, 4, 5
Cooke, Sam, 12
Cousin Brucie, 6, *6*, 53, 81, 89–93, *94*; as The Beatles take stage, 133–34; in concert opening acts, 125, 126, 128; on documentary, 171
Coward, Noel, 61
Cox, Maureen, 43; birth of child of, 167; at Cavern Club, 45; as expectant mother, 55; marriage proposal to, 38, 44; new home of, 77; wedding of, 45–46, 158
Crosby, Bing, 3–4
Curtis, King, 105, *106*; as concert opening act, 126, 128; on documentary, 171

The Daily Howl, 65
Daily Mirror, 22
Dalton, David, 55
Dancing out of Darkness (Nikirk), 185
the Dave Clark Five, 26, 78
Davis, Sammy, Jr., 61, 99

The Dean Martin Show, 78
death threat, 35
Decca Records, 11
Dee, Sandra, 2
Denning, Chris, 74
DeShannon, Jackie, 125
deWilde, Brandon, 50
Disciples of Soul, 186
Discotheque Dancers, *67*, 68; at concert, *126*, 126–28, *127*; on concert day, *111*
"Dizzy Miss Lizzie," 117
documentary. *See The Beatles at Shea Stadium*
the Doors, 97
"Downtown," 45, *45*
the Dozier Holland, 46
duck blind, at concert, 102, *102*
dugout, at concert, 122, *122, 124*; Lennon, John, to, *131*
Dylan, Bob, 60; on Hardy, 74; at Newport Folk Festival, 76; at Warwick Hotel, 96

Eamonn Andrews Show, 55
Early Beatles, 49
Eastman, Linda, 54–55, 101; as The Beatles take stage, 139
Eastman, Marjorie, 139
Edmund, Lada, Jr., 40, *41*
The Ed Sullivan Show, 2, 5–15; Calandra of, 19–20; the David Clark Five on, 78; the Supremes on, 158; taping of, 96–98; Walsh and, 140
Eight Arms to Hold You, 45, 48
"Eight Days a Week," 49, *49*
"Eleanor Rigby," 59
Ellington, Duke, 17
EMI: Cogan and, 62; Martin, George, at, 24

INDEX

Epstein, Brian, 23–25, *24*; as The Beatles take stage, *136*; Bernstein and, 23, 29, 38; Cogan and, 62; concert and, 29–30, 53, 72, 100; on concert day, 116; concert experience and, 152; drug use by, 39, 77; *Eight Arms to Hold You* and, 48; on helicopter flight, 114; on holiday shows, 35; on *Hullabaloo*, 39, *39*; media blackout and, 77; NEMS and, 55; Northern Songs Ltd. and, 39, 47; sexual liaisons of, 77; at Starr wedding, 45–46; on truck to concert, 115; at Warwick Hotel after concert, 158; Yankee Stadium and, 28

E Street Band, 186

European Tour, 73–76, *75*

Evans, Mal, 48, 52, 93–94, 97; as The Beatles take stage, 133; on helicopter flight, 114; on US tour, 166; at Warwick Hotel after concert, 158

the Everly Brothers, 6

"Everybody's Trying to Be My Baby," 34, 74; at concert, 117, 175; on documentary, 172

the Exciters, 158

Fabian, 82

"Fingertips," 130

Flying Cow, 77–78

Forsyth, Bruce, 61

Freddie and the Dreamers, 33, 34; on *Hullabaloo*, 39

Freed, Alan, 38, 42, *42*

Frost, David, 77

Gabarini, Peter, 73

GAC. *See* General Artists Corp

Gale, Geraldine "Gerry," 21, 22, 28, 31, 79

Garland, Judy, 17

Garrity, Freddie, 34

Gay, Marvin, 58, 68, *68*; on concert day, 129, *129*

Gazzarri Dancers, 186

General Artists Corp (GAC): Bernstein and, 21, 22, 26; on concert day, 103

Genkins, Harvey, 73

"Get Off My Cloud," 167

Gilmore, Mikal, 8; as The Beatles take stage, 141

Ginsberg, Allen, 60, 65

Glyde, David, 11–14, *12*, 93, 96, 130; on *The Beatles' Christmas Show*, 33–34; on changes to The Beatles, 180; on concert day, 105, 129; on cultural change, 177; on US tour, 164, 166; at Warwick Hotel after concert, 160

Godfrey, Arthur, 5

Goldberg, Whoopi, 9, 85, 183; on concert day, 111; on concert experience, 142

"Good Lovin'," *16*

Goodyear Blimp, at concert, 143, *143*

Gordon, Elliott: on Bernstein, 25, 26, 27, 28, 31; on concert experience, 142

Graham, Bill, 17

Graham, Peter, 162

Grammy Lifetime Achievement Award, of McCartney, 186

Grammys, 55

Grant, Cary, 61

Greer, Charlie, 130

haircuts, 92

hair dryers, 165

"A Hard Day's Night," 34, 74; at concert, 117; Grammy for, 55

A Hard Day's Night! (album), 45

A Hard Day's Night! (film), 35, 49–51

Hardy, Françoise, 74

Harrison, George, 12–13; on *The Beatles' Christmas Show*, 33; on Bicknell, 94; on concert day, 121; concert experience of, 142, 153, 157; estate of, 43; on evil of fame, 36; on fame, 35; as favorite Beatle, 83, 141; in *A Hard Day's Night*, 50; on helicopter flight, 112–13; in *Help!*, 56; Indian music and, 56, 71; jelly beans and, 34–35; the Lovin' Spoonful and, 174; LSD and, 57, 166; marriage of, 172–73; on MBE, 70; Northern Songs Ltd. and, 47; Page, Jimmy, and, 34; on planned ticker tape parade, 35; sitar of, 56; spirituality of, 50, 56; on truck to concert, 114–15; on US tour, 163, 164; Van Zandt on, 141; Wilson and, 159

Harrison, Pattie, 43; marriage of, 172–73

Haslam, Michael, 33

Having a Wild Weekend, 78

helicopter, for concert, 52, 112–14

"Help!," 76, 86; at concert, 117; on *The Ed Sullivan Show*, 97

Help! (album), 71, *71*, 76, 77

Help! (film), 45, 56, 58–63

Hendrix, Jimi, 141

Hepburn, Audrey, 61

Herman's Hermit, 26, 119

heroin, 36

The History of Rock and Roll, 85

Holland, Eddie, 46

Hollingshead, Michael, 57

INDEX

Holloway, Brenda, 12, 49, *49*; as concert opening act, 125, 126, 129; on US tour, 164, 165, *165*

Hollywood a Go Go, 186

Holmes, Alan, 12

"Honey Don't," 34

Horton, Jack, 73

"House of the Rising Sun," 27

Howard, Ron, 36

Howes, Arthur, 70

Hullabaloo, 38; Bernstein and, 39; dancers on, 40–41, *41, 68,* 68–69; Epstein on, 39, *39*

Hunter, Wes, 12

Hutchins, Chris, 119

Hyman, Walter, 26, 27

"I Can't Help Myself," 129

"I Feel Fine," 34, 38, 74; at concert, 117; on *The Ed Sullivan Show*, 97

"If You Want to Make a Fool of Somebody," 13

"I'm a Loser," 34, 74

"I'm Down," *71,* 72, 86; at concert, 117, 152; on *The Ed Sullivan Show*, 97

Indian music, 56, 71

"In the Hall of the Mountain Kings," 130

"I Saw Her Standing There," 8

"It's Only Love," 72

"I've Just Seen a Face," 71

Ivor Novello Awards, 77

"I Wanna Be Your Man," 74

"I Want to Hold Your Hand," 7, *7,* 8, 9, 11

Jackson, Hal, 129

Jackson, Michael, 157

Jagger, Mick, 51; as The Beatles take stage, 136; on day of concert, 119–22; on Hardy, 74; on rivalry, 64. *See also* the Rolling Stones

James Bond (fictional character), 37

James, Dick, 39; Northern Songs Ltd. and, 47

Jaramillo, Bobby "Rabbit," 138, 146. *See also* Cannibal and the Headhunters

jelly beans, Harrison, G., and, 34–35

Johnson, Lyndon B.: at Shea Stadium, 52; Vietnam War and, 45, 65, 76, 78; Voting Rights Act and, 78

Jones, Brian, 51; the Lovin' Spoonful and, 174

Jordan, Tony, 103

Kane, John, 161–62; on technology, 178

Kane, Larry, 152; on changes to The Beatles, 180; on US tour, 166, 167

Katz, Sidney, 168, 171

Katzenberg, Jeffrey, 85, 103

Kaye, Danny, 61

Keeley, Charles, 51

Kennedy, Jacqueline, 1

Kennedy, John, 1–2

King, Ben E., 12

King, Martin Luther, Jr., 37, 49

the Kinks, 26; at Ad Lib Club, 44

Kinnear, Roy, 49

Kirchherr, Astrid, 13

Klein, Allen, 86, 99; on concert day, *132*; Vinton and, 119–21

The Knack (and How to Get It), 64

Kohan, Buz, 3, 4–5; on concert filming, 168, 169, 170, 172

Kottke, Leo, 177

Kraft, Mark, 40

LaFlamme, Linda Baker, 84, *84,* 92, 100, *100,* 184, *184*; as The Beatles take stage, 137, 141; on concert day, 108

"Land of 1,000 Dances," 45, *45,* 128

Lane, Michael, 18

Larcher, David, 65

Laszlo, Andrew, 73, 82; as The Beatles take stage, 135; on concert day, *102,* 102–4; on concert experience, 144, 145; on concert filming, 167–68; hearing loss of, 156–57

Leary, Timothy, 37, 57

Led Zeppelin, 162

Lee, Brenda, 9, 12

Lefsetz, Bob, 7, 14–15; on changes to The Beatles, 181

Lennon, Cynthia: on Cogan, 62; on drug use of Lennon, John, 46–47; at estate, 43; new home of, 77–78; on Starr marriage proposal, 44; on Starr wedding, 46

Lennon, John, 1; on *The Beatles' Christmas Show*, 33; as The Beatles take stage, *136*; Bicknell and, 59–60; Bron and, 59; Cogan and, 62; on concert experience, 142, 153, 157; drug use of, 46–47; to dugout, *131*; on Epstein's changes to band's image, 24; estate of, 43; on evil of fame, 36; Ginsberg and, 65; on *A Hard Day's Night*, 49; on helicopter flight, 113; independence of, 13; Ivor Novello Awards of, 77; the Lovin' Spoonful and, 174; LSD and, 57, 166; on MBE, 60, 71; new home of, 77–78; Northern Songs Ltd. and, 39, 47; Pelletier and, 177; on piano, 98, 152; *Rubber Soul*

INDEX

and, 43–44; runners and, 146; *A Spaniard in the Works* by, 65, *65*; on US tour, 163, 164; "We're more popular than Jesus" by, 173, *173*
Lennon, Julian: at estate, 43; kidnapping threat to, 35
Lerner, Max, 22
Lester, Richard, 35–36, 48, 49, 56, 64, 77
Levitt, Steve, *67*, 68; at Warwick Hotel after concert, 160
Little Richard, 12
Lociano, John, 114, 115
Lockhart-Smith, Judy, 43
"Long Tall Sally," 34, 74
Lopez, Richard "Scar," 128–29
"Love Me Do," 11, *11*
Lovin' Spoonful, 2–3, *3,* 174
LSD, 37, 56–57, 77; on US tour, 166

Madison Square Garden, 28, 29; Jackson, Michael, at, 157
Malcolm X, assassination of, 45
Manfred Mann, 26
Margaret, Princess, 61, 77; at Ad Lib Club, 44
Margolis, Abe, 26, 27
Margolis, Gert, 27
marijuana: acceptability of, 47; Bicknell and, 87
Marotte, Linda Ghigonne, 83, 99; as The Beatles take stage, 136, 138, *138*; on concert day, 107–8, 110, 123, 124; on concert experience, 144, 145, 146; screaming of, 145
Martha and the Vandellas, 58
Martin, George: broken foot of, 43–44; on documentary, 172; Epstein and, 24; "I've Just Seen a Face" and, 71; Lockhart-Smith and, 43

Martin, Giles, 178–79
Martin, Mary, 21
Martin, Tony, 67, *67*
the Marvelettes, 58
MBE. *See* Members of the Order of the British Empire
McCartney, Paul: with Asher, J., 43; on *The Beatles' Christmas Show*, 33; on Bicknell, 43; Bron and, 59; Cogan and, 61, 62; Cohen and, 183; on concert day, *117*, 118; on concert experience, 142, 157; on documentary, 171; on European tour, 76; as favorite Beatle, 83; Grammy Lifetime Achievement Award of, 186; on *A Hard Day's Night*, 49; heroin and, 36; Ivor Novello Awards of, 77; the Lovin' Spoonful and, 174; LSD and, 166; Mourges and, 165–66; new home of, 78; Northern Songs Ltd. and, 39, 47; Pelletier and, 177; as pop star, 13; runners and, 146; at Shea Stadium Concert, *135*; Streep and, 186; on US tour, 163, 164, 165–66; at Warwick Hotel after concert, 160; "Yesterday" and, 34, 63, 65, 78, 97, 167
McCarty, Jim, 34, *34*
McKechnie, Donna, 40, *41*
McKern, Leo, 49
media blackout, 76–78
Melody Maker, 22
Members of the Order of the British Empire (MBE), 60, 64, 70–71
merchandise, *81*, *98*, 99
Merman, Ethel, 61
Mersey Beat, 23
Michaels, Dawn, 40, *40*, 41, *41*, 66, *66*, 67, *67*, 68, 69, 186, *186*; on concert day, 105, *105*, 111, *111*,

126, 127; on US tour, 163, *163,* 164, 165; at Warwick Hotel after concert, 159–60
Miles, Barry, 65
Miller, Bill, 19
Miller, Jimmy, 19
Mills, Hayley, 44
the Miracles, 58
Molina, Bobbie, *8*, 8–9, 54, 69, 184, *184*; as The Beatles take stage, 136–37; on concert day, 106, 107, 124; on departure from concert, 153–54; on helicopter flight, 113
Monck, Chip, 177–78
Monterey Pop Festival, 176, 178
Montgomery, Joyce, 70
the Moody Blues, 26
Moon, Keith, 174
moon landing, 14
Morrow, Cousin Brucie. *See* Cousin Brucie
Mourges, Denise, 66, 67, *67*, 69, 184, *184*; on changes to The Beatles, 179, 180; on concert day, 105, *111*, 126, 127; on US tour, 164–66; at Warwick Hotel after concert, 160
Muir, Jean, 44
Murray the K, 126, 128
Musical Express, 23

Namath, Joe, 38
Nehru jackets, 117
NEMS. *See* North End Music Store
Newman, Tony, 12, 130
New Musical Express Awards Live, 55
Newport Folk Festival, 76
Newsweek, 10
New York World's Fair, 55, 113
Nikirk, Susan Silva. *See* Silva, Susan

INDEX

North End Music Store (NEMS), 23, *23*, 24, 55

Northern Songs Ltd., 39; on stock exchange, 47

"Norwegian Wood," 44

"Now Lady Now," 128

Nyro, Laura, 27

Oldham, Andrew Loog, 38–39

Old Wave, 186

Ono, Yoko, 65

opening acts, for concert, 125–32; Cannibal and the Headhunters as, 126, 128–29; Cousin Brucie in, 125, 126, 128; Curtis as, 126, 128; Holloway as, 125, 126, 129; Murray the K in, 126, 128; Sounds Incorporated as, 126, *130*, 130–31

Orsino, George, 82, 85–86, 118–19, 185, *185*; on concert day, 107, 109, 131, 132; on departure from concert, 155; runners and, 146

"Out of Sight," 128

Page, Jimmy, 34

Page, Joey, 51

Parker, Colonel, 162

Parlophone, 24

Parsons, Gram, 50

payola, 42

Peace Corps, 1–2

Pelletier, David, 177–78

Perst, Buddy, 54, 83

Perst, Renee, 83, 84, 185–86; as The Beatles take stage, *138*, 138–39; on concert day, 107–8, 109, 123; on concert experience, 144–45; on concert opening acts, 130

Peter and Gordon, 3, *3*

piano, Lennon, John, on, 98, 152

Pickett, Wilson, 141

Precht, Bob, 5–6, 7, 72–73; on Bernstein, 18; on concert day, *102*, 102–3, *121*, 122, *123*; on concert experience, 144, 156; on concert filming, 168; on Harrison marriage, 173

Precht, Vincent, 6, 7

Presley, Elvis, 4, 6, 12; glamor of, 10; rebellious style of, 8; at sports stadiums, 28; on US tour, 166; Van Zandt on, 141

Preston, Billy, 12

Prichard, Peter, 7

Procol Harum, 177

"P.S. I Love You," *11*

Pulp Fiction, 171

Quant, Mary, 44

the Rascals, *16*, 18, 69; as The Beatles take stage, 135; Bernstein and, 79, 108–9, *109*, 116; at concert, 103, 108–9, 116, *124*; flashing sign for, 116

Rayhack, Michael, 73

Ready, Steady, Go!, 55, 174

Redding, Otis, 141

Revolver, 175

Richard, Cliff, 12

Richards, Keith, 119, 120; as The Beatles take stage, 136; on concert day, *132*

the Righteous Brothers, 14

Riley, John, 56–57

"Rock and Roll Music," 34, 74

the Rolling Stones, 3, 76, *76*, 167; at Academy of Music, 38–39; at Ad Lib Club, 44; as bad boys, 51, 78; Bernstein and, 27, 63–64, 122; Calandra on, 97; on day of concert, 119–22; Eastman, L., and, 55; on *Hullabaloo*, 39; Oldham and, 38–39; Pelletier and, 177; rivalry with, 63–64

the Ronettes, 128; departure from concert by, 154–55

Ross, Diana, 177

Ross, Scott, 128, 154

Rothenberger, Warren, 102

Roxon's Rock Encyclopedia, *85*

Rubber Soul, 43–44, 167, 175

runners, at concert, 146, *146*

Rydell, Bobby, 82

"Satisfaction," 76, *76*, 129

Savile, Jimmy, 34

Schneider, Ronnie, *21*, 65, 68, 86, 99; as The Beatles take stage, 138; on Bernstein, 21; on concert day, 120–21, 131; on the Rolling Stones, 64

Schwartz, Ronnie, *67*, 68; on concert day, 105, *105, 111*; on US tour, 163, *163*; at Warwick Hotel after concert, 159–60

Science Newsletter, 10

"Scrambled Eggs," 72

SDS. *See* Students for a Democratic Society

the Searchers, 3

Sebastian, John, 174

Sedaka, Neil, 86

Sgt. Pepper, 175; album cover of, 70

the Shadows, 63

"Shake," 129

Shannon, Del, 158

Shea Stadium concert, *101*–5, 101–11, *107, 110, 111*; advance ticket sales for, 32; advertising for, 30–31; aftermath of, 161–81; arrival in U.S. for, 89;

INDEX

Beatlemania at, 152; The Beatles changes after, 179–81; Bernstein and, 29–31, 37; concert plans for, 51–53; as cultural defining moment, 176–77; departure from, 153–57; Discotheque Dancers at, *126*, 126–28, *127*; duck blind at, 102, *102*; dugout at, 122, *122*, *124*, *131*; Epstein and, 53, 72, 100; flight from England to, 87–88; Goodyear Blimp at, 143, *143*; guarantee for empty seats, 30; heat wave at, 102; helicopter for, 52, 112–14; leaving Warwick Hotel for, 112; night before, 98–100; opening acts for, 125–32; police at, *103*, *121*, *122*, 124–25; radio station ticket contest for, 70; the Rascals at, 103, 116, *124*; runners at, 146, *146*; behind the scenes of, 116–19; screams at, 135–44, 172; security issues of, 51–52; as sellout, 33; set list for, 117; stage for, 51; Sullivan and, 116, *121*, *122*, *123*, 128, 134, 135; taking stage at, 133–53, *134–38*, *140–44*, *146–51*; technology from, 178–79; ticket for, *123*; ticket prices for, 31; truck to, 114–16

"She Loves You," 11

Shenson, Walter, 48

"She's a Woman," 34, 74; at concert, 117, 175; on documentary, 172

Shindig, 78

the Shirelles, 12

Sid Bernstein Calling (Bernstein), 22

Silva, Susan, 40–41, 66–67, *67*, 68, 93, 185, *185*; on concert day, 126, 128; identification pass of, 126, *126*; on US tour, 163, 164

Silver, Charles, 47

Simon and Garfunkel, 27

Sinatra, Frank, 3–4, 83; glamor of, 10

sitar, of Harrison, G., 56

16 Magazine, 54, *54*

Skelton, Red, 22

Sklar, Rick, 89

Snowdon, Lord, 77

The Sound of Music, 21

Sounds Incorporated, 11–14, *12*, *96*; on *The Beatles' Christmas Show*, 33; as concert opening act, 126, *130*, 130–31

A Spaniard in the Works (Lennon, John), 65, *65*

Spector, Phil, 161

Spector, Ronnie, 154–55

Spinetti, Victor, 48, 49

Spitz, Bob, 178

Springfield, Dusty, 9

Starr, Ringo, 8, 13; All-Starr Band of, 186; on *The Beatles' Christmas Show*, 33; as The Beatles take stage, 137; birth of child of, 167; on concert day, 116; on concert experience, 142, 152; death threat of, 35; on European tour, 76; as expectant father, 55; as favorite Beatle, 83; in *A Hard Day's Night*, 49; Holloway and, 165; LSD and, 166; marriage proposal by, 38, 44; on MBE, 60, 70; new home of, 77; Northern Songs Ltd. and, 47; on US tour, 163, 164, 165; Van Zandt and, 186; Walsh and, 186–87; at Warwick Hotel after concert, 160; wedding of, 45–46, 158. *See also* Cox, Maureen

Stewart, Rod, 177

Stickle, Frank, 128

St. John, John, 12

Streep, Mary Louise (Meryl), 54, 65, 82, 86, 99, 176, 186; as The Beatles take stage, 137; on concert day, 108, 124; on concert experience, 144

Streisand, Barbra, 27

Students for a Democratic Society (SDS), 55

Sullivan, Ed: concert and, 53, 72, 116, *121*, 122, *123*, 128, 134, 135; Epstein and, 25. *See also The Ed Sullivan Show*

Summer of Love, 175

Sunday Night at the Palladium, 61

Sunny Heights, 77–78

the Supremes, 9, *9*, 38, 46, *47*, 57, 57–58, 167; on *The Ed Sullivan Show*, 158; at Warwick Hotel after concert, 158–59

Sutcliffe, Stuart, 13

Switzer, Dawn Michaels. *See* Michaels, Dawn

the Talking Heads, Pelletier and, 177

Talley, Nedra, 128; departure from concert, 154

Taylor, Alistair, 23

Taylor, Derek, 35

Taylor, Elizabeth, 37

the Teddy Bears, 92

the Temptations, 58

Thank Your Lucky Stars, 55

"There! I Said It Again," 11

"This Bird Has Flown," 44

Thompson, Jim, 29, 30

Thurman, Uma, 171

ticker tape parade, 35

ticket, for concert, *123*; prices of, 31

"Ticket to Ride," 57, *57*, 74; at concert, 117; on *The Ed Sullivan Show*, 97

INDEX

Tomasky, Michael, 14
Top of the Pops, 11, 55; Savile of, 34
touring end, 173
Travolta, John, 171
truck, to concert, 114–16
Tudor, Anthony, 40
"Twist and Shout," 34, 74, 128; at concert, 117, 137
A Twist of Lennon (Lennon, C.), 43
Tycobrahe Sound, 178

US tour, 163–65, 163–67

Van Zandt, Steve, 27, 141, 186
the Ventures, 12
Vietnam War, 37; escalation of, 45, 76; protests against, 55, *55*
Vincent, Gene, 12, 13
Vinton, Bobby, 1, 11, 78, 86, *119*; on Bernstein, 18; on concert day, 131, 132, *132*; on concert experience, 143, 157; Klein and, 119–21; on sports stadium concerts, 28
Vishnu Devananda, 50

Voormann, Klaus, 56
Voting Rights Act, 78

Walsh, Joe, 139–40, 186–87
Warwick Hotel: arrival at, 89–96, *90*; after concert, 158–60; leaving, 112; on night before concert, 98–100
Watts riots, 37, 79
Wayne, John, 2
"The Way You Do the Things You Do," 128
Weinstein, Marc, 79–81, *80*, 100, 186; on concert day, 106, 111, 124–25, 128; on concert experience, 142–43, 152, 153; on departure from concert, 153
Weintraub, Jerry, 19
Welch, Bruce, 63
"(What Are You Gonna Do) When I'm Gone," 49, *49,* 129
"What'd I Say," 128
"Where Did Our Love Go," 46, *47*
the Who, 174; Pelletier and, 177
"The William Tell Overture," 130

Willis, Gordon, 73, 102
Wilson, Mary, 9, *9*, 46, 58; at Warwick Hotel after concert, 158–59
Winters, David, 40
WMCA, 128
Wonder, Stevie, 58
Woodstock, 171
Woodstock Festival, 18, 176
Wyman, Bill, 51

Yankee Stadium, 28
Yanovsky, Zal, 174
the Yardbirds, 33, 34, *34*, 74
"Yesterday," 34, 63, 64, 65, 78; on *The Ed Sullivan Show*, 97; release of, 167
Yesterday and Today, 173
"You Can Cry on My Shoulder," 129

Zimmerman. Seth: on Bernstein, 19, 20, 21, 25, 26, 162; on changes to The Beatles, 180; on concert day, 103

QUOTES

Unless otherwise noted, all quotes are from author interviews.

CHAPTER 1

"That concert in 1965": John Lennon, quoted in Sid Bernstein and Arthur Aaron, *It's Sid Bernstein Calling* (New York: Jonathan David Publisher, 2002), xvi.

"It's like that sort of perfect storm": *The Beatles: Eight Days a Week—The Touring Years*, directed by Ron Howard (2016).

"When people think of him": Stephanie Nolasco, "Then and Now," August 11, 2019, Foxnews.com.

"Maybe having The Beatles on": Vincent Precht, "John, Paul, George, and Me," *New York Times*, February 9, 2014, section SR, page 3.

"I know they're important": Precht, "John, Paul, George, and Me," *New York Times*.

"Fifty years ago, our nation": Bob Lefsetz, "Beatles 50th Anniversary Special," *The Lefsetz Letter* (blog), January 28, 2014.

"Their American debut, on *The Ed Sullivan*": Mikal Gilmore, "Why This Band Plays On," *New York Times*, August 24, 2005, www.nytimes.com/2005/08/24/opinion/why-this-band-plays-on.html.

"I remember the": *The Beatles: Eight Days a Weeks—The Touring Years* directed by Ron Howard (2016) with permission from Ms. Goldberg.

"The Beatles are not merely awful"; "Visually they are a nightmare"; "The Beatles follow a line of glamorous figures"; "Don't let The Beatles bother you": Cary Schneider, "What the Critics Wrote about The Beatles in 1964," *Los Angeles Times*, February 9, 2014, www.latimes.com/opinion/commentary/la-oe-beatles-quotes-20140209,0,1146431.story#ix zz2sz93LgMw.

"In that first wave": Michael Tomasky, "Cute? Hardly. The Beatles Subverted the American Way of Life," *Los Angeles Times*, February 9, 2014.

"We were becoming adults": Lefsetz, "Beatles 50th Anniversary Special."

QUOTES

CHAPTER 2

"The British Invasion was the most important": Steven Van Zandt, https://quotes.thefamouspeople.com/steven-van-zandt-9636.php.

"In the heyday, the mad days": George Harrison, *I Me Mine* (New York: Simon and Schuster, 1980), 36.

"The first big American trip, when": Harrison, *I Me Mine*, 39.

"I saw it happen to Paul": Philip Norman, *Shout!* (New York: Simon and Schuster, 1981), 244.

"There was more good": Harrison, *I Me Mine*.

"We were only trying to play rock": *The Beatles Anthology* (San Francisco: Chronicle Books, 2000), 143.

". . . We were . . . surrounded": *The Beatles Anthology*, 143.

"Beatlemania was not just": Promotion for *The Beatles: Eight Days a Week—The Touring Years*, directed by Ron Howard (2016).

CHAPTER 3

"It was beyond": Sid Bernstein and Arthur Aaron, *"It's Sid Bernstein Calling . . ."* (New York: Jonathan David Publisher, 2002), 190.

"It was during this time": Beatles Music History, www.beatlesebooks.com/norwegian-wood.

"'Norwegian Wood' is my song": David Sheff, *All We Are Saying: The Last Major Interview with John Lennon and Yoko Ono* (New York: St. Martin's Griffin, 2000).

"The Ad Lib Club was": Alasdair Ferguson and Alf Bicknell, *Ticket to Ride* (Glitterbooks of London, 1999), 36.

"Alf was special": Ferguson and Bicknell, *Ticket to Ride*, 36.

"I loved Maureen": Lennon, *A Twist of Lennon*, 132.

"We were not at all": Tony Barrow, *John, Paul, George, and Me* (New York: Thunder's Mouth Press, 2005), 143.

"It was just a drag": Barrow, *John, Paul, George, and Me*, 143.

"Two down": Barrow, *John, Paul, George, and Me*, 143.

"Every single thing they": Lennon, *A Twist of Lennon*, 142–43.

"We smoked": *The Beatles Anthology*, 167.

"I realize, looking back": *The Beatles Anthology*, 167.

QUOTES

"We were pretty disinterested": *The Beatles: Eight Days a Week—The Touring Years*, directed by Ron Howard (2016).

"They were high all": Norman, *Shout!* 244.

"a nice guy who was": Lorraine LoBianco, Brandon deWilde profile, www.fold3.com/memorial/527812386/a-dewilde-1942/stories.

"They took us up": *The Beatles Anthology*, 169.

"Absolutely bursting to go": Bill Wyman, *Stone Alone: The Story of a Rock 'n' Roll Band* (Boston: Da Capo Press, 1997).

"I am arranging to have the": Brian Epstein, press release, BeatlesBible.com.

"It was an incredible time": Linda McCartney, *Linda McCartney's Sixties Portrait of an Era* (New York: Little, Brown and Company, 1992), 10.

"We were waiting to": *Billboard*, December 1992.

"I felt as though I knew": Norman, *Shout!* 644.

"There are various stories": Ferguson and Bicknell, *Ticket to Ride*, 125–26.

"It was terrifying": *The Beatles Anthology*, 177, 180.

"John and I spent": *The Beatles Anthology*, 177, 180.

"All of us"; "With John you only got": Ferguson and Bicknell, *Ticket to Ride*, 46–47, 52.

"We all agreed"; "We had to do": *The Beatles Anthology*, 181.

"They were very nice"; "I took it round to Alma": https://sentstarr.tripod.com/beatgirls/almacog.html.

"In the flesh she": DailyMail.com, April 4, 2015, www.dailymail.co.uk/femail/article-3026005/Yes-lost-John-woman-WASN-T-Yoko-25-years-ago-Beatle-s-former-wife-Cynthia-shared-secret-biographer-told.html.

"I knew about Alma": Michael Thornton, "John's Secret Lover," *Daily Mail*, November 8, 2006.

"John was potty about": Thornton, "John's Secret Lover."

"The five of them": Ferguson and Bicknell, *Ticket to Ride*, 50.

"I knew it was magic": Mark William Harding, "All Our Yesterdays," September 7, 2021, https://portugaltravelguide.com/paul-mccartney-in-portugal.

"We had sort of a lot": excerpt from Mick Jagger's speech inducting The Beatles into the Rock and Roll Hall of Fame in 1999.

"You don't do that": BeatlesBible.com.

"The biggest thing The Beatles": Hunter Davies, *The Beatles* (New York: McGraw-Hill, 1968), 212.

"Some old soldiers": *The Beatles Anthology*, 183.

"I brought it home": *The Beatles Anthology*, 183.

"Your Majesty": Peter Brown and Steven Gaines, *The Love You Make* (New York: McGraw-Hill, 1983), 334.

"Most people think it's": Barrow, *John, Paul, George, and Me*, 146.

"Just moving around": Andrew Laszlo, *It's a Wrap!* (Los Angeles: ASC Press, 2004), 178–79.

"The thing I remember about": BeatlesBible.com.

"I remember playing": BeatlesBible.com.

"When there was no": Laszlo, *It's a Wrap!* 179.

"I heard about": *The Beatles: Eight Days a Week—The Touring Years* directed by Ron Howard (2016) with permission from Ms. Goldberg.

"In August 1965": 32nd Grammy Awards, February 21, 1990, with permission from Ms. Streep.

"Put musical director": Ferguson and Bicknell, *Ticket to Ride*, 52.

CHAPTER 4

"The whole airport was": Ferguson and Bicknell, *Ticket to Ride*, 55–56.

"Alf was a friend": Ferguson and Bicknell, *Ticket to Ride*, 4.

"It was heaving wall to": Barrow, *John, Paul, George, and Me*, 153.

"Ringo, what are you gonna name": audio of conference, http://beatlesinterviews.org.

"Saturday's rehearsal took": Barrow, *John, Paul, George, and Me*, 154–55.

"Most people can do": Murray Schumuch, "Fans Put on Show to Rival Beatles," *New York Times*, August 15, 1965, 82.

"I had a": 32nd Grammy Awards, February 21, 1990, with permission from Ms. Streep.

CHAPTER 5

"I loved The Beatles": McCartney, *Linda McCartney's Sixties Portrait of an Era*, 144.

"So this is": *The Beatles: Eight Days a Week—The Touring Years* directed by Ron Howard (2016) with permission from Ms. Goldberg.

"We flew in by": Barrow, *John, Paul, George, and Me*, 155.

QUOTES

"Thousands of flashbulbs": Barrow, *John, Paul, George, and Me*, 156.

"I didn't think Wells": Paul Du Noyer, "Remembering Shea," *TV Guide*, August 24, 2005, 26.

"As we lazed on": Chris Hutchins and Peter Thompson, *Elvis Meets the Beatles* (London: Neville Ness House, 2016).

"We went down this long": Ferguson and Bicknell, *Ticket to Ride*, 66.

"I remember I": 32nd Grammy Awards, February 21, 1990, with permission from Ms. Streep.

"Jackie DeShannon did their": Tom Meros, YouTube interview, December 2019.

"The audience didn't go": Steve Pond, "Being There," *TV Guide*, August 24, 2005, 31.

"Oh my God, I'll": Tom Meros, YouTube interview.

"It was bedlam": Pond, "Being There," 31.

"One of our": *The Beatles at Shea Stadium* directed by Bob Precht, 1965.

"Honored by their": *The Beatles at Shea Stadium* directed by Bob Precht, 1965.

"Ladies and gentlemen": *The Beatles at Shea Stadium* directed by Bob Precht, 1965.

"Keith and Mick were": Chris Hutchins and Peter Thompson, *Elvis Meets the Beatles*, Google ePub edition, 1994, 160.

"As indelibly as": 32nd Grammy Awards, February 21, 1990, with permission from Ms. Streep.

"We were standing right": Pond, "Being There," 32.

"Linda was also there": BeatlesTrivia.com, Beatlestrivia.com/category/Linda-McCartney.

"She was crazy": Jordan Runtagh, "Ringo Starr's Wife Barbara Bach First Saw Her Future Husband as a Teenager at a Beatles Concert," People.com, September 25, 2017.

"I took one look": Cameron Crowe, "Joe Walsh," *Rolling Stone*, February 27, 1975.

"I was in New Jersey": Steven Van Zandt, https://quotes.thefamouspeople.com/steven-van-zandt-9636.php.

"That August in 1965": Gilmore, "Why This Band Plays On."

"I never felt": Maria Lalonde, "The Beatles' Epic Performance at Shea Stadium in 1965," Rare, November 2, 2020, https://rare.us/entertainment-and-culture/the-beatles-shea-stadium/.

"When you're competing": Pond, "Being There," 33.

"It was like being": Du Noyer, "Remembering Shea," 26.

QUOTES

"It was like": *Tomorrow with Tom Snyder*, NBC, April 25, 1975.

"It's what they": *The Beatles: Eight Days a Week—The Touring Years* directed by Ron Howard (2016) with permission from Ms. Goldberg.

"Long before The Beatles": Laszlo, *It's a Wrap!* 183.

"They're psychos!": Murray Schmuach, "55,000 Fill Shea to Hear Beatles," *New York Times*, August 16, 1965, 29.

"We went backstage": Pond, "Being There," 32.

"Brian Epstein's face": Barrow, *John, Paul, George, and Me*, 156.

"Brian was very relieved": Pond, "Being There," 32–33, and Larry Kane, *Ticket to Ride* (Penguin Books, 2003), 182.

"John just went": *The Beatles Anthology*, 187.

"I felt naked": *The Beatles Anthology*, 187.

"They came off": Pond, "Being There," 34.

"We had just enough": Ronnie Spector, *Be My Baby* (New York: Crown Publishers, 1990), 82.

"After that day": Spector, *Be My Baby*, 83.

"I put the top down": Pond, "Being There," 34.

"To say that": Laszlo, *It's a Wrap!* 184–85.

"I've never felt": Hutchins and Thompson, *Elvis Meets the Beatles*, 160.

"Once you know you've": "New York City—Sunday, August 15, 1965," The Paul McCartney Project, www.the-paulmccartney-project.com/concert/1965-08-15/.

"That concert in 1965": Bernstein, *"It's Sid Bernstein Calling . . ."*, 16.

"The four boys expressed": Barrow, *John, Paul, George, and Me*, 157.

CHAPTER 6

"We turned down the": Bernstein, *"It's Sid Bernstein Calling . . ."*, 193–94.

"We were on the plane": Tom Meros, YouTube interview, December 2019.

"One time the crowd": Tom Meros, YouTube interview, December 2019.

"Women came and went": Larry Kane, *Ticket to Ride* (New York: Penguin Books, 2003), 152–53.

"After fifteen performances watching": Larry Kane interview, *The Beatles: Eight Days a Week—The Touring Years*, directed by Ron Howard (2016).

QUOTES

"If I'd said television": Jordan Runtagh, "When John Lennon's 'More Popular Than Jesus' Controversy Turned Ugly," RollingStone.com, July 29, 2016.

"Did we play Shea twice?": Eddie Deezen, "The Night The Beatles Rocked Shea Stadium," Mental Floss, August 15, 2012, www.mentalfloss.com/article/31470/night-beatles-rocked-shea-stadium.

"They were expected, maybe": "An Interview with Dave Glyde aka Major Griff West," October 9, 2013, www.youtube.com/watch?v=NcVu8NlrU5s&t=1s&ab_channel=Powerhouse.

"It forever changed": interview with Bill Littlefield, *Only a Game*, WBUR, August 8, 2015.

"It's hard to think, now": Bob Boilen, "All Songs +1: The Beatles Are Live and Sounding Better Than Ever," NPR, August 25, 2016.

"They were suddenly playing": Michael K. Bohn, "A Pop Music Milestone: The Beatles Meet Elvis," Tribune News Service, August 7, 2015, https://fredericksburg.com/entertainment/music/a-pop-music-milestone-the-beatles-meet-elvis/article_c4898e6e-4eaa-539f-8b97-6b11dd964d01.html.

"They were very, very sensitive": Larry Kane interview, *The Beatles: Eight Days a Week—The Touring Years*.

"Just four guys, no support": Bob Lefsetz, "A Hard Day's Night Live at The Hollywood Bowl," *The Lefsetz Letter* (blog), August 25, 2016.

CAST OF CHARACTERS

"The Beatles gave": *The Beatles: Eight Days a Week—The Touring Years* directed by Ron Howard (2016) with permission from Ms. Goldberg.

"He's not just the greatest": Branden C. Potter, "A Look at Joe Walsh and Ringo Starr's Relationship," Grunge, May 11, 2021, www.grunge.com/406748/a-look-at-joe-walsh-and-ringo-starrs-relationship.